EPONYMISTS IN MEDICINE

── **William Heberden** ──

Physician of the Age of Reason

Ernest Heberden

Editor-in-Chief: Hugh L'Etang

Royal Society of Medicine Services Limited

Royal Society of Medicine Services Limited
1 Wimpole Street London W1M 8AE
8 East 60th Street New York NY 10022

© 1989 Royal Society of Medicine Services Limited

British Library Cataloguing in Publication Data
Heberden, Ernest
    William Heberden, 1710-1801.
    1. Great Britain. Medicine. Heberden, William *1710-1801*
    I. Title   II. Series
    610'.92'4

    ISBN 1-85315-117-3
    ISBN 1-85315-116-5 (pbk)

Editorial and production services by Diane Crofter-Harris, Devizes, Wiltshire

Design by Mehmet Hussein/Medilink Design

Phototypeset by Dobbie Typesetting Service, Plymouth, Devon

Printed in Great Britain by Henry Ling Ltd at the Dorset Press, Dorchester, Dorset

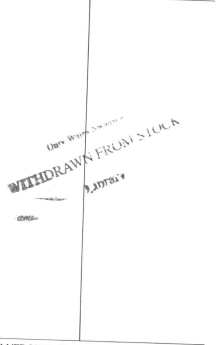

Contents

List of Illustrations

Notable Events

William Heberden

1710 Born in Southwark

1717 Entered St Saviour's Grammar School

1724 Entered St John's College, Cambridge; BA, 1728; MA, 1732; MD, 1738.

1740 Delivered the first course of lectures on materia medica

1741 *The Athenian Letters* printed for private circulation; *An Introduction to the Study of Physic* completed

1745 'Antitheriaca or an Essay on Mithridatium' printed

1746 Elected FRCP

1748 Left Cambridge and settled in London

1749 Delivered Goulstonian Lectures

1750 Elected Fellow of the Royal Society

1752 Married Elizabeth Martin

1754 Son Thomas born; wife died

1759 Published *A Collection of the Yearly Bills of Mortality*; wrote *Plain Instructions on how to Perform Inoculations*

1760 Married Mary Wollaston

1761 Declined invitation to be physician to Queen Charlotte; elected FRS

1767 Proposed the publication of *Medical Transactions*

1768 First volume of *Medical Transactions* published by RCP; read paper 'Some account of a Disorder of the Breast' (angina)

1770 Elected Fellow of the Society of Antiquaries; moved to new house in Pall Mall

1772 Supported Petitions seeking increased toleration

1774 Attended inaugural meeting of Royal Humane Society

1782 Bought house in Windsor; completed *Commentaries on the History and Cure of Diseases*

1783 Began attendance on Dr Johnson

1788 Attended George III

1792 Wrote *Strictures upon the Discipline of the University of Cambridge*

1801 Died at his house in Pall Mall

1802 *Commentaries* published in Latin and English versions

Acknowledgments

My thanks are due to the following institutions for permission to make use of unpublished manuscript material; I am grateful also to the Librarians and their staffs for their friendly and expert assistance.

The Wellcome Library of the Royal College of Physicians, London
The Library of the Royal Society
The British Library
The Library of the Wellcome Institute for the History of Medicine
The Library of Lambeth Palace
The Greater London Council Record Office
The City of Westminster Reference Library
The Guildhall Library
The Library of St John's College, Cambridge
The Cambridge University Library
The Hampshire Record Office, Winchester
The Francis A Countway Library, Boston, Massachusetts

Many of my notes on the minor characters in the story are drawn from the *Dictionary of National Biography*—my source if this is not acknowledged elsewhere.

Amongst the many people who have helped me with information and advice, I am specially indebted to Dr Roy Porter, Senior Lecturer in the Social History of Medicine at the Wellcome Institute for the History of Medicine, who found the time to read earlier drafts of my typescript and to make invaluable criticisms and suggestions.

Foreword

I began my researches for this book out of a natural desire to discover more about an ancestor who, though obviously a man of unusual distinction, had for nearly two centuries eluded the attentions of a biographer. Separated from him by five generations and possessing no family archives, my knowledge of William Heberden was virtually limited to what I had read in the *Dictionary of National Biography* and in a short essay published in 1879 by a surgeon's assistant at St Bartholomew's Hospital, London. These sources, which conveniently listed the authorities consulted, were enough to convince me that there must be ample material, if I could locate it, for constructing a more adequate picture of my subject's life and character.

My search for facts began among baptismal registers in Record Offices and continued in the British Library and at St John's College, Cambridge; at the Wellcome Institute I was introduced to the work of present-day medical historians, and at the Royal College of Physicians I was able to read some of William's unpublished letters and other manuscripts; from the Royal Society I learned about his wider scientific interests and from the Countway Library in Boston, Massachusetts I received xerox copies of items from their Heberden archive.

It is mainly from this mass of scattered material that I have attempted to build the first rounded portrait of an illustrious medical pioneer.

Ernest Heberden

Richmond-on-Thames   1989

William Heberden the Elder, aged 86; a mezzotint by James Ward, after the painting by Sir William Beechey.

Introduction

'What a glorious country is ours! Where Talent and Conduct are sufficient to draw mean Birth and original Poverty out of the Shadow of Life and set their Merit open to the Sun.' When writing these words in 1786, Mrs Piozzi—the former Mrs Thrale—was paying tribute to the English social system which, for all its glaring defects, compared favourably with the arrangements in many continental countries—those 'wretched nations where pride and prejudice chain up every liberal idea and keep the mind enslaved'.

A perfect illustration of Mrs Thrale's thesis is the physician William Heberden the elder (the subject of this book), who rose from humble beginnings to fame and fortune, making in the course of his long career many lasting friendships among the most celebrated figures of his time. If it was Talent that secured him his early admission to St John's College, Cambridge, Conduct played a crucial part in his progress thereafter.

Son of an innkeeper who died when he was seven, William's escape-route from obscurity was provided by his Southwark grammar school, where the curriculum, firmly based on the Classics and the religion of the Established Church, opened doors to the learned professions. Arriving in Cambridge at the tender age of fourteen, he found himself in a different world—mediaeval in many of its customs and ceremonies, but responding to new ideas in the realms of science, philosophy and religion; this was the ambience in which he grew and matured, becoming first an accomplished classical scholar and then, after his election to a Fellowship, a student of Medicine.

William's new field of inquiry involved a knowledge of the ancient medical writers from Hippocrates onwards, all of whom he could read with ease; but by now he was more than merely a proficient scholar; he had absorbed the messages of the pioneers of the Age of Enlightenment—such as Francis Bacon and John Locke—who rejected the uncritical acceptance of 'authority' and advocated the inductive method of reasoning from experience. It was this new attitude towards the physical world that had stimulated important advances in many branches of science, including the spectacular discoveries of Isaac Newton. Progress in medicine (by comparison with other disciplines) had been slight but by no means negligible: Harvey had discovered the circular movement of the blood; Thomas Sydenham raised the level of medical practice by his accurate observations of the symptoms of disease in his individual patients; and Hermann Boerhaave, teacher of medicine at Leyden University, initiated modern methods of clinical instruction, including demonstrations of autopsies.

The increase in scientific knowledge had been accompanied by a gradual rise in the status of physicians and by the time George I had arrived on the scene several of them—notably Richard Mead and Sir Hans Sloane—had amassed large fortunes. On the negative side, the new knowledge had brought few benefits to the patient and the standard of medical education at the two English Universities remained lamentably low. Nevertheless, for an ambitious young man, intent upon putting poverty behind him, a career as a learned physician offered promising prospects and if there were innumerable problems concerned with the causes and treatment of disease that still remained to be solved, they at least provided a worthwhile challenge to William's acute intelligence.

At all stages of his career he had to contend against the formidable obstacles that stood in the way of progress; the scientific attitude still had to battle against widespread ignorance and superstition; quackery flourished unhindered by any 'ethical' controls, and basic medical facilities—drugs, anaesthetics, antiseptics, diagnostic aids and so on—were almost totally lacking. It was the nature of these obstacles that determined the direction of William's efforts both as teacher and practitioner. The booklet he wrote for his Cambridge students provided them for the first time with an up-to-date introduction to their duties and responsibilities and a critical assessment of the books they should read; in his public lectures he was remorseless in exposing and ridiculing false beliefs and useless therapies; and even before his election to Fellowship of the prestigious Royal College of Physicians, he had brought his influence to bear on the revision of their pre-scientific *Pharmacopoeia*. Later he demonstrated his belief in medical glasnost by persuading the College to publish papers recounting its members' observations and experiences.

In his practice the absence of effective drugs obliged him to stress the healing powers of nature and to dispense advice that was often (in Dr Johnson's words) rather prudential than medical; no less important was his manner and personality, which gave his patients confidence and hope. His skills and attitudes can be gauged from his major work *Commentaries on the History and Cure of Diseases*, completed near the end of his active career.

If we knew nothing of William apart from his role as physician, he would still make a strong appeal to the modern reader; medicine was in the pre-specialist era; technical jargon was minimal and we can all appreciate his penetrating observations and sympathise with his inevitable failures. But this appeal is enhanced by the width of his interests and the personalities of his friends, patients and acquaintances. In the early days of his practice he came to know the shy, retiring poet Thomas Gray and his fellow Etonian Horace Walpole; the novelist Samuel Richardson was both his dinner-guest and patient; and the well-connected Mrs Delany consulted him and introduced him to members of the Court. Later in his career William attended members of Dr Johnson's circle—including the Thrales—and became both physician and friend to the great Lexicographer himself during the last eighteen months of his life.

It was an age in which it was common for men of talent to make their mark in more than one field of endeavour and William as a Fellow of the Royal Society was associated with several of the most brilliant of them. One example was Stephen Hales, who conscientiously performed his parish duties as Perpetual Curate of Teddington (publicly reprimanding any backsliding sheep before the assembled congregation) and at the same time pursued his other roles as physiologist, inventor and campaigner for good causes. Another was Joseph Priestley, Unitarian minister and theologian, whose patient scientific researches into the constituents of air led to the discovery of oxygen. A third was Benjamin Franklin, with whom William co-operated in promoting inoculation against smallpox in America. As for the activities that William himself pursued outside the strict limits of his profession, we find him at one moment helping the scholar Jeremiah Markland with the publication of Greek plays, and on other occasions carrying through a lengthy experiment concerning rainfall, supporting petitions to Parliament on religious toleration and testing (by astronomical observation) the accuracy of Thomas Mudge's chronometer.

The first half of William's life roughly coincided with the age depicted by Hogarth, whose pictures—such as Gin Lane—referred to scenes all too familiar to him during his Southwark schooldays. But as his personal circumstances were gradually transformed, so too were the social conditions of the country at large; military and naval successes, science, exploration, commerce and industry—all had helped to make Britain wealthier and (through improvements in diet and hygiene) healthier. Meanwhile the efforts of social reformers had awakened dormant consciences and had resulted in the foundation of many new hospitals, dispensaries and other charitable institutions. By the end of the century (and the closing years of William's life) we have arrived at the age of Wordsworth and Jane Austen.

William was married twice, his first wife dying soon after the birth of their son; his second wife outlived him and though domestic details are sparse, their homes—first in Cecil Street off the Strand, and later in Pall Mall and Windsor provide the essential though unobtrusive background to his varied activities.

Although William has been the subject of at least three brief memoirs and is frequently referred to in medical literature, no attempt has hitherto been made to bring together all the material now available.

In this biography I have quoted extensively from William's own works and from many other contemporary sources; material previously unpublished includes extracts from his lectures and private correspondence. In order to dispel confusion with his physician son and namesake, I have briefly sketched the career of William 'the younger' in an Appendix. He deserves to be remembered on at least two counts: first for translating and publishing his father's *Commentaries*, and secondly for his untiring (though unavailing) efforts to secure for his patient George III more humane and enlightened treatment during the long period of his derangement.

To my wife

Chapter 1

Years of Promise

William Heberden's forebears came from West Sussex and the family name,[1] under a variety of spellings, appears in the county records from the thirteenth century onwards. His first identifiable ancestor was a certain Nicholas Heberden who in 1568 became a copy-holder on the manorial estate of Idsworth on the Sussex-Hampshire border,[2] and founded a line of yeoman farmers who remained there for more than two centuries. William's knowledge of his ancestry was sketchy and when he was asked to furnish the College of Arms with his 'pedigree', the details he provided were extremely sparse: he recorded his great-grandfather as Edward Heberden of Idsworth Park and his grandfather simply as Thomas of Chichester. In the absence of any other contenders of the same name, we may assume that this was the Thomas who settled at Boxgrove, a village only three miles from the town, and whose son Richard, born in 1663, was William's father.

The next evidence of Richard's existence is his marriage licence or 'allegation' dated 29 September 1698.[3] His bride was Elizabeth, daughter of William Cooper of Brightling, Sussex; she was nearly twenty-six and was living in Rye, the small seaport at the extreme eastern edge of the county; how Richard met her can best be explained by his occupation: he was a coachman[4] and it would not be surprising if Rye was the terminus of some of his journeys.

For the first two years of their marriage the couple lived in the parish of St Brides on the south side of Fleet Street, but by 1701 they had moved to Southwark, where Richard soon abandoned coaching and settled down as an innkeeper in the parish of St Saviours. In due course he was elected by the Vestry to serve as an Overseer with responsibility for such matters as repairs to church property and poor relief. The work was voluntary but as it attracted some useful perquisites vestrymen usually held their offices for several years; Richard however, for some unexplained reason—perhaps the time-consuming nature of his business at the inn—relinquished his office after only nine months.[5]

There were six children; the first two died in infancy; Thomas, the future surgeon and naturalist was born in 1703 and was followed two years later by Sarah, who died unmarried aged thirty-five. William was born on 13 August 1710[6] and the youngest child John, who became an attorney, arrived in 1712. The inn that was their home can no longer be identified, but whatever its size or style, the children would have been expected to do some small share of the work from an early age.

St Saviour's Grammar School, Southwark, c 1700.

All three boys attended the Free Grammar School, founded in the reign of Elizabeth, which stood in the precincts of St Saviour's church (now Southwark Cathedral). The school had been burnt down in 1676, but was quickly rebuilt; in 1691 a new and well-qualified headmaster—William Symes of Balliol College, Oxford—was appointed and it was under his régime that the brothers received their education. William was admitted in June 1717.[7]

The school statutes[8] are illuminating: the Headmaster had to be chosen 'with the advice of the Bishop of Winchester, or in his absence some learned man at the Governors' discretion'. He was required to be an MA and be 'sounde in christian religion according to the lawes of this land . . . well skilled in the Latin tongue and able to teach grammar oratorye and poetry and the Greeke, as also the principles of Hebrewe'. The two upper forms 'shall onelye speak latine in the schole'. Moreover 'the Scholars of the highest form shall be every year carried to the Merchant Taylors School and to Westminster upon their election days, that there they may see the manner and fashion of the scholars, orations and exercises which may serve for good directions to them either to do the like or better approve their own'. Repetition was not to be a mere exercise of memory, but a lesson in deportment and elocution 'to frame the presence, good grace, countenance, standinge, pronunciation and everythinge that may commende their carriage all their lives'. On play days 'the highest forme shall declaim and some of the inferior formes act a scene of Terence or some dialogue . . .'

The statutes, last revised in 1614, were still, after a century's use, a realistic and imaginative expression of the school's purpose; for an intelligent boy without money or social advantages, proficiency in the classics opened the door to the learned professions; while the emphasis on those accomplishments which would 'commende their carriage' increased the pupils' chances of all-round success. Though the hours spent in mastering the elements of the ancient languages occupied the greater part of William's days in the classroom, the school statutes left no doubt that religious instruction was of prime importance, and the time devoted to this subject was supplemented by regular attendance at the services in St Saviour's.

William left no written record of his early life in Southwark, though he must have retained many lasting recollections of it. Symbols of Established Religion were much in evidence. In addition to St Saviour's, the Bishop of Winchester's palace was close at hand; and across the river rose the spires and cupolas of Wren's new churches—dominated by the magnificent structure of St Paul's Cathedral, completed in the year of William's birth.

In his own parish two prominent buildings were being erected, both of them hospitals: the first, St Thomas's, replaced the mediaeval building, which had fallen into ruin; the second was a brand new foundation, bearing the name of its benefactor, the wealthy bookseller and philanthropist Thomas Guy.

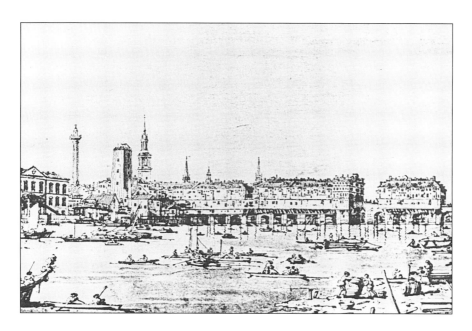

The Thames above London Bridge viewed from Southwark bank; a drawing by Canaletto, c 1750.

But Southwark owed its special character to London Bridge—the only bridge linking London to the Thames's south bank until Westminster Bridge was constructed in 1750. All roads bringing travellers to London from the south and south-east converged on Southwark, which thus became the great terminus for coaches and the place where inns of every description abounded.

Houses lined the Bridge itself and it was natural that Southwark came to be regarded as almost part of the City and was described as the Ward of Bridge Without. Other objects of interest included the busy market just south of St Saviour's and the colourful spectacle of Southwark Fair, an annual event that became the subject of one of Hogarth's paintings.[9]

But perhaps the prospect that offered the greatest fascination was the ever-changing scene of the River—thronged with craft of all sizes and shapes, from small rowing boats to sizeable merchant vessels; and if the largest of these had to berth below London Bridge, the remainder, continually passing to and fro between the Bridge and Westminster, were sufficient to prove that the Thames was London's greatest thoroughfare.

There were plenty of grim reminders that life could be brutal and harsh, and was always precarious—especially for the very young. Burials at St Saviours were a daily occurrence—there were 582 of them in 1708, many of them children, of whom only one quarter would be expected to survive their fifth birthday.[10]

One cause of this appalling wastage was filth; sanitation was primitive and there was little regard for personal cleanliness. For the inevitable fevers and infections that abounded, remedies were ineffective, and nature took its course. The situation had been aggravated by various Acts of Parliament designed to help landowners to obtain a good price for their cereal crops, even in years of surplus. The business of distilling the grain for gin and brandy (once the monopoly of the Distillers Company) was, after the Revolution of 1688, thrown open to anyone who could pay a modest excise duty, and gradually nearly all restrictions on retailing the spirits were also lifted. By 1720 gin was so cheap and so readily available that it was being consumed in vast quantities, particularly by the poorer classes, with devastating effect.[11] Children were also put at risk by lack of adequate housing; indeed the building of houses outside the limits of the City was restricted by law. Many houses were therefore erected without official permission in courts and alleys, without regard for standards of construction or materials, and were then occupied by several families, the poorest living in the damp cellars or draughty garrets.[12] To add to the general distress, these ramshackle tenements frequently collapsed or caught fire.

These were not the only inconveniences that Londoners had to contend with; heat for houses, offices and workshops was provided by coal and the smoke from thousands of chimneys polluted the air with soot, veiling the sunlight, blackening buildings and injuring lungs. Another nuisance was noise—caused partly by the incessant traffic of horse-drawn carriages, carts and wagons with iron-rimmed wheels, and partly by the shouting of the drivers, the efforts of itinerant musicians and the cries of street vendors.

Behaviour, at least among the strong and healthy, tended to be boisterous and aggressive, with much shouting and laughter—an expression of the feeling that as life was extremely precarious every moment should be enjoyed to the full. Appetites were hearty; gambling was a common passion. People were stoical in enduring pain and callous towards the suffering of others. Public executions were regarded as exciting theatrical events. For many children, life was an education in brutality.[13]

We do not have any contemporary description of day-to-day life at the school, but it is clear that William was an extremely able pupil and that Symes wanted him to continue his education at a University; but this plan was nearly frustrated.

The year before William's admission to the school, Thomas had been apprenticed to a Surgeon[14] in Rotherhithe, some two miles away to the east, for a fee of £50—equivalent to at least £3000 today. This was surely a sign that Richard's affairs were going well, and that he looked forward to launching his two younger sons on equally worthwhile careers when their schooldays were completed. He did not however live to see his ambitions realised, and by October of the following year was dead. As he left no will, it is probable that his death was sudden and unexpected. Under these circumstances his widow might reasonably have hoped to obtain letters of administration within a few weeks, but in fact four years elapsed before matters were settled, and although no details of the estate are provided in the brief record,[15] we may surmise that Richard left very little; indeed, if the money needed for Thomas's apprenticeship fee had been borrowed, the unfortunate widow was probably saddled with a substantial debt.

At all events, it seems that she continued to manage the inn; but money was still so short in 1724 that she intended, when William left school, 'to put him behind the counter.'[16]

It was at this point, when his whole future was in the balance, that a solution was found—doubtless by the initiative of Mr Symes—which enabled William to proceed to the next stage of his career at St John's College, Cambridge. According to a memorandum in the school accounts, a certain Mr Ralph Carter had left money in his will to provide an exhibition (i.e. a maintenance allowance) for a needy scholar; its value was £7 per annum and the school, having awarded it to William, continued the payments until he was elected Fellow of his college seven years later.

Cambridge from the first milestone on the road to London, in 1809.

His last recorded appearance as a schoolboy was at the annual meeting of former pupils, held on 17 November, 1724. The programme of events included a service in St Saviours with a special preacher and a presentation by some of the senior scholars of the last two scenes of the Latin comedy *Phormio* by Terence. Of the four actors listed, William is the first. The following month he took the road to Cambridge.

This brief account of William's background and childhood leaves many questions unanswered. If our impressions of Richard are vague and ill-defined, Elizabeth's personality must have been strong and determined. That she succeeded in rearing four of her six children was in itself no mean achievement; but besides this, she provided the sole parental support throughout her younger sons' schooldays, and her positive influence on their development must have been considerable. Meanwhile, she kept the business going (probably helped by her daughter Sarah); and though she must have been very hard pressed when William's future was in the balance, she was later able to support John when he began his training as an attorney. One of her attributes must surely have been robust good health; she survived to the age of 86.

William's first journey to Cambridge—probably by the public coach—would have been a test of endurance. The state of England's roads, even many of the main highways, was abysmal; long stretches were little better than farm tracks, deeply rutted and pot-holed. Progress seldom exceeded five miles an hour and the perpetual jolting and swaying of the vehicle added to the tedium and discomfort. William's coach set out long before the dawn of the chill December morning and only reached its destination after darkness had closed in, perhaps fourteen hours later.

The town (as distinct from the University) of Cambridge was unimpressive; a visitor some years earlier had found it 'abominably dirty' with 'miry, narrow streets'. Many of the buildings 'were so little and so low, that they looked more like huts for pigmies than houses for men'.[17] But whatever its outward appearance, the town was a vital adjunct to the University; and besides its numerous inns, ale-houses and coffee-houses, it provided the printers, booksellers, stationers, builders and all the other crafts and services upon which every college depended. Most of the provisions were brought in from the surrounding fenland by river barges. It was this water-borne traffic that made possible the most extraordinary event in the Cambridge calendar, the annual Sturbridge Fair, held on the outskirts of the town, where merchants from all over Britain and from many continental countries as well displayed an amazing variety of wares on a site covering some four acres. The goods, on arrival at the port of Kings Lynn, were transferred into barges and completed their journey via the Ouse and the Cam. Booksellers were present in large numbers and set up their stalls in Cooks Row, 'the scholars' chief rendezvous'.[18]

By contrast, the colleges and other university buildings offered many notable examples of fine architecture dating from mediaeval times to the present. Not far from the soaring edifice of King's College Chapel, a brand new building—the Senate House—was, at the moment of William's arrival, in course of construction and it was there that he was later privileged to sit while fulfilling his role as senior medical doctor on the 'caput' or controlling committee. The architect was James Gibbs, designer of St Martin-in-the-Fields, William's parish church when he moved to London. His own college, St John's, had been founded in 1511 by the bounty of Lady Margaret Beaufort, Henry VII's mother. Consisting originally of a single court, it had been gradually extended until by the end of the seventeenth century two more courts had been built and the college had become the largest in the University. But events in the comparatively recent past had left scars that were still remembered. In the Civil War, Cambridge had been a Cromwellian stronghold; churches and chapels had been despoiled, and St John's chapel had lost much of its furniture, its pictures and its organ; even the statue of its patron saint on the gateway had been removed. The accession of William and Mary had brought problems of another kind: all University Fellows were expected to swear allegiance to the House of Orange—a demand that gravely offended the consciences of those who felt that they still owed loyalty to the Stuarts. At St John's no fewer than twenty-eight Fellows refused to take the oath and after many delays

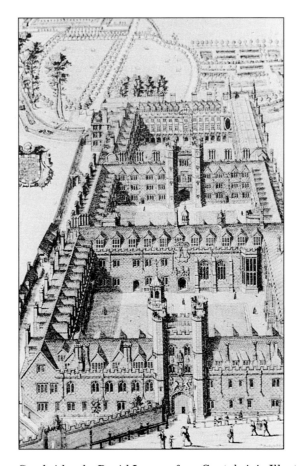

St John's College, Cambridge, by David Loggan from Cantabrigia Illustrata, *1688.*

any 'non-jurors' who were still living in the college were ejected. The sole exception was Thomas Baker, whom we shall meet in the next chapter.

The majority of undergraduates were described as 'pensioners'; they enjoyed no special privileges and simply paid the modest fees required for board, lodging and tuition. Sons of the wealthy and aristocratic might be admitted as 'fellow-commoners'—a status which entitled them to take their meals at the Fellows' table in Hall. The third category, to which William belonged, comprised those who were too poor to pay the normal fees; these 'sizars' performed certain domestic tasks such as waiting in Hall and in return received free accommodation, free or cut-price tuition, plus a small allowance towards the cost of food. Thus it was possible for a sizar to live extremely cheaply—indeed the printer Bowyer, who was at the University earlier in the century, reckoned his expenses at only £20 a year.[19] But William could not have subsisted very long merely on his Exhibition, and we can assume that his mother was able to make some additional contribution towards the cost of basic necessities. Fortunately the College had its own traditional methods of helping hard-pressed students who showed promise of academic success and on 9 November 1725 William was admitted Foundress Scholar 'for the bell' — a description denoting his duty to ring the chapel bell for the daily services. His emoluments included a weekly payment of about 2 shillings for commons, and to this was added a sum estimated at roughly £8 a year, paid out of a fund derived from the sale of corn given to the College by the tenants of its farms in lieu of rent — an interesting sidelight on one of the most important sources of college income.

Whatever academic benefits the students hoped to gain depended largely on the quality of teaching and discipline; but the senior members of the university who were responsible for these matters were all too often ineffective and negligent. The majority of the Fellows were ordained clergymen; they could not marry without forfeiting their Fellowships and their social status was generally greatly inferior to that of their twentieth century counterparts. Advancement depended on patronage and much effort was expended on currying favour with those who held positions of power and influence.

It was an age of heavy eating and drinking, and gluttony was no disgrace. Dr Ogden, a Fellow of St John's (whose sermons were warmly commended by Dr Johnson) remarked that the goose was a silly bird, being too much for one person and not enough for two; and in 1760 the poet Gray reported that Dr Chapman the Master of Magdalene had eaten about a week before his death 'five large mackerel, full of roe, to his own share, but what gave the finishing stroke was a turbot on Trinity Sunday, of which he left very little for the company'.[20]

The instruction of students was frequently neglected: lecturers might hold their appointments without delivering a single lecture; and it was possible for a Professor to know nothing of the subject he was supposed to teach.

Among the student body were many who had no serious intention of taking a degree; riotous behaviour was common and discipline ineffective. In 1716, the Vice-Chancellor and Heads of Houses had been obliged to issue a decree calling attention to 'late divers disorders among several scholars of the university, tumultuously meeting together, provoking and exasperating one another by invidious names, opprobrious words, hissing and shouting one against another, throwing of stones and other great irregularities'.[21]

Incidents like these were comparatively mild, but on more than one occasion the disturbances between 'town and gown' led to serious rioting. Under these conditions, a student who wished to do well needed a conscientious tutor and plenty of self-reliance.

Although William was well below the usual age for admission, many arriving for their first term would have been boys of only sixteen or seventeen. To maintain some measure of order and discipline, it was the custom to allocate each student a room on the same staircase as his tutor. Accommodation was often cramped and the student might find himself sharing a room with one or two chamber-fellows or 'chums'. The tutor was responsible under the statutes for his pupils' general welfare as well as for the direction of their studies. In practice this meant that he was expected to be guide, friend, guardian, treasurer and instructor—a formidable task for even the most versatile academic. He could, and did, delegate some of the teaching to assistants, but he was still obliged to collect the fees due to them; and if a pupil omitted to pay a college bill, the tutor could be held responsible. William's tutor was John Newcome, Doctor of Divinity and future Master of the college, who taught a variety of subjects including philosophy, mathematics, rhetoric and Greek.

The syllabus for William's first major objective, the degree of Bachelor of Arts, demanded three areas of study: classics, divinity and philosophy. Under the first heading at least nine Latin and nine Greek authors had to be read, and these included poets, dramatists, orators and historians. The divinity course included the reading of

John Locke.

sermons in English and (for those who were capable) pursuing biblical studies in Greek and Hebrew. But if these subjects were traditional, the content of the 'philosophy' course had undergone far-reaching changes within living memory. For much of the seventeenth century there was still a reluctance to question the fundamental principles upon which intellectual enquiry was based and although 'reason' was admired, its activity was often quite unrelated to everyday experience. Now, students could read John Locke who, in his *Essay Concerning Human Understanding*, argued that we should distinguish between two different classes of 'knowledge': the first, which includes the revealed truths of religion, is derived from unquestioned *a priori* assumptions; while the second class—the kind of knowledge we need to perform our day-to-day occupations—can only be derived from personal observation and experience. In effect Locke recommended that men should look at the facts and use the intelligence that God had given them to solve their problems. This empirical attitude of mind was shared by Isaac Newton, who had employed it to spectacular effect in his numerous observations and experiments, which demonstrated that the universe moved in accordance with explicable physical laws. His *Opticks* and *Principia Mathematica* were on many of the more serious students' reading lists and in the 'philosophical' section of the syllabus mathematical subjects held a dominant place. The new attitude ushered in the Age of Enlightenment and William lost no time in absorbing its spirit.

Although many of the fellow-commoners and pensioners had no serious intention of taking a degree and were more interested in enjoying themselves, sizars were strongly motivated to take their studies seriously; their aim was to leave poverty behind, to get on in the world, to win status and if possible make a fortune. There were plenty of models to emulate: Isaac Newton had been a sizar, and so too had Richard Bentley, the greatest classical scholar of the century. With men such as these to inspire him, the sizar could willingly accept his temporary status as 'charity boy' for the possibility of a golden future.

Much of William's daily routine consisted of attendance at lectures, doing exercises for his tutors and reading the set books. There were no organised games and few facilities for entertainment; as William was by nature sociable, much of his leisure would have been spent in the company of friends, exploring the countryside or visiting each other's rooms for argument and discussion.

Although the syllabus reflected the influence of new ideas, the mode and conduct of examinations had hardly changed since the far-off days when the mediaeval schoolmen held their disputations. They were entirely oral and were conducted in Latin. The most important element took the form of a series of debates in which a candidate had to participate twice as the proposer of a motion and twice as the opponent. These requirements, called respectively 'acts' and 'opponencies' were controlled by senior Fellows known as Moderators. A fortnight prior to an 'act' the proposer or 'respondent' had to submit three propositions, at least one of them on a mathematical subject, and when the fateful day arrived, he was expected to defend them against three opponents, nominated and forewarned by the Moderator. The arguments in this verbal combat had to be advanced in syllogistic form according to the rules of logic.[22]

The exercises were not the only test the undergraduate had to face; there was also the 'accustomed examination' ordained in the Elizabethan statutes. This was a straightforward oral test in question and answer form, conducted as usual in Latin; but because the test was considered less important than the exercises, the questioning was often perfunctory.

However bizarre these routines seem to us today, there were plenty of enlightened men at the time who had no doubts about their value, mainly on the grounds that they encouraged a most beneficial contest of mental acuteness. But even many of their supporters admitted that their usefulness would have been increased if they had been conducted in English. William took his BA in 1728. The names of the successful candidates were listed in the *Grace Book*[23] (which contained the official record of the Senate's decisions); the total number, a mere twenty-seven, casts an interesting light on the size of the student population. Annual admissions in the 1720s hardly exceeded 170, and if we make allowance for the proportion of men who left without taking any degree, the brevity of the BA list is understandable. William's name is seventeenth on the list; the order however was not according to merit but to seniority—an arrangement that could cause no offence to the titled or privileged.

His next target was the senior degree of Master of Arts, which required as much or as little effort as the candidate was prepared to make. Nominally he had to perform further acts and opponencies, but these could be evaded by payment of a fine. A BA however had to wait a minimum of four years, and although William took his MA as soon as this period had expired, a significant event had occurred in the interval: on 6 April 1731 he was elected to a St John's Fellowship and from that time began to study medicine.[24]

It is impossible to say how long the idea of a medical career had been maturing in William's mind—or indeed why a career in the Church (of which he was a devout member) failed to attract him. He may well have felt that many of the clerics in the University provided a poor advertisement for the 'sacred profession' and that their total dependance on patronage was demeaning. If his decision was influenced by any single individual, the obvious candidate is his elder brother Thomas, who had proved himself the very pattern of the Industrious Apprentice. His master, Lancelot Copplestone had twelve children; the tenth, named Hackell after her mother, attracted Thomas's eye and after completing his apprenticeship, he married her and qualified as a Liveryman of the Guild of Barber-Surgeons.[25] Although Surgery was regarded as a craft rather than a profession and was thus lower in status than Physic, Thomas, after several years' experience of treating wounds and injuries, was well placed to appreciate the contribution that his more talented brother could make to the treatment of diseases; and as Hackell had died childless in the year that William gained his Fellowship, one can imagine Thomas hoping that his brother might one day have the skill and knowledge to reduce the toll of such bereavements.

By his election to Fellowship William became a full member of a self-governing society, with all the privileges and responsibilities this entailed. He received a stipend of roughly £41 a year, derived (like his earlier scholarship) from agricultural rents and leases. He had a suite of rooms with separate accommodation for the young students under his supervision; he dined with his colleagues at the High Table and discussed college affairs with them in the spectacular senior combination (or common) room—a long pannelled gallery in the second court dating from 1602. Whenever a Master of the college died or for some other reason relinquished his office, it was the Fellows who elected his successor, and when a vacancy arose in 1736, William did some active and successful lobbying on behalf of his former tutor Dr Newcome.[26] The outcome was of some significance politically as Newcome was a Whig and the college had previously been regarded as the home of Anglican Toryism.

William could not have held his fellowship indefinitely without taking Holy Orders. Happily this problem was overcome in July 1734 by his election to a medical fellowship, the tenure of which made ordination unnecessary. In the same year he was appointed Linacre Lecturer in Physic.[27] The lectureship was the oldest medical endowment in the University, but the founder's original intentions were no longer observed and the appointment provided William with a welcome supplement to his income, without requiring him to undertake any duties.

Although we have little direct information about the course of William's medical training, it clearly depended very largely on his own initiative. The medical faculty was small and generally despised; most serious students, if they had some cash to spare, could find better training elsewhere—for example at Leyden, where the illustrious Boerhaave taught, or at Edinburgh where his influence was being transmitted by his former pupils. But if William could not afford (and perhaps had no wish) to travel, he could still obtain his theoretical knowledge through books and his practical training by making the right personal contacts. The latter inevitably included Christopher Green, the Regius Professor of Physic; others were Russell Plumptree, who later succeeded him, and Edmund Waller, a Fellow of St John's who had obtained his MD twenty years earlier. It was probably in the company of one of these men that William visited his first patients.

Two other men were available to give William tuition in their special subjects; the first was the Professor of Chemistry John Mickleborough who managed to combine this office with his business as an apothecary. Such simple chemical reactions as were useful in medicine often required a furnace and the Professor's laboratory was equipped with a convenient model introduced some years earlier by his predecessor Vigani. In his role as apothecary Mickleborough would have shown William his stock of drugs and other materials and demonstrated how they were processed and combined to make up the physicians' prescriptions.

Of equal importance to William was John Morgan, Professor of Anatomy—a subject which posed peculiar problems: the emotional and religious objections to the dissection of human corpses were widespread and deep-seated. For centuries the Church had forbidden the practice and when Henry VIII permitted the Guild of Barber-Surgeons to 'anatomise', the bodies on which they could operate were limited strictly to those of executed felons. The numbers too were limited—originally to four a year, later increased to six.[28] A similar licence had in due course been granted to the University of Cambridge, but in view of the paucity of medical students, the number of bodies permitted must have been very small. This was a serious drawback for the keen anatomy student and the demand for extra bodies gave rise to the activities of the 'resurrectionists'. Occasionally (as we shall see below) a student might find and 'take up' the body of a vagrant, without attracting any awkward questions.

In his *Introduction to the Study of Physic* William lists the many branches of knowledge that a medical student should pursue and leaves us in no doubt that he had pursued them all himself; but as he left no record of his day-to-day activities, we must rely on the diaries of another medical student, William Stukeley,[29] to provide a plausible picture. Stukeley came up to Bene't College (as Corpus Christi was then known) in 1703 at the age of sixteen, and when he had turned his mind 'particularly to the study of physic' he began 'a diligent and near inquisition into Anatomy & Botany', searching the countryside for plants and fossils, and dissecting frogs, dogs and cats. Soon he contracted acquaintance 'with all the lads in the University that studyd Physic'. There were nine of them and 'we used to have sett meetings at our chambers to confer about our studys, try Chymical experiments, cut up Dogs, Cats & the like . . . We took up old Hoyes that hangd himself & was buryd in the highway, & dissected him, & afterwards made a sceleton of his bones, & put them into a fine Glass case with an inscription in Latin . . . We saw too, many Philosophical Experiments in Pneumatic Hydrostatic Engines . . . & some Chymical Experiments with

Mr Stephen Hales . . .'[30] Stukeley's tutor encouraged him by giving him a room in College where he could carry out his dissections and experiments; it 'had a very strange appearance with my Furniture in it, the wall was generally hung round with Guts, stomachs, bladders, preparations of parts & drawings'. He also visited 'the Apothecarys shop to make myself perfect in the knowledge of Drugs & Official Compositions & exercised a little Gratis Practise among the poor people that depended upon the College, & such lads as would trust themselves to my Care'.

There is ample evidence from William's works that he too botanised, dissected and experimented but there is no record of his having enjoyed Stukeley's advantage of working in a group with other medical students.

Later in his life William stated that his training was received partly in Cambridge and partly 'at a hospital in London'.[31] Although we cannot identify the hospital with absolute certainty, there are good reasons for supposing that it was St Thomas's in Southwark. In the early years of the century many Cambridge medical students trained there under the celebrated Richard Mead and the close link between hospital and university was maintained for many years after his death. In the 1730s, one of the eminent Physicians teaching at St Thomas's was Sir Edward Wilmot (1693-1787), a former Fellow of St John's and Physician in Ordinary to the King. As he knew William during his Cambridge days and thought well enough of him to recommend him to settle in London, it would not be surprising if William was one of his hospital pupils. It is perhaps significant that in the *Commentaries*, St Thomas's is the only hospital to be mentioned by name.

One of the requirements of the University statutes was that a Doctor of Medicine must be 'of seven years' standing from the degree of MA'—in other words, as William had obtained his MA in 1732, he could not claim his Doctorate until 1739. By 1737 however he felt confident that he had learned enough to begin practising and took the unusual step of writing a formal letter in Latin to the Senate,[32] pleading that the five years of medical studies that he had completed since obtaining his MA 'may suffice for him to practise in that same faculty provided that his erudition is first examined and approved by the Regius Professor of Medicine, Dr Green, and that he be presented by the aforesaid Professor to the Vice-Chancellor in the Senate.' William's plea was read, accepted and signed on 27 April 1737, and in the summer of the following year, Green examined and approved him.[33] There is no record of William's presentation to the Vice-Chancellor, but we may assume that all the formalities which usually attended the conferment of a Doctorate were completed within a few days of the examination. In the College's *Buttery Books* his name appears as Dr Heberden from the first week of August 1738.

Chapter 2

Building a Reputation

Having achieved his coveted Doctorate, William might have been tempted to leave the University and set up a practice elsewhere. But the arguments against such a venture were overwhelming; quite apart from his lack of capital and practical experience, his living expenses at St John's were minimal, he was surrounded by friends and if his patients at first were few, he could confidently expect their numbers to increase as his reputation grew. Meanwhile the University offered him ample opportunities for exercising his talents as teacher and lecturer and provided a stable and congenial base where he could accumulate experience and widen his contacts.

During the seven years that had elapsed since his election to Fellowship, William had come to know many of the men in other colleges—both the birds of passage and the more permanent figures who occupied positions similar to his; dining in each other's halls was a common event and there were parties from time to time to celebrate a success or an appointment. His favourite relaxation was conversation—the cheapest and most fascinating of diversions—in the company of his friends; and it was his gift for making and keeping friends that was a crucial factor in the development of his career. Some of them make their first appearance in a coffee-house.

Since the turn of the century coffee-houses had gradually established themselves as favoured rendezvous outside College precincts for the exchange of news and ideas. They were quieter than taverns, were usually supplied with newspapers and provided a pleasant and relaxed atmosphere in which friends could discuss their common interests.

William was a member of a group who met for literary discussions and corresponded with a similar group of friends in London. The leader—or secretary—of the Cambridge circle was Daniel Wray, who was to remain one of William's closest friends for the next forty-five years. He had gone to school at Charterhouse (a stone's throw from his home), then to Queens' College, where he took his degrees and lived, apart from a prolonged visit to Italy, until about 1740. Although an asthmatic, he was an active member of the Royal Society and later became a trustee of the British Museum.

The group included two men of an older generation: the first was Thomas Baker the 'non-juror' who had written a history of St John's and was held in such respect that he had been allowed to retain his rooms in college. The second was the unorthodox cleric, the Revd Conyers Middleton, Fellow of Trinity. His character was flawed by a tendency to indulge in futile quarrels and one of these (with the Master of Trinity, Richard Bentley) led to an expensive libel action which he lost. Fortunately his friends persuaded the Senate to create a new post for him with the formidable title of Protobibliothecarius (chief librarian of the University Library) at a salary of £50 per annum. The most successful of his literary works was *A Life of Cicero*, published in 1741, which brought him enough money to buy a small estate at Hildersham near Cambridge, where he spent his summer vacations.

The name of the Cambridge coffee-house is not recorded, but the London circle met at Rauthmell's in Henrietta Street, Covent Garden. The secretary there was the prolific, if somewhat uninspired, historian Thomas Birch, a young man of thirty-three who had been brought up as a Quaker. However, he soon decided (for whatever reasons) to join the Established Church and after being baptised in 1730 was almost immediately ordained. He was fortunate in having as his patron the influential Earl of Hardwicke, who secured for him a succession of ecclesiastic preferments; these entailed very little work and enabled Birch to pursue his many literary interests. He was a keen collector of letters and in one of these Wray, writing to him on 5 October 1738, playfully compares their respective 'congregations' and mentions William for the first time:[1]

> We have, you must know, a kind of conventicle here, a faint imitation of the Established Church in Henrietta Street. To give you some idea of its proportion, I reckon myself to fill the same place in one, that you fill in the other . . . Mr Baker, Dr Middleton and Dr Heberden are much obliged to you for their respective paragraphs in your letter; and our whole coffee-house was no less entertained with your literary advices, which I communicated.

William had several other literary friends besides those who were members of the 'conventicle'. One of them, Zachary Gray, sought his help in the production of a new edition of Samuel Butler's *Hudibras*. The poem, originally published during the early years of the Restoration, had already gone through several editions and its popularity was still assured. Packed with erudite allusions, many of them to the Greek and Latin classics, the work required copious explanatory notes to satisfy a new generation of readers. When the new edition appeared in 1744, the editor duly acknowledged William's 'large annotations'.

None of the men we have so far mentioned ever attempted to write a considered account of William's life and we must turn to the work of another friend—the Revd William Cole—for more first-hand information. Cole (1714-1782) had been admitted to Clare College in 1733, but two years later migrated to Kings, where he lived, apart from periods of travel, for the next sixteen years. During this time he began collecting material for a series of biographical sketches of members of the University entitled *Athenae Cantabrigienses*, an uncompleted project that occupied him for much of his life. He was no respecter of persons, and as he was aware that much of what he had written would cause offence, the ultimate disposal of his unpublished papers caused him some perplexity. 'To give them to King's College', he wrote, 'would be to throw them into a horsepond.' In the end, he decided to bequeath them to the British Museum, on condition that they should not be opened until twenty years after his death. His observations on William—sometimes critical or ironic—provide us with valuable insights into his subject's character and activities.[2] He describes him as 'a tall, thin, spare man' with 'a most clear and healthy countenance', and was often in his company:

> He [William] and I constantly almost spent our evenings at poor Dr Middleton's, where, if ever we staid to supper, was never anything besides a tart and bread and cheese, both Dr Heberden and Dr Middleton being persons of the greatest abstemiousness I ever met with, rarely drinking more than one glass of wine.

The enjoyment of meals in congenial company was in fact an important part of William's lifestyle and judged by present-day standards, his intake of food and drink was probably quite normal. In his own day, however, meals were often mountainous and the flow of wine was measured by the bottle rather than the glass.

Another visitor to Middleton's house was the poet Thomas Gray, whose friendship with William may have originated there. Gray had come up to Peterhouse from Eton in 1734, but left after four years without taking a degree. After returning from the Grand Tour as the companion of Horace Walpole, he resumed residence at Peterhouse as a fellow-commoner in 1742. He mentions William for the first time in a letter to his physician friend Wharton dated March 1747 in which he refers to a party given by Dr Chapman (of the robust appetite) soon after his election as Master of Magdalene. Gray was one of 'a very brillant (sic) Assembly' including William, Middleton and several others.[3]

Perhaps Walpole should be classed among William's acquaintances rather than his friends; what is certain is that he too came under the influence of Middleton and after the latter's death composed, with William's co-operation, a collection of 'Anecdotes' concerning him. In character and physique Horace Walpole was the opposite of his robust father Sir Robert and wisely decided that instead of attempting to be an active man of affairs, he would be a spectator and chronicler of events. The results of this decision can be seen in his memoirs of the times and in his voluminous correspondence (much of it carefully composed with a view to later publication), where William is mentioned on several occasions.

In or about 1739 the energetic Dr Birch had hatched a project which was to have a significant effect on William's future. His patron Lord Hardwicke had two sons, Philip and Charles Yorke, who were now both at Cambridge. In spite of their youth, they were already competent scholars, and Birch no doubt felt that if he could help them to achieve a reputation in the world of literature, he might hope to gain further advancement through the family's patronage. He therefore proposed that they should produce a work of historical fiction in the form of a series of letters supposedly translated from documents (conveniently discovered in a library) written during the war between Athens and Sparta in the fifth century BC; the epistolary form would enable the brothers to share the labour with any of their friends who had the necessary talent and imagination. The idea was taken up with enthusiasm and the work was entitled *The Athenian Letters: or the epistolary correspondence of an Agent of the King of Persia residing at Athens during the Peloponnesian War*. Although the brothers wrote most of the letters themselves, there were ten other contributors, among them Birch (who also edited the completed work), Daniel Wray and William. The other seven were not, as we might have expected all men; the exception was Mrs Catherine Talbot, born in 1717, fluent in Latin, Greek and Hebrew and in the process of mastering several modern languages as well. She had already published a volume of poems and was a member of the Blue Stocking Circle, the group of well-educated ladies who held evening receptions entirely devoted to conversation.

For William's contribution, history had conveniently provided a perfect theme: Hippocrates had been alive at the relevant time and William accordingly settled down to write 'Cleander to Alexias on Hippocrates and the State of Physic in Greece.' But the fictional Cleander, while giving proper weight to the many achievements of the revered Father of Medicine, found much to criticise; he begins his letter with an account of Hippocrates' background on the island of Cos and his efforts to discover everything he could about illnesses and their cures; he then continues:

> It is hard to say whether he has most advanced the knowledge or the usefulness of physick, by introducing a practice, which was not common before his time, of constantly visiting the sick in their beds; by which careful attendance to the whole course of the distemper, he has not only been able to give a timely assistance against every inconvenient or dangerous accident, but is become superior to all other physicians in the knowledge of diseases, and in foretelling their events. From this practice he has got the name of a Clinic physician.
>
> From the philosophers he not only learned the reasons and foundations of his practice, but was also enabled to write with method and elegance; which has justly gained him the reputation

of being the first who collected the scattered precepts of physick into an art, and delivered them in a clear and elegant manner . . ..

Now come the criticisms; the writer points out that the art of physic is still in its infancy and that

> . . . this great man has only begun what cannot be perfected without the accurate observation of many ages. In particular, he is not master of a sufficient number of simples for all the various purposes of physick, and does not perhaps fully understand the true uses and qualities of those he has; for too much stress seems to be laid on some ineffectual ones, while others, more violent in their effects, are used with too little caution. The study of anatomy is still less advanced; all that is known of it is derived, either comparatively from the animals that are sacrificed, or from the Aegyptian embalmers of human bodies; and I much doubt, whether Hippocrates ever saw a human body dissected . . .
>
> He knows nothing of the causes and hidden nature of distempers, and in other matters he has been too hasty in forming his axioms, and in reducing to a certain rule things depending on too many circumstances to be fixed by the observations of one man, if not too uncertain to be ever fixed at all.
>
> Indeed I could not help thinking myself, that the common stories which are told of him are very idle; and that there is nothing so miraculous in this great physician . . .
>
> As to morality, his reputation is very high: he is superior to a love of money, and freely communicates his art for the relief of the necessitous and strangers. The oath which he enjoins his followers . . . forbids them to procure abortions, to administer poison, to make any ill use of the free access they have to houses, or betray the confidence reposed in them . . .
>
> Yet on one occasion he procured an abortion for a dancing-girl 'though in direct contradiction to his oath' . . .

William's approach to his chosen subject is of special interest as it contains the earliest expression of the view which he affirmed throughout his life—that even the most revered physicians of the past were subject to the limitations of the times in which they lived, as well as to their own human frailties; and that the 'modern' physician can never evade his individual responsibilities merely by referring to some ancient authority.

There were some two hundred letters in the collection; when they appeared in 1741, they were printed for private circulation in an edition limited to ten copies—fewer even than the number of contributors. But the *Letters* were not forgotten and later editions were published towards the end of the century.[4] No doubt William could have composed more letters; but no other theme could have been as relevant to his professional concerns; in any case, his single contribution was enough to give him the entrée into the Yorkes' circle and to establish a friendship with both the brothers that lasted throughout their lives.

The long-term effect on William's career of this introduction is impossible to assess; what is certain is that it brought him within the orbit of two men of great power and influence. The Yorkes' father, the 1st Earl of Hardwicke had had a meteoric career in the Law, becoming Lord Chancellor at the age of forty-six. Among his confidants was the Duke of Newcastle, who became High Steward of Cambridge University in 1737 and later Chancellor. He exercised enormous powers of patronage and was largely responsible for the practice of granting degrees by royal mandate to fellow-commoners who were unable or unwilling to acquire them by examination.

Hardwicke's sons had both been admitted to Corpus Christi College. Philip was in due course appointed Teller of the Exchequer and employed Wray as his deputy. On his father's death he succeeded to the title. His younger brother Charles became Attorney-General and looked forward to becoming Lord Chancellor, like his father, but he died the day after receiving the appointment.

At some time during the years of preparation for his MD William became aware that his wide reading of medical literature, both ancient and recent, could provide him with ample material for a course of lectures. If he could carry through such a project successfully, it would establish his own reputation, reflect credit on the Medical Faculty and at the same time earn him some extra income.

The aspect of his studies that William selected was Materia Medica—the almost inexhaustible range of substances which had, at one time or another, been credited with the power to heal or avert sickness or injury. Even though the use of many of these substances had long been discredited, they could still form an instructive and often entertaining element in an historical survey. There was another important consideration: no Cambridge lecturer had dealt adequately with the subject before—at least not for many years—and William had the field to himself.

Having organised his formidable mass of notes into no less than twenty-six lectures, William delivered his opening discourse on Wednesday 9 April 1740, thus inaugurating the first of a series that was to be repeated each year until he left Cambridge in the autumn of 1748. He publicised the course with printed handbills setting out the subjects to be covered in each lecture, and four of his own annotated copies are preserved in his college library. After an introductory account of the 'rise and progress of the Materia Medica', the course fell under four main headings: the first 'Of Fossils' dealt with such substances as waters, earths, sulphurs, bitumens, metals and stones. In the next nine lectures 'Of Vegetables' William

The Order of a Courſe of LECTURES on the
MATERIA MEDICA.

3: 1745
May 18

Lect. I. INTRODUCTORY Lecture, giving a general account of the Riſe and Progreſs of the Materia Medica.

OF FOSSILS.

II. Of Waters.
III. Of Earths.
IV. Of Sulphurs, Foſſil Oyls, Bitumens and Ambar.
V. Of Sea-Salt, Alum, Nitre, Borax and Vitriol; Of the Ores of Metals and, Of Semimetals.
VII Of Quickſilver, and the perfect Metals.
VIII Of Stones.

OF VEGETABLES.

VIII. Of the Aromatic Flowers, Seeds, Barks, Woods and Roots.
IX. Of the Acrid Fruits, Seeds and Roots.
X. Of the Aſtringent Flowers, Fruits, Seeds, Barks, Woods and Roots.
XI. Of the Peruvian Bark; and the Emollient Fruits, Seeds and Roots.
XII. A general account of the uſe of Purging Medicines; Of the Purging Herbs, Leaves, Flowers, Fruits, Seeds, Barks, Woods and Roots.
XIII. A general account of the uſe of Emetics; Of the Emetic Herbs, Seeds, Barks and Roots: Of Diuretics.
XIV. Of Opium and Narcotics.
XV. Of Vulneraries &c.
XVI. Of Gums, Balſams, Turpentines and Reſins.

OF ANIMALS.

XVII. Of Inſects, Fiſhes and Birds.
XVIII. Of the Serpent-kind, Quadrupeds and Man.

OF CHEMICALS.

XIX. Introductory Lecture explaining the Terms.
XX. Of the ſimple and compound Waters, Eſſential and Fixed Salts, Soaps, Cauſtic Stones, Expreſſed and Eſſential Oyls.
XXI. Of the Preparations of Turpentine; Of Spirit of Wine, Spirituous Waters of Vegetables, Vinegar, Tartar and its Preparations, Tinctures and Chemical Reſins.
XXII. Of Ammoniac Salt, Spirit of Ammoniac Salt and Hart's Horn, Salt of Hart's Horn, Spiritus Volatilis Oleoſus, Animal Oyl and Phoſphorus.
XXIII. Of Spirits of Sea-Salt, Nitre and Vitriol; Of the Preparations of Ambar, Sulphur, Steel, Lead, Tin, Silver and Copper.
XXIV. Of the Mercurial and Antimonial Preparations.
XXV. General Rules for Preſcribing.
XXVI. Of the Antidotes proper to all the known Poiſons.

In this Courſe a Specimen of each Particular will be ſhewn, and every Thing is intended to be mentioned that is uſeful or curious regarding its Natural Hiſtory, Introduction into the Materia Medica, Adulterations, Preparations, Virtues, Doſe and the Cautions neceſſary to be obſerved in its uſe.

Theſe Lectures will begin on   at 2 o'Clock in the Afternoon, in the Anatomy-Schools; and will be read every Day,

By W. HEBERDEN, M.D.

The Firſt Courſe is Two Guineas; the Second One Guinea; ever after, Gratis.

Thoſe Gentlemen, who intend to go, are deſir'd to ſend in their Names.

Handbill of the lectures on Materia Medica, with Heberden's annotations, (St John's College).

described the properties of flowers, fruits, leaves, seeds, barks, woods and roots, grouping them according to their qualities—e.g. astringent, aromatic or emollient. The section 'Of Animals' comprises only two lectures, one on 'Insects, Fishes and Birds', the other 'Of the Serpent-kind, Quadrupeds and Man'. The final heading 'Of Chemicals' begins with an introduction explaining the terms; and the next five lectures deal with such topics as salts, soaps, caustic stones, spirits of sea-salt, nitre and vitriol and with preparations of turpentine, antimony, mercury and other metals. The penultimate lecture gives general rules for prescribing and the course ends with an account 'Of the antidotes proper to all known poisons.'

Beneath this summary the handbills announced that:

> In this Course a Specimen of each Particular will be shewn, and every Thing is intended to be mentioned that is useful or curious regarding its Natural History, Introduction into the Materia Medica, Adulterations, Preparations, Virtues, Dose and the Cautions necessary to be observed in its use.
>
> The First Course is Two Guineas; the Second One Guinea; ever after, Gratis. Those Gentlemen, who intend to go, are desir'd to send in their Names. These Lectures will begin at 2 o'clock in the afternoon, in the Anatomy-Schools; and will be read every Day.

As regular attendance for several weeks would have been difficult for even the keenest student, William's concessionary fee made good sense; but to take up his offer of free re-entry would have required the patience to wait for two years! The audience was not restricted to students of Physic and the Revd William Cole was among those who attended.

The construction of the course reflects the special importance attached at the time to certain procedures and substances; thus purges, emetics and pain-relievers (opium and narcotics) each occupy a complete lecture, and so too do vulneraries, which promoted the healing of wounds. A substance of outstanding importance was Peruvian Bark, to which by 1745 William was devoting a full two-hour discourse. 'The Bark' was the source of quinine and was used extensively in the control of fevers; it came from the South American cinchona tree and had originally been called 'Jesuits' Bark' in honour of the missionaries who had introduced it into Europe in the seventeenth century; but in Protestant England this was considered an offensive title for a substance with such power for good, and the name was abandoned.

As the years went by, William gradually increased the number of lectures from 26 to 31, so as to allow for the inclusion of new material. Each lecture was carefully timed; the normal length was one and a half hours; three lasted for two hours and at the end of the final lecture for 1747 William noted '2h¼ & went on heavily'.

There was one external event in the calendar with which no lecturer could hope to compete and William identifies it on his 1747 programme: 'Left off a week between the 10th and 11th lecture for Newmarket Races.' The racecourse, only thirteen miles away, was a compelling attraction and it would be interesting to know whether William himself attended the meetings. It seems very unlikely; his recorded amusements or diversions were all intellectual and although (like Stukeley before him) he would have explored the countryside to increase his understanding of nature, it is harder to imagine him enjoying a passive role at a spectator-sport.

William had gathered his information from many sources, though a proportion of it had already been collected together by authors whose works—such as Dale's *Pharmacologia* and Geoffroy's *De Materia Medica*—he recommended to his students. He may also have been influenced by a course of lectures delivered on the same subject in Oxford some fifteen years earlier by a certain John Pointer, who exhibited 'a specimen of each particular' to his audience.[5]

William never published the text of his lectures, but at least one copy survived for a century after their delivery, and Dr Thomas Pettigrew who wrote a memoir of William in 1839[6] possessed a copy of them 'twenty-nine in number'. He made no effort however to describe the content of the course and the few extracts he quotes seem to be selected as much for their entertainment value as for any useful information contained in them; two of them are as follows:

ANTIMONY. Dioscorides mentions that it had a vogue in physic, but it was not of long date, because it is very dangerous . . . Among the ancients Antimony was used to dye the Supercilia, or eyebrows, black; and accordingly we read in Scripture that the wicked Queen Jezebel, in order to charm the King, her husband, painted her eyes, (by which I suppose is only meant the eye-brows,) with Antimony, and the women who used that practice were also reproved by the Prophets . . . It acquired the name of antimony in the opinion of some from [a monk named] Valentine who, in his search after the Philosopher's stone, was wont to make much use of it for the more ready fluxing his metals; and throwing a parcel of it to some swine, he observed that they were violently purged by it after they had eaten it, but afterwards grew the fatter upon it, which made him harbour the opinion that the same sort of cathartick exhibited to those of his own fraternity, might do them much service; but his experiment succeeded so ill, that every one who took of it died. This therefore was the reason it was called Antimony, as being destructive to the Monks.

CINNAMON is the inner bark of a tree, which comes from the remotest part of the East Indies. That which the ancients had, is very probably the same; but it was so very rare with them that they thought it a present fit for princes. We read that Cleopatra burnt it with her greatest rarities, that Augustus might not get it. Though the bark of cinnamon is so excellent a spice, yet the wood of the tree has neither taste, smell or virtue in the least degree. Cinnamon is not only aromatic, but also an excellent astringent.

Fortunately our knowledge of the lectures is not confined to Pettigrew's quotations. William kept his bound volumes of notes in his library and eventually handed them on to his physician son. All but one of these volumes were later lost or destroyed; but the one that has survived[7]—with most of the later pages torn out—still contains the whole of the Introductory lecture. William begins:

The Materia Medica is generally understood to signify all those natural substances which are either used themselves for the recovery of health, or from which any medicinal preparations are made. This Collection was undoubtedly begun by the first man, whom accident alone must have acquainted with the changes that many Drugs are able to effect in the human body & their uses. We must suppose that all knowledge of this kind was very rude & imperfect in the first ages of the world, consisting only of a few family medicines handed down from Father to son. As soon as men had formed themselves into Societies & had invented Letters & Architecture, these private observations being all brought into their temples & there registered were soon enlarged into a considerable science which had its Professors in the earliest times ... If Mankind had continued faithfully to deliver their observations to Posterity, Physic would have been advanced by this time much nearer to Perfection: but covetousness & Ambition soon prevailed on those who had the keeping of these Registers ... to lock them up declaring they were Mysteries, which were to be inspected by none but themselves, in order to gain Riches & Influence over the rest of Mankind, by the superior knowledge which these records gave them of the effects of natural causes. Thus was this useful knowledge in a great measure at a stand ...

After referring briefly to Hippocrates and Galen, William describes some of the important contributions made by the Arabs, who introduced spices such as cloves and nutmeg and demonstrated how sugar could be used 'for preserving the virtues of herbs in syrups and conserves'. An equally significant development was their application of chemistry to medicinal purposes.

In a digression on the origins of chemistry, William suggests that its appearance was hastened 'by a boundless desire after gold', which led to the delusive belief in a chemical preparation called the Philosopher's Stone. At a later date, this delusion was expanded to include the notion of 'an universal medicine' or 'Catholic remedy'—

he Materia Medica is generally understood to sy
ll those natural substances which are either us'd
es for the recovery of health, or from which any
al preparations are made. This Collection was un
y begun by the first Man, whom accident alone mus
uainted with the changes that many Drugs are able
in the human body & their uses. We must suppose
knowledge of this kind was very rude & imperfect
first ages of the world consisting only of a few
medicines handed down from Father to Son. As soon
had form'd themselves into Societies & had invented
architecture, these private observations being all
into their Temples & these register'd were soon
into a considerable science which had its Professo
earliest times, [for such were those who in Scrip
e said to have embalm'd Joseph's Bodys. These
sort of Physicians, whose art of embalming then
fell in the virtues of aromatic Drugs as can
be equall'd at this day.] If Mankind had con
faithfully to deliver their observations to Poste
ysic would have been advanc'd by this time muc
to Perfection: But Covetousness & Ambition soo
'd on those who had the keeping of these Register
particularly did with the books of Hermes Tris
in Egypt, to lock them up, declaring they
ysteries, which were to be inspected by none but
lves: in order to gain Riches & an Influence
e rest of Mankind, by the superior knowledge
hese Records gave them, of the effects of natural

First page of the introductory lecture on Materia Medica, (Francis A Countway Library of Medicine, Boston, Massachusetts).

another 'absurd fiction' which gives William an excuse for launching into a highly coloured and entertaining account of the sixteenth century German physician and alchemist Bombastus von Hohenheim, who styled himself Paracelsus:

> Paracelsus . . . was a bold, vain, illiterate enthusiast; yet as it was the fate of chemistry to be promoted by Absurdities, this unpromising character greatly contributed to its present perfection: for his enthusiasm & vanity incited him to make several processes, which had been untry'd before, & he was bold enough to apply them at random to his patients . . .

The Lues Venerea (syphilis) was raging at the time and as the Physicians were unable to treat it, 'every patient was sure to dye in the most miserable and loathsome condition. This was a happy juncture for Quacks' and patients came to Paracelsus 'who was such a notoriously illiterate drunkard, that at any other time few would have ventured to trust him'. Luckily for him he was able to bring off some remarkable cures by using preparations of mercury (with which all alchemists were familiar) and these preparations 'as is now well known, are peculiar antidotes to almost all the external & internal symptoms of the Lues'.

> By this he got great reputation & riches and so was enabled to pursue his chemical labours and to continue making his experiments upon mankind; many of whom we may suppose he kill'd & many he had the good luck to cure . . .

William next considers how the virtues of medicinal drugs have been discovered and how far they can be depended upon. After dismissing amulets as irrational, he warns his audience against all those simples whose credit depends on signatures:

> . . . for some have taken it into their heads to imagin that Nature has been so kind as to point out the virtues of drugs by certain signs impress'd upon them, as that yellow things are useful in a jaundice, scarlet in an inflammation; and a stone containing another stone & as it were big with it, will promote the birth of a child; with many other such trifles, which all depend upon the groundless supposition that Nature design'd these external marks of things for the characters of their virtues. Lastly we must absolutely reject the notion of similar parts, by which some have been betray'd into a belief that the sound or diseased parts of an animal have some secret correspondence & sympathy with the like parts in another: hence the stone of the bladder & worms of the intestines have been recommended as efficacious in curing or preventing these diseases.

To the question what 'cautions' should be used with regard to these medicines that have some foundation in Nature, William's answer is that:

> . . . the first of these is Experience, with which Mankind, as we have seen, set out, but soon grew weary of this tedious but safest method of finding the true effect of medicines. Tho' this may justly be called the most unerring guide, yet even this may prove an useless or dangerous one unless followed with caution. Experience is either that of our own, or what we receive from the testimony of others. In original experience many have been misled by coming to a conclusion before they had a sufficient number of tryals to ground it upon. Almost every one thinks himself able to pronounce what was the cause of a disease, & to what the recovery was owing. But those who are aware of the difficulties of coming at truth in this matter will agree that it may be very false reasoning to conclude that such a medicine cured a man because he took it & recovered. It is not therefore a single fact, but facts repeated in a variety of circumstances that can establish the just reputation of a remedy . . .
>
> If we are thus liable to be misguided by original experience, much more are we so by traditional; for first, the original experimenter might be mistaken; 2dly, the constitution of Human Bodies has been found to be very different in different ages and nations; and lastly the names of druggs alter or are misunderstood & defeat the experience of former times . . .

It is deplorable that the scripts of William's other lectures have been lost, but the above extracts give us some idea of the probable quality of the whole series. Although he succeeds in making his discourses entertaining as well as instructive, humour is always subordinated to the serious purpose of conveying information and drawing thoughtful conclusions, as in his observations on Experience. As to the doctrine of 'signatures' and the 'notion of similar parts', these are mentioned not merely as historical curiosities, but as harmful superstitions that still lingered on and therefore had to be exposed.

The specimens used by William to illustrate his lectures may still be seen housed in a large cabinet which he later presented to the college. They are all catalogued under appropriate headings, most of them in Latin, with occasional comments in English.[8] Although William never ventured overseas, his specimens came from many different countries: Lignum Agallochum (a soft resinous wood) was 'given by P Burrel Esq, whose relation brt it as a great variety from China, where it is used as incense'; from China too came ginseng and from the Americas a variety of nuts and seeds besides a sample of the renowned Peruvian Bark. In drawer 18 there is some 'Sulphur ex Vesuvio'—a title which William believes to be mistaken. 'By what right', he says in a Latin note, 'it is called Sulphur, I don't know; it doesn't smell like sulphur; it doesn't ignite from fire or liquefy; I tested it 10 Feb 1742/3'.

The catalogue also tells us some of the places where William collected items himself—several of them in Yorkshire, where he spent some summer vacations:[9] alumina—ore from Whitby, 1742; some transparent rock crystals called Bristol Stones, 'gathered at Leppington'—a hamlet some twelve miles north-west of York; petrified moss and twigs from Knaresborough, and an unidentified substance 'found plentifully near the stinking well at Harrogate'. Nearer home he collected specimens of ivy 'from an old tree near the Abbey of Bury St Edmunds', and Cambridge provided a 'chalky substance from the water of Trinity College'.

Since the day when the 14-year-old William made his first uncomfortable coach trip to Cambridge, there had been some marginal improvement in the state of the roads; so long as he was a student, he would have been unable to afford any long journeys, apart from his trips to and from his home in Southwark. But once he had secured his Doctorate, it is clear that he was determined to be more mobile. For short journeys—for example to Bury St Edmunds—he could have hired a nag or light chaise; when setting out on his more adventurous summer tours to Yorkshire, probably by stage coach, he would not have been pressed for time and would no doubt have been happy to break his journey at any places en route that took his fancy.

Chapter 3

Precept and Practice

Having successfully delivered his first course of lectures, William turned his mind to providing a remedy for one of the most glaring deficiencies in the system of University medical training—the lack of any modern syllabus to which the student could turn to discover what books he should read and what other steps he should take to equip him for his future responsibilities. The result was a short work, completed in 1741, entitled *An Introduction to the Study of Physic*. William made no attempt to publish it; instead, he encouraged his students to make their own copies. But as this involved a risk that his original manuscript might be damaged or lost, he took the precaution of writing out a second version, virtually the same as the first, but embodying some stylistic changes and a few other minor alterations.[1] It was this second 'original' that his students borrowed and their transcriptions were copied by later generations of students over the next forty years. One such copy (full of errors and omissions) was the source of the first and only published version which eventually appeared in 1927.[2]

In a short 'Preface' William points out that existing books written to introduce beginners to the study of medicine are now largely obsolete. 'Hence appears the necessity of new directions of this kind, and it is to be wished for, that these may share the fate of the former, and that every celebrated author may be eclipsed by the superior excellence of succeeding physicians.'

The first chapter 'Of Introductory Books' leaves the student in no doubt about the demands that are going to be made on him; he must be a scholar ('for every physician is expected to be such') and should be able to read not only Greek and Latin but one or two modern languages as well, so that he can appreciate the 'rise and progress and present state' of the medical art. Moreover he should not 'be ignorant of geography, chronology, history, logic, metaphysics, ethics, mathematics and natural philosophy'—especially the last two 'if he would be secure from error and superstition, from mistaken theories and ill grounded practice'. William's readers may have felt somewhat disconcerted by this list of demands, yet no item was irrelevant: some knowledge of geography would be helpful in assessing the merits of the many items in the materia medica that came from overseas, and in diagnosing imported diseases. Chronology and history illustrate the vital importance of time and experience. Logic provides an intellectual scaffolding which helps the physician to arrive at sound conclusions based on evidence rather than

An Introduction to the Study of Physic. *The first page of the 'Preface', (Francis A Countway Library of Medicine, Boston, Massachusetts).*

on superstition. Ethics and metaphysics expose the student to theories of right behaviour and to the problems of the nature of knowledge.

In a brief chapter on botany the student is advised to learn to recognise all the medicinal plants; to learn chemistry he should attend lectures at an 'elaboratory' and then 'by means of Vigani's temporary furnace' perform most of the common operations himself.

Next comes a chapter on Materia Medica:

> ... The knowledge of the various adulterations to which simples are
> liable, & which of them are most exposed to fraud, with the ways of
> discovering them, must sometimes be of service to all practitioners;
> tho' it is of more common use to the druggist & apothecary,[3] to
> whose skill & integrity the physician generally trusts, & unless on
> some particular occasions, does not trouble himself with the inspec-
> tion of the drugs. But then the virtues of drugs, their proper doses,
> the method and cautions to be observed in using them, are the chief
> business of the physician without which his enquiry into the causes
> and symptoms of diseases will be an empty useless speculation.
> Here therefore we can never take too much pains, but for every
> superstitious & false virtue we reject, & for every true one that
> we find out, we shall become the better physicians, less likely to
> tease our patients with useless medicines, and to fail in
> endeavouring to relieve them with those that are really efficacious.

Pharmacy is defined as 'the art of preparing and compounding
medicines so as to exalt their virtues, obviate their ill qualities and
render them less nauseous'. Although this is the business of the
apothecary, the young physician should learn how it is done by
frequenting the apothecary's shop. A study of the various
pharmacopoeias (published in Edinburgh and Dublin as well as in
London) is also recommended.

The chapter on Anatomy is much longer and as we would expect,
William stresses the vital importance of carrying out dissections as
well as studying the relevant literature; after the student has begun
to practice, he will have few opportunities of improving in anatomy,
'but must live upon the stock of his early studies'.

Under the heading 'Of Institutions' William comments on various
treatises dealing with physiology and systems of medicine. He did
not however have a very high opinion of 'systems', as the authors
often adapted their facts to fit in with their theories, thus producing
'a medley of fact and fiction.'

The following chapter—'Of the History of Diseases and their
Cure'—brings us:

> ... to the great business of the physician, to which all that has
> hitherto been said is only preparatory. In this pursuit he is to set
> himself no bounds, but must be perpetually adding either to his
> own observations by those of others, or enlarging what others have
> done by what he himself observes, nor must his study in this part
> end except with life.

Two authors are particularly commended for their description of
diseases: the first is Thomas Sydenham (born 1624) who grew up

Thomas Sydenham.

during the Civil War. Though he studied medicine at Oxford and took his MB, he found the curriculum overburdened with theory and largely irrelevant to the curing of patients; and when he set up his practice in Pall Mall soon after the Restoration, his treatments were based on his own clinical (i.e. bedside) observations, rather than on the theories of such ancient writers as Galen. His work was admired and supported by the physicist Robert Boyle and by John Locke (physician as well as philosopher) and when he published his most important work *Observationes Medicae*, his future reputation on the continent as well as at home was assured. His merit in William's opinion is that he is an original author

> ... giving only what he himself observed of diseases; and in doing this is judged to have come nearer to the true Idea of a practical writer than most other authors; as he has mixd but little of hypothesis & speculation with what he says, being generally contented with relating an exact history of the rise & progress of the disease, & of that method of treating the patient, which was found most effectual in conducting him easily to a speedy recovery.

The second medical writer to receive William's unstinted approval was the Dutch physician Hermann Boerhaave, an accomplished

Hermann Boerhaave. A portrait in chalks, c 1725, by Jan Vandelaar, (Medical and Pharmaceutical Museum, Amsterdam).

linguist and scholar, whose lectures attracted students from all over Europe to Leyden where he taught medicine, chemistry and botany. He held Sydenham in great veneration and gave his students instruction at the bedside; but in addition to this he gave post-mortem demonstrations and by thus combining physiology with pathology, he laid the foundations of the modern medical curriculum.

Surgery is dismissed in a few sentences, as the subject does not fall within the physician's province. Three text-books, however, are listed 'to provide some little acquaintance with the modern practice of it'.

In discussing books of medical observations, William is ready to commend them, provided they have been compiled from first-hand experience and he makes reference to the various

> . . . journals & transactions of learned societies, which last are repositories of much rare & valuable knowledge to a physician, tho' defended from common use by the immoderate price of such books, & oppressed with the heaps of other learning; I think it is much to be wished, that the medical papers were collected out

of these volumes, & published separately, digested into their proper heads, that so they might more easily come into the hands of those for whose use they were designed.

Among the publications he had in mind were the *Philosophical Transactions* of the Royal Society, which included articles of medical interest mixed up with a variety of other subjects. It was not until 1767 that the Royal College of Physicians, acting on William's recommendation, agreed to publish its *Medical Transactions*.

William envisaged a course of study lasting at least six years; he stresses the importance of note-taking and the indexing of subject-matter and concludes this section with a few words on the physician's proper address and behaviour towards his patient. In the final chapter he gives his candid assessment of the ancient Greek and Latin medical writers:

Andreas Vesalius. A woodcut from his book De humanis corporis fabrica, *1543. (Wellcome Institute Library, London).*

... They had made but very little progress in botany, & had not found out such a method of characterizing plants as to deliver them down with any certainty to posterity ... This affects a considerable part of their materia medica . . . Their pharmacy or art of preparing & compounding simples ... must be very uninstructive and consequently tedious; which they do not seem to be aware of, for these books are clogged with a great number of these obsolete unintelligible receipts. There is great reason to believe that they very rarely dissected a human body, & accordingly there was scarce anything known of it, till the great Vesalius taught us to leave disputing about the anatomy of the ancients & to study nature . . . Their natural philosophy was very little better . . . Now upon anatomy & natural philosophy is founded physiology, for the use of the parts. What therefore can we expect from the ancients on this head, but a heap of wild notions, such as are the usual product of an imagination let loose upon those subjects without any help from observation & matter of fact. All these defects in the above-mentioned branches of study, which can hardly be disputed by anyone, must therefore be abundantly compensated by their merit in the history of diseases, which alone remains to support their character.

Referring to the limitations imposed on Hippocrates by the times in which he lived, William makes this comment:

Knowledge in nature is justly called the daughter of Time & Experience, & indeed of much longer time & experience than we are apt to imagine after the discovery has been made. It is a great while before men are capable of making any use of what passes before them unless they are put upon the observing of it. When they first enter upon a new field of knowledge, they are struck with many insignificant appearances & pass over others of the greatest importance: they are too impatient to wait for the slow production of nature for the formation of their system, & so help it forward by the warmth of their fancy: they are too hasty in coming to general conclusions & aphorisms from too small a number of facts; which sort of knowledge, like the ill-gotten possessions of those who make haste to be rich, seldom thrives, moulders & comes to nothing with their posterity.

To round off his treatise, William appends a catalogue of some 114 books mentioned in the text. The list includes the most recent editions available at the time, and William's desire to keep the list up-to-date is evident from several entries he added later on the blank left-hand pages, for example: 'Linnaeus' Method—generally adjudged to be superior to those of all former Botanists'; 'Macquer's *Chemical Dictionary*—a very useful work which has been published since this chapter was written'; and 'Haller's *Physiologia* (on Anatomy)—contains all the useful knowledge contained in these books with very great improvements upon them.'

Several of William's pupils distinguished themselves in later life; Sir George Baker demonstrated that the 'Devonshire colic' was caused by the leaden vessels used in cider-making; in due course he was elected President of the Royal College of Physicians and was appointed to attend the King. Dr Thomas Gisborne became physician to St George's Hospital, followed Baker as President of the Royal College of Physicians and, like him, attended the King. Robert Glynn,[4] well known for his learning, benevolence and wit, followed William's example by giving regular lectures and became the first physician to Addenbrooke's Hospital in Cambridge when it was opened in 1766.

The 'Introduction' is more than a blue-print for the training of medical students in the 1740s; it is the testament of one who believed, like Wilmot, Mead and many others, that the physician could not be equipped for his responsible and demanding task unless he had acquired the background of scholarship and culture which would enable him to employ his talents with the maximum of wisdom and understanding. The 'Introduction' also tells us, by implication, a great deal about William's own training and methods. His later works leave us in no doubt that he had studied and practised everything that he recommended to the attention of his readers. His extensive knowledge of anatomy, for instance, could only have been gained by employing the knife and scalpel himself, rather than by mere attendance at demonstrations; and we can be equally confident that he experimented with Vigani's furnace and quizzed the apothecary on the mysteries of pharmacy.

But one of the most important lessons that he taught and practised concerned the keeping of case-notes and other records; and it was these disciplines that enabled him near the end of his career to bring all the authority of a lifetime's experience to the composition of his major work, the *Commentaries on the History and Cure of Diseases*.[5] His case-notes, he tells us in the 'Preface', were taken 'in the chambers of the sick' and any significant features were later transferred to an index alphabetically arranged according to the Latin names of the illnesses or complaints. All cases seem to have been given voucher numbers, running in one unbroken sequence throughout the whole length of his career. The vouchers themselves (of which none has survived) presumably recorded fees due and fees received and indicated those patients who were treated free of charge.

William's note-taking was not of course confined to his bed-ridden patients, and he was just as meticulous in recording the relevant facts about the many others—perhaps the majority—who were able, despite their complaints, to come and see him.

His records thus provided an accumulating body of documentation
which was the best possible guide to the solution of future problems.
If William attended an individual patient more than once, he could
refer to his notes of earlier visits; if on the other hand he wished
to reflect on the best treatment for a particular ailment, his 'Index'
provided him with a summary of the significant facts on all similar
cases he had treated previously.

No physician could have done his job without holding some general
view of the nature of the human body; and although William was
prepared to abandon any system or theory when it conflicted with
his own personal observations and experience, it was the Hippocratic
doctrine of the four 'humours' that most frequently dictated the forms
of treatment he prescribed. When the body was healthy, the humours
were in balance; but in times of sickness this balance was disturbed,
and it was the function of the physician to restore the equilibrium
by enabling or encouraging the 'peccant humour' to escape. William's
attitude to the theory can be gauged from his discussion of 'The
Method of Curing Diseases (Ratio Medendi)' in the second chapter
of the *Commentaries*. He begins:

> One of the first considerations in the cure of a disease is, whether
> it require any evacuations; that is, whether it have been the
> general opinion of practical authors, that emetics, cathartics,
> diuretics, bleeding (by leeches, cupping-glasses,[6] or the lancet),
> sudorifics, blisters, issues,[7] sternutatories, or salivation, have in
> similar cases been found to be beneficial.

As for remedies or 'specifics' which were reasonably reliable,
William's list is all too brief:

> . . . Peruvian bark for the cure of agues; quicksilver for Venereal
> disorders; sulphur for the itch; and perhaps opium for some
> spasms; and Bath waters for the injury done to the stomach by
> drinking.

Besides these there were perhaps a dozen other remedies which
were widely used but were too uncertain in their effects to be
regarded with complete confidence. Under this heading William
includes squills for asthma, soap-ley for gravel and stone, hemlock
for cancers, electrification for blindness[8] and antimony for continual
fevers. With such a minute and inadequate armoury of medicines
at his disposal, we can sympathise with his view that

> Though, among the pretended specifics, some have very little
> virtue, and others may be inconstant in their operations; yet, if
> a physician be satisfied that they are safe, there may be many
> occasions when he may with propriety employ them.

The above quotations from the *Introduction* and the *Commentaries* help us to form some idea of the methods William employed in treating his patients. The pattern of his practice was largely determined by the University Calendar; during term-time the number of his potential patients was at its maximum and besides meeting their demands, he had to fulfil his roles as teacher and lecturer. Additional duties are revealed in the *Grace Books*: in 1739 he was appointed to the panel of examiners who assessed candidates for the degrees of MB and MD; and a few months later he was elected Senior Medical Doctor for the following year on the 'caput' or controlling committee of the Senate.

Fortunately most of his patients were near at hand; those with minor ailments could see him at the coffee-house or in his College rooms, and he could visit the more serious cases without time-wasting journeys. From the evidence of the *Index* it seems that the most frequent complaint was abdominal pains (*intestinorum dolores*). Of the many possible causes, the commonest must surely have been contaminated food; standards of personal hygiene were low and apart from the dangers wrought by the dirty hands of kitchen staff, there were genuine difficulties (in pre-refrigeration days) in preserving food in fresh condition. Headaches too were common—some no doubt the penalty of alcoholic carousals, others perhaps brought on by eye-strain from too much reading by feeble candle-light. Affections of the skin, coughs and chest complaints made further substantial contributions to William's case-load.

But in the vacations the population of the University sank dramatically and at the conclusion of the summer term many of the Fellows and tutors—as well as the entire student body—dispersed, leaving the colleges almost deserted. William's trips to Yorkshire while Cambridge was dormant were not undertaken merely to collect specimens for his lectures. His intention was to spend some profitable and agreeable weeks widening his experience at a spa, where the well-to-do congregated during the season. The resort he chose on two or three occasions was Scarborough, the only spa in England that offered the pleasures of the seaside in addition to its 'medicinal waters'. The mineral springs had been discovered in the 1620s and by the time that William paid his first visit, the town had a fine spa-house and enough boarding-houses to attract 'the nobility, quality and gentry'.[9] There were plenty of patients prepared to pay for his advice and he 'met there' according to Cole 'with abundant success'.

The names of his Scarborough patients are not recorded, but one of them may have been Thomas Pape, who taught navigation and studied botany. At all events, the two men became acquainted and Pape in due course presented William with his considerable collection of dried plants, which was added to the cabinet of materia medica. As the cabinet's catalogue indicates that William visited

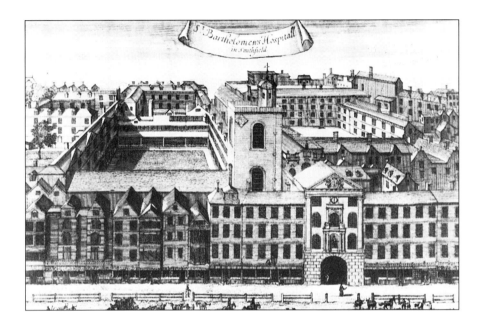

St Bartholomew's Hospital, Smithfield, c 1720.

another flourishing spa—Harrogate—we may perhaps assume that
he spent a season there treating patients, and this seems to be
confirmed by several references in the *Index* to the powers of the
waters which sometimes appeared helpful and in other cases useless.

According to Cole, William often visited London, where his friend
Sir Edward Wilmot probably allowed him to accompany him on his
rounds of the wards at St Thomas's. This would explain the fact that
William was able to visit the hospital in later years, although he
held no official position there. One such visit is described in chapter
49 of the *Commentaries*, and William sets the scene dramatically:

> 26 June 1764, in St Thomas's Hospital, I saw a woman of six-and-
> thirty years of age motionless with a fit of the catalepsy.

He also acted as a temporary assistant at St Bartholomew's.[10] In
both hospitals he would have gained an insight into many conditions
which he would seldom, if ever, have encountered at his University—
an exclusively male preserve, where opportunities for treating female
patients were few and far between.

Of his Cambridge patients, only three can be positively identified.
One was the Revd Thomas Baker (of the coffee-house circle) who died
in 1740 following a stroke. His case-history is, in a sense, unique,
as it is the only one among the thousands that William wrote to
have survived in its original form, complete with the patient's name
and other personal details. Its preservation was due to an enquiry

from Cole who, in October 1777 was still seeking fresh items to include in his *Athenae Cantabrigienses* and wrote to William to ask for information about Baker's parents and 'the nature of his departure whether by a long or lingering illness or more sudden'.[11]

In spite of the years that had elapsed, William was able to turn up his case-notes and send Cole a copy of a short memorandum, with the assurance that it 'was taken at the time and you may depend on every particular there mentioned'. The memorandum was as follows:

> The Rev Mr Baker was found by his Bedmaker on Sat 28 June 1740 at five in the afternoon lying upon his floor where he was judged to have fallen about 2 hours before, by the circumstance of a clean pipe which laid broken beside him, which he generally went to fetch at 3 o'clock. His face was so much convulsed that part of what he said was with difficulty understood; a great stupor hung upon his senses and one side of him was helpless and dead. Sometimes he seemed to disregard what was doing about him and talked incoherently; at other times he would recollect himself and know those who were with him, recommending himself to their prayers for an easy death; expressing with great resignation that he perceived the time of his departure was come and thanking his friends for their good offices with his usual humanity. He continued in this way till a little after seven on Wednesday evening, when he expired. He seemed incapable of swallowing and therefore hardly took anything, either food or physic, all the time of his short illness. Whatever was offered to him to take or to be done for him (except changing his linen with which he was pleased) gave him great uneasiness as if he thought it was disturbing him to no purpose, and every trouble of this kind was forborne, as much as could be without neglecting him. His death was such an one as he had often talked of and desired, being preceded by a very short sickness and attended with little or no pain. It was rendered more fortunate from the circumstance of his executor and near Relation happening to be with him a day or two before he was taken ill and staying to take care of him during his illness and settle his affairs.

No doubt the memorandum contained certain details of a kind that would have been omitted from many of William's case-notes on dying patients; but in this case William was writing in a dual capacity— both as physician and friend, and the personal details were therefore no less important than the clinical. Baker's attitude of resignation was typical of many educated Anglicans of his time;[12] the old terrors of damnation and hell-fire were giving way to less uncomfortable views; although death was so often arbitrary and unpredictable, it was no longer so widely regarded, as it had been in earlier times, as divine punishment, but rather as a natural event with a natural cause—even if the cause might not be immediately discoverable. Moreover, as earthly life was so full of pain and sorrow, a rational man—particularly one as elderly as Baker—might well be resigned to (or even positively welcome) death as a door to a new dimension, free of this world's anguish.

If William was present, as the memo suggests, when Baker expired, he was there as a friend; in his professional capacity he would not have been expected to remain at the bedside once it had become clear that nothing more could be done; from that point onwards the responsibility was borne by Baker's executor and near relation. As for Baker's hopes for an 'easy death', William would certainly have been ready and willing to administer an opiate draught if the patient had been in pain; his revered predecessor Sydenham had frequently done so, and William fully endorses the practice in the *Commentaries*.

Another patient was Conyers Middleton, with whom William enjoyed discussing religious topics at his house adjoining Caius College. Middleton's second wife died in 1745 and the following summer William advised him to take a holiday. Accordingly he set off with a group of friends to stay at the spa of Hotwells, overlooking the river in the Avon Gorge near Bristol. His letter to William dated 10 August 1746[13] gives a lively picture of the company in the Pump Room:

> For my own part I drink the waters for the sake of fashion; but by fits only, as fashionable folks do: & when I want to see company; who examine all new comers like fresh criminals brought to a jail with What are you sent hither for? & indeed our dayly examination of one another is just the reverse of the true Christian kind, not of what good we have done but of what we have received each day; but whether these polite inquiries procede from benevolence or curiosity or the mere want of something else to say, is a problem which your experience of Scarborough will enable you to solve.

The third in the trio of William's patients who are known to us by name was Richard Bentley.[14] Born in Yorkshire in 1662, he had been admitted (like William) to St John's as a sizar at the age of fourteen and had soon been elected to a scholarship. After taking his BA he spent some years employed as a private tutor and later moved to Oxford where he delivered the lectures named after the scientist Robert Boyle. Although the lectures aroused fierce controversy, Bentley was recognised as a man of exceptional brilliance and in 1699 he was elected Master of Trinity College, Cambridge. Unfortunately he was arrogant and high-handed and the Fellows of the college (including Middleton) were frequently at odds with him; yet he was the most outstanding scholar of his age; he promoted scientific studies by building a college observatory and by fitting up a laboratory for Vigani; and besides these accomplishments he was active in landscaping the 'backs'—the grounds between the colleges and the river. He died of 'pleuritic fever' in July 1742; William attended him in his final hours and refused to bleed him 'though the aged patient pressed him'.[15]

Bentley's biographer would hardly have recorded this detail if he had not thought it significant; bleeding after all had been recognised as an important therapeutic routine since ancient times, and as it was in conformity with the doctrine of humours and had been firmly supported by Galen, many patients would have expected to be bled by their physician, regardless of the nature of their complaint. However, William recognised that bleeding was likely to be helpful only for certain conditions—such as the 'plethora' caused by over-indulgence—and that in other cases, including Bentley's, the procedure was useless, if not positively dangerous.

Amongst the influential physicians who gave William their encouragement very early in his career was Sir Richard Mead (1673-1754), whose daughter had married Sir Edward Wilmot. Mead was regarded as one of the most distinguished physicians of his day, and was certainly one of the wealthiest. As a young man he had attended the Universities of Leyden, Utrecht, Padua and Rome; he was elected FRS in 1703, took his MD at Oxford and became FRCP in 1716. Having established a lucrative practice in London, he indulged his enthusiasm for classical learning by gradually amassing an impressive collection of books, manuscripts, statuary, coins, gems and drawings. The house in which these treasures were displayed was in Great Ormond Street, on the site of the present Children's Hospital. Mead regularly held levées (with breakfast included) at which persons with suitable introductions were welcomed and shown round the exhibits. William accepted an invitation to view the great man's antiquities in 1741 and shortly afterwards sent him a carefully composed letter[16] beginning:

> I return you many thanks for your obliging reception of me when introduced to see your celebrated collection of the valuable remains of antient Greece and Rome. Your goodness will, I hope, excuse me if upon being only thus slightly known to you, I take the liberty myself of introducing another stranger to your acquaintance, the inclosed essay.

This was entitled 'A dissertation to show that the Daphne of the Greeks was the Lauro-cerasus of the Romans or our Laurel and not the Bay Tree' and William excuses himself for straying from the proper business of his profession into realms of classical learning by citing Mead himself as his authority 'who is confessed to be the first physician of the age and yet is as well known for his taste and skill in Greek and Roman literature . . .'

The central argument of the dissertation was that as the poets and even the naturalists of the ancient world often gave the same name to different plants, confusion was inevitable; and this confusion could have dangerous consequences when many plants (including the laurel) were poisonous, and others (like the bay tree) were harmless.

To prove his case, William produces a battery of quotations from ancient authors which clearly identify the daphne by its effects; it has, for example, 'a power to disturb the mind and to transport it into extasies'. By contrast, the bay tree has no poisonous qualities, and 'we use both the leaves and the berries in physic'.

Taken together, the essay and the introductory letter must be regarded as something more than a rather over-elaborate expression of thanks to Dr Mead for his hospitality. William had only recently received his MD; the goodwill of a physician as distinguished and influential as Dr Mead could in the future lead to many valuable introductions and William accordingly set out to make an impression that would not be forgotten.

Several of William's acquaintances, including Mead and Wilmot were Fellows of the Royal College of Physicians, a small but prestigious society which admitted to its ranks only those Doctors of Medicine who were members of the Established Church and had obtained their degree from Oxford or Cambridge. One of the College's responsibilities was to publish the *London Pharmacopoeia*, which provided doctors with ready-made prescriptions for a wide range of ailments. Many of the remedies listed in the volume were at best completely useless, if not positively dangerous, and a revised edition was long overdue. In December 1738 the College set the wheels in motion by appointing a committee (which included Wilmot) to consider what revisions might be desirable and to make proposals.[17]

The work proceeded at an unhurried pace and in 1742 the committee printed a 'Draught' of their proposals and presented copies both to the Fellows and to 'some other gentlemen likewise', inviting their comments and suggestions. In an introduction of some thirty pages the committee described their suggested revisions which included the deletion of certain items no longer in use, the addition of some new ones, and the simplification of others. In this third class were two preparations which the committee felt should be retained though they 'might be much reduced without any diminution of their virtues'. Both had been invented before the time of Galen: the first, Theriaca Andromachi or Venice Treacle had 65 ingredients including dried vipers; the other, Mithridatium, named after an ancient King of Pontus, could only boast 50 components, but made up for this by including the bellies of lizards. The general tone of the introduction was cautious, although the committee seemed aware that at least a few of the traditional remedies might owe more to superstition than to science.

The next development was the publication in 1744 of an anonymous work called *Pharmacopoeia Reformata*, in which the author gave a summary of the committee's Draught, adding his own caustic comments and damning the proposals for their timidity.

Up to this point it is impossible to say what influence, if any, William had had on the committee's views; but he would certainly have been aware of the 'Draught' and may have been one of the 'other gentlemen' whose comments had been invited. He now decided that he must come out clearly in support of radical revisions, and in the following year he printed a pamphlet[18] for circulation among the Fellows, in which he argued forcefully for the deletion of Mithridatium and Theriac from the new edition. As he was aware that he himself might be proposed for Fellowship in the near future, he was careful to cast his essay in a form that could cause the College no offence. He begins innocuously by demolishing the traditional notion that Mithridates was an expert in the use of poisons and antidotes; in fact, when Pompey defeated him, the only items found in his medicine cabinet were 'twenty leaves of rue, one grain of salt, two nuts and two dried figs'. It was some artful people in Rome who invented the preparation they called Antidotum Mithridatium and who promoted it as 'a most powerful preservative from all kinds of venom. Whoever took a proper quantity in a morning, was insured from being poisoned during that whole day. This was confirmed by the example of its supposed Inventor; who was farther said, by using it in this manner, to have been at last so fortified against all baneful Simples, that none would have any effect, when he wanted their assistance to dispatch himself.'

Various alterations were made to the components and the name of the reformed mixture was changed first to Galene and later to Theriaca.

> Now whether Mithridates was or was not the author of this celebrated composition, it was manifestly founded in error, since it was chiefly intended as a counterpoison: for nothing can be more false than the notions which have generally prevailed about the force and number of Poisons, and consequently of Antidotes.
>
> In the ruder ages of the world, before experience had furnished mankind with any considerable knowledge of nature, they seem to have been under perpetual alarms from an apprehension of poisons. They had probably seen the ill effect of some few substances on the human body, and, like people in the dark, immediately made their dangers more and greater than they were; hence came that great number of Antidotes, which we meet with

in the writings of the old Physicians, whose chief use was against poisons. What ignorance or an immoderate fondness for life had thus begun, was carried to a much greater height by that strong passion which the Vulgar have ever shewn for prodigies and miraculous stories.

In fact, the only poisons known to the ancients were 'the cicuta, Aconitum and those of venemous beasts' and 'they knew of no antidote whatever to these poisons'. Thus, of the many tales of poisonings in earlier ages, very few were credible. As for Mithridatium, the experience 'of near two thousand years' had completely failed to confirm any of its alleged virtues, with the result that it was no longer used for its original purpose as an antidote but merely as 'a Diaphoretic, which is commonly the virtue of a medicine that has none'.

Persuasive as this argument was, the importance of the essay in the history of pharmacology depends primarily on the attack that William now proceeds to mount against 'polypharmacy'—the notion that a medicine made up of many different ingredients would necessarily retain the virtues of each. The manner in which numerous items have been united together as in Mithridatium 'has by many been called a piece of mere jumble and chance-work without any footsteps of order, proportion or design, without any regard to the known virtues of Simples or to any rules of artful composition'.

Moreover, the constituents have been so frequently altered that there are many different formulae and methods of preparation; thus

> . . . their use is attended with a good deal of danger. As many people busy themselves with the practice of Physic, who are unqualified to know what they are doing; it may be advisable for the sake of such as fall into their hands, to discountenance a medicine which . . . is often applied at random and, by means of the Opium, does much mischief . . . for Opium or any powerful drug, mixed up into an electuary with so many other things, is against all rules of pharmacy.

This statement, written at a time when polypharmacy was a common practice and its dangers generally ignored, helps to make the essay a key text in eighteenth century medicine; it lays down sound principles for determining the safety and efficacy of drugs, it warns the reader of the danger of including potent remedies in mixtures and reminds him that drugs when mixed together may be incompatible or unstable.

In his conclusion William pays a tactful (if somewhat undeserved) compliment to the College; after noting that the power and fame of Mithridatium has of late been declining, he hopes that its reign will not last much longer . . .

Perhaps the glory of its first expulsion from a public Dispensatory was reserved to these times and to the English Nation; in which all parts of Philosophy have been so much assisted in asserting their freedom from antient fable and superstition; and whose College of Physicians in particular hath deservedly had the first reputation in their profession. Among the many eminent services which the authority of this learned and judicious Body hath done to the practice of Physic, it might not be the least that it had driven out this medley of discordant Simples; which perhaps has no better title to the name of Mithridates, than as it so well resembles the numerous, undisciplined forces of a barbarous King, made up of a dissonant crowd collected from different countries, mighty in appearance, but in reality, an ineffective multitude, that only hinder one another.[19]

The new edition of the *Pharmacopoeia* duly appeared in 1746; Theriac and Mithridate were retained, but in the long introductory narrative of more than a hundred pages there were some surprises; here were passages far more robust than the tentative words of the 'Draught', and the source of these passages was unmistakable: they had come directly from William's introductory lecture on materia medica. His references to chemistry, to Paracelsus and many other subjects reappear in the 'narrative'. As for the following paragraph, the whole of it—apart from the final sentence—repeats the message of *Antitheriaca*:

It would be a disgrace and a merited reproach to us if our *Pharmacopoeia* abounded any longer in discordant and random mixtures introduced by primitive ignorance or thrust into it by fear of poison and by perpetual suspicion. To meet these dangers the ancients bent almost all their energies to the search for antidotes, for which, in their superstition and foolish naivete, they had recourse to oracles, dreams and the fictions of astrologers. Relying on the futile hope of devising compound antidotes designed in their individual elements to check the action of any kind of poison, they added to the mass everything which they imagined resisted the infection. Thus the simplicity of medicine was lost. Thus the riotous excess of mixing, adding and heaping drug upon drug became fairly established. This stain on medicine has lasted to our own times. We, so far as has been permissible, have attempted to remove this accumulation, but yielding to the force of custom, we have left some prescriptions for our successors to remove.[20]

If William was disappointed at the committee's refusal to jettison Theriac and Mithridate, he still had every reason to be pleased at the extent of the influence he had exerted. Moreover, he knew that

'the force of custom' could not be lightly dismissed; patients, at least
the fee-paying variety, regarded themselves as customers who were
entitled to be given the medicine they asked for, and if they
demanded Theriac or some equally absurd preparation, their
physicians would be reluctant to refuse it.

The College lost no time in showing its appreciation of William's
contribution. His name had already been put forward as a candidate
for Fellowship and at the beginning of June 1745 he had made his first
appearance before the Censors to be examined *in parte physiologica*.
The secretary noted in the minutes that 'in consideration of his
business at Cambridge he was appointed to take his second examination
(*in parte pathologica*) on the tenth instant at five in the afternoon'.
This took place as arranged and after a third examination—*in parte
therapeutica*—held on the 25th, he was approved. But the ritual was
not yet complete; first he had to produce his Diploma from Cambridge
as evidence of his Doctorate; then the Comitia met and the President
formally proposed Dr William Heberden to be admitted candidate;
he was then 'ballotted, elected, admitted and gave his faith'. Exactly
a year later he was elected FRCP.[21]

An important section of William's lectures on materia medica was
concerned with the properties of vegetables and some of his audience

*The Royal College of Physicians in Warwick Lane, London: engraving by J Mynde,
(Wellcome Institute Library, London).*

may have wondered why the University had no garden for the cultivation of medicinal plants; Oxford had had its Botanic Garden since 1632, and the Physic Garden in Chelsea, planted in 1676, had more recently received generous support from the distinguished physician and natural historian Sir Hans Sloane.[22]

Soon after receiving his FRCP William made a serious attempt to establish a similar garden in Cambridge. His efforts did not have any immediate effect, but in 1762 Dr Richard Walker, the Vice-Master of Trinity, bought part of Austin Priory 'with near five Acres of Garden about it' and presented it to the University for use as a public Botanic Garden in perpetuity. William's part in promoting the scheme was later acknowledged as follows:[23]

> About 15 years ago the learned physician Dr Heberden was so kind as to oblige the University with a course of Experiments upon such plants as he then found amongst us in order to show their use in Medicines. This was entering into the practical and principal part of Botany to which we had been strangers . . . But this Doctor's great abilities in his profession soon after called him from us, much lamenting the want of a Public Garden, furnished with a sufficient variety of Plants for making the like experiments. These considerations, particularly Dr Heberden's most useful attempt, put the present Vice-Master of Trinity College upon finding a proper situation for such a garden.

The garden flourished in its 'proper situation' for some 70 years, until it was removed to its present more extensive site by the Trumpington Road. There it continues to fulfil William's original hopes by providing teaching material for the University courses in botanical studies.

Since gaining his coveted FRCP William had become increasingly aware that Cambridge could only be a prelude to a more spacious career elsewhere. Within the University the prospects for advancement were virtually nil; there was only one position—the Regius Professorship of Physic—which might have attracted him, but that was unattainable as on Green's death in 1741, it had been awarded to the well-connected Russell Plumptre. A spur to his ambitions was his natural desire to get married—although under the University statutes matrimony would have involved the loss of his fellowship.

Cole remarks that he 'practised with so great success his profession at Cambridge', that he was often urged to move to London by, for example, his young friend Richard Hurd (the future Bishop of Worcester) as well as by Sir Edward Wilmots.

If Wilmot was prepared to recommend him, so too was Sir Richard Mead, to whose levées William could now introduce his younger friends.[24] Another supporter was Sir Edward Hulse, Physician-in-Ordinary to three monarchs, who had been present at the meeting which approved William's candidature for FRCP.

On the other hand a move to London would involve a number of hazards which needed careful calculation and assessment. Any physician contemplating such an enterprise in 1748 would have been aware that competition in the medical field was keen. The capital was a magnet to the ambitious, and therapies were on offer not only from qualified physicians, but from surgeons, apothecaries, unlicensed practitioners, midwives, bone-setters, wise-women, clergymen and quacks.[25] From Simmons's *Medical Register*, published in 1783, it appears that there was one doctor (i.e. a physician, surgeon or apothecary) for roughly every 850 members of the population, and there is no reason to suppose that this proportion was substantially different a generation earlier. The total number of FRCPs was 54, and although many of them had country practices, there were at least 24 other physicians, who, however excellent their qualifications, lacked two of the basic requirements for Fellowship—membership of the Established Church of England and an MD degree from Oxbridge. These were the Licentiates who practised in London, subject to the College's approval.

In view of his solid reputation, his patrons, friends and connections, William had every reason to feel that he could enter this competitive *mêlée* with confidence; but there was one question that still had to be resolved: had he enough money to acquire and furnish a suitable house and to maintain a reasonable standard of living while the practice was still in process of being firmly established? At the outset of his career his sole source of income had been his Fellow's stipend; extra guineas began to flow in with the inauguration of his annual course of lectures, and to these could be added the fees from his growing list of patients. By living in College, his day-to-day expenses were kept to a minimum, and the opportunity to save for the future greatly enhanced. Satisfied that he could overcome any financial obstacles that might arise, he was now ready to move to the capital as soon as a suitable opening presented itself.

The advice that William finally adopted came from Sir Edward Hulse—but the story has a curious twist: when Hulse was on the point of retirement, he decided to invite William to take over his London practice. We would have expected him to send this very important piece of information by letter, but for some unaccountable reason he confided his intentions to another doctor whom he asked to deliver the message verbally. The messenger however decided to cash in on this opportunity himself and instead of delivering the message, reported back to Hulse that William was not interested. As soon as Hulse realised that he had been misled, he wrote to William (on 14 July) explaining what had happened and how in the intervening weeks the scene had changed:[26]

What shall I say to you now? . . . When I left London, I had, as
far as I could, recommended Dr Shaw[27] to my business; so it
stands now, except that Dr Shaw has too much business, more
than he can possibly do, upon which account I have endeavoured
to assist Dr Taylor, who came from Newark. He is greatly
supported by some noble families, and has already wonderfully
succeeded. I have set before you the difficulties that I lie under,
of recommending any body at present. I don't intend to flatter
you, when I say, I make no doubt you will be able to support
yourself by your own merit; and as far as shall be consistent with
honour, jointly with my power, which is now very little, you may
depend upon the friendship of, Sir,
                    Your most affectionate humble servant, E Hulse.
PS Since the writing of this, I am certainly informed that Dr Shaw
is gone over to Hanover with the Duchess of Newcastle.[28] I
believe you will never have a fairer opportunity of settling in this
town than the present.

William replied:

                                                30 August 1748
I take the opportunity of returning my thanks for your most
obliging letter. No one can be ignorant that your assistance and
recommendation must be of the highest advantage to any person
who was beginning the practice of physic in London; and I am
persuaded they would at any time have determined me to fix there,
though I had otherwise no such intention. But I never was rightly
informed that I had such a valuable opportunity in my power.
By what accident or mistake it happened, I do not know, but the
person you mention never acquainted me with it at all, nor indeed
any one else with authority from you. I had only heard
accidentally, that you had expressed yourself with great civility
on a supposition of my moving to London. There was no reason,
when I first heard such reports, to imagaine that they amounted
to anything more than your good wishes. As soon as I could believe
there was the least probability of your intending to assist me with
your interest, I immediately took the liberty of writing to you.
I must reckon it among my greatest misfortunes that this
application came too late: though I shall always think myself
under the same obligations to you, as if I had enjoyed the benefit
of your kind intentions. My best acknowledgments are due for
the assurances of your disposition to assist me still, where your
other engagements have not put it out of your power; and it is
with the highest satisfaction that I find myself possessed of a place
in your friendship. I propose seeing London some time in October,
in order to consult with some friends about the advisableness of
my settling there, when I hope to have the pleasure of paying my
respects to you.

As William was meticulous in answering letters promptly, it is difficult to understand why he allowed six weeks to elapse before sending a reply; but whatever the reasons for this delay, the letter leaves no doubt about his acute disappointment at the loss of a unique opportunity. Hulse's PS offered a handsome consolation prize, but the note of caution in the final words of William's letter suggests that the new prospects, however promising, were not quite as radiant as those of which he had been defrauded.

None the less, William had made his decision; by October he had moved to London and a new phase of his life had begun.

Chapter 4

Cecil Street

For almost twenty-four years Cambridge had been William's home; it had given him the key to the world of learning and a friendly ambience in which he was able to determine the direction of his career; and if he found the system of medical education to be sadly deficient, the defects had stimulated him to offer something better to the students that came after him. His physical separation from the scene of so many happy and fruitful experiences may have caused him some pangs of regret, but any such feelings were mitigated by his continuing contacts with the University and by the presence in London of many of his Cambridge contemporaries.

Birch and Wray were among the first to welcome him on his arrival; both were members of a dining club founded in 1743 with the grandiose title of The Club of the Royal Philosophers,[1] which met weekly at the Mitre Tavern, Fleet Street. On 13 October William accepted his friends' invitation to attend as a guest and during the months that followed he was present on no less than fifteen occasions before being elected to membership at the AGM in July. The names of the members and guests, together with the menus, were recorded in a series of 'dinner books' by the club's Treasurer Josiah Colebrooke, who held office from the club's inauguration until his retirement thirty years later. Dinners were held on Thursdays at 4pm 'at 1s.6d. per Head Eating. A Pint of wine to be paid for, everyone that comes.' At William's first guest-attendance, nineteen men were present and tucked into soup, cod, plaice, herrings, calves head, chickens with oyesters, chine of mutton roast, turkey roast, pear pye and apple pye (both creamed), plumb pudding, butter & cheese. Colebrooke (to keep the club in profit) encouraged members to make gifts of 'viands' from time to time and when anyone did so, his health was drunk in claret and the fact recorded. On one occasion William contributed venison and a turtle.

For William, these convivial meetings were events of major importance: besides the strong appeal they made to his sociable nature, they offered him unique opportunities to make friendly contacts among many of the most distinguished men of his time.

But his most immediate concern was to find a house; it must, if possible be near his friends and within easy reach of the wealthy West End residences from which he might hope to earn the greater part of his income; and as he was keen to get married, the house had to be suitable for bringing up a family. These needs were met by a vacant property in a terrace of houses 'fit for persons of repute', built at the end of the previous century in Cecil Street[2] which used to run down from the Strand towards the river, but is now buried beneath the Savoy Hotel. There were friends nearby: Birch lived only a few minutes walk away to the east, and closer still was Rauthmell's Coffee House which still flourished as a meeting place for gossip and business. By Christmas 1748 William had installed himself in his new home.

In the stimulating atmosphere of the metropolis, William throve and Cole could not resist the temptation to make a sly comment:

> I thought it remarkable that he should ever establish himself in London, because whenever he had occasion to go thither from Cambridge, as he had frequent calls of that sort, I have heard him say often and often that the air was so dissimilar to his constitution and lungs that he could never sleep there, but always lodged at some miles distant. Great Genii deal often in paradoxes. He soon reconciled him to an air that so amply filled his pockets.

In fact, William's pockets were by no means empty when he first arrived in London, and if he needed a loan to supplement his savings, he was not short of friends who would have been happy to oblige him. But although the records are silent on this point, there is no doubt that within a few months of acquiring his house, he had furnished, equipped and staffed it, so that his patients who called on him for consultations could be received in proper style and his friends could be offered hospitality—and if necessary a spare bed.

Cole was among his early dinner-guests and noted 'I have dined with him several times while I was Rector of Hornsey'—a living he briefly held from 1749 to 1750; and soon afterwards William himself provides clear evidence[3] that his bachelor establishment was efficiently managed and could run smoothly even in his absence. In a note to Birch evidently written while attending a patient at the Tudor mansion of Dorney Court, near Maidenhead, William apologises for his absence:

> 11 o'clock 13 July 1751
>
> Dear Sir, I am forced against my will to stay here too long to have any hopes of dining with you in Cecil-street. It distresses me to the last degree to think of having such friends at my house without being able to enjoy their company. Let me beg of you, dear Sir, to do the honours of my table, and excuse me to my worthy friends. By that time you have dined, I hope to be with you. I dare say that everything will be taken such care of, that you will have nothing to do but to eat and drink, and see that our friends do so too. Ever yours
>
> W Heberden

Soon after moving into Cecil Street, William received a letter[4] from Middleton who, having lost two wives, had recently married a third:

                                                            Camb 3 Apr 1749
Dear Dr
I ought to have thanked you long ago for your friendly & entertaining letter; yet I persuaded myself from my long experience of your candor that you will not charge the omission to any sort of neglect or disregard on my part towards one whose constant friendship and favours to me I have so much cause to remember & whose loss is felt & regretted almost every day at my fireside; which is made however the easier to us by hearing, as we do, of your growing fame & success & that the change is likely to answer all our wishes.

We propose to be in London in the beginning of the next week, which will afford me the greater pleasure by affording me the opportunity of your company . . .

As to the news of this place, you will hear it always from others who are better informed of it than myself & whatever I can recollect of that sort, I shall now reserve to a personal conference & open to you perhaps at the same time in our old free manner, what new heterodoxies I have been meditating & sketching out in this interval of your absence. In the meanwhile I can only add our joint & sincere wishes of everything prosperous to you and am, with great truth, Dear Dr,
                        Your affectionate friend & faithfull servant
                                        Conyers Middleton

Middleton's letter reminds us that in his day a man often found his most lasting emotional ties in the company of other men of similar tastes and interests and would have no inhibitions in expressing his feelings. His special affection for William was no doubt partly due to the latter's open-minded and unprejudiced attitude to his religious 'heterodoxies', which had brought showers of abuse from other clerics. In his next letter[5] Middleton again emphasises the pleasure that William's company had given him:

                                                        Camb 4 Feb 1749-50
Dear Sr,
Next to the pleasure of writing books, I esteem that of writing to my friends, & I know none whom I have more reason to value, or to whom I would sooner write than to yourself; yet the perpetual interruptions which I suffer in that first & capital pleasure of my life scarce leave me any leisure to indulge myself in the second, but as my study was always open to you, while you continued in the University & your company which I might then have enjoyed

in a vacant hour was ever welcome to me in the busiest; so in our present distance, your letters will find the same reception from me & instead of interrupting, will be an agreeable relief to my studies, by recalling to my mind those easy & philosophic conversations which I used so frequently to enjoy with you & to which I have been a stranger ever since.

Middleton ends his letter by referring to the topic in which he and his contemporaries took an almost obsessional interest—health:

My wife has for some time past been free from that sort of complaint which she had in London but has long been troubled with an ugly dry cough attended with a constant uneasiness in her breast which gives her pain as oft almost as she draws her breath. I advise her to bleed for it, but she waits for proper weather to take the benefit of the air & gentle exercise which she has wholly omitted; & scarce stirred out of the house since we came last from Hildersham; for domestic cares have much confined & disturbed us of late; two servants taken with the small pox, one of whom died lately in the house; a maid fresh from Hildersham, a sister to the two whom you formerly cured with us; the other our coachman, who for several days past has been given over, but is struggling still for life at a Nurse's house, whither we sent him . . .

I am much obliged by your friendly offer of a lodging at your house if I should happen to come to town alone . . .

Middleton's readiness to prescribe treatment for his wife's cough illustrates the view commonly held by educated laymen that as far as the more familiar ailments were concerned, they knew almost as much as the physicians. This attitude was often justified; in any case a gentleman grounded in the classics would have found nothing esoteric in medical jargon and would have felt more competent than his counterpart today to discuss symptoms and treatment on an equal footing.[6]

A physician's advice was not usually sought for minor upsets; apart from the matter of expense (a guinea a visit could be expected), illness was generally regarded as some kind of bodily malfunction (rather than the result of some external influence or invasion) and the individual was held responsible for keeping himself in good fettle. Thus for primary health-care families looked to their medicine-chests, well stocked with purges, emetics and a wide variety of drugs and remedies. For information on their proper use—and on all other aspects of health—dozens of books were readily available to tell the reader not only what measures he should take if he fell ill, but (equally important) how he could keep illness at bay by following a prudent 'regimen'. This included the so-called 'non-naturals' (some, if not all, of which Mrs Middleton clearly favoured)—diet, evacuations, exercise, fresh air, sleep and the control of the passions.

In addition to books, there were regular advertisements (of doubtful trustworthiness) in the newspapers extolling the amazing virtues of patent remedies. Perhaps the most respectable and respected source of advice for the educated reader such as Middleton were the articles of medical interest which appeared each month in the *Gentleman's Magazine*, founded by Edward Cave in 1731. Several of William's contributions to the *Medical Transactions* of the Royal College of Physicians were later to be summarised in its pages, and Middleton would have read several discussions of his own controversial works in the columns devoted to history and theology.

The reference to the two maids 'formerly cured' clearly indicates that William was prepared when necessary to treat all the members of a household including the servants and retainers. Although we have no positive evidence that this was a regular feature of his London practice, it would certainly have made sense for a gentleman of means with a large establishment to try and insure against the inconvenience of sickness among his staff by paying the family physician to care for them.

Although Middleton gives no hint of being worried about his own health, his condition in fact soon began to deteriorate and in July he made the journey to London to seek William's advice. The latter probably recognised that his friend was beyond help, but understandably refrained from saying so. A day or two later Horace Walpole wrote from his town house in Arlington Street to his friend George Montagu:[7]

> Dr Middleton called on me yesterday: he is come to town to consult his physician for a jaundice and swelled legs, symptoms which the doctor tells him, and which he believes, can be easily cured; I think him visibly broke, and near his end.

Walpole's forecast proved correct, and Middleton, having struggled home to Hildersham, died there on 28 July.

Had William foreseen this outcome? And if, as we must assume, his prognosis was the same as Walpole's, should he not have told his old friend the truth?[8] Certainly traditional medical etiquette required that a dying patient be fully informed of his condition; but William would have regarded etiquette as a matter of very minor importance compared with the needs of the individual under his care. Middleton had at least been able to make the journey to London and was not literally at death's door; and William, knowing that optimism was therapeutically valuable, kept his forebodings to himself. The following day Russell Plumptre sent William an account of their friend's last hours:[9]

I was on Friday sent for to Mrs Middleton, who was under the greatest affliction & disorder on account of the Drs approaching end; when there, I went up to the Dr who was sensible & talked a little while with me; amongst other things he told me he had designed to write to you, but feared he was too weak to do it: I asked him if I could write for him, he thanked me & said he should be obliged if I would; the sum of what he said was as near as I can remember to this effect: that he had left off taking his medicines as they were disagreeable to him & because he was fully sensible that his cause was such as would admit of no remedy, that he was resigned & even desirous of dying & therefore you must excuse him if he took nothing more . . . This was about six o'clock on Thursday evening & at three the next morning he died. You have lost a valuable friend; the world a great & worthy man & the University its brightest ornament . . . I am, Dear Sr,
your most humble servant, R Plumptre.

After the funeral Middleton's widow gave her late husband's papers to William, so that he could decide what items might be suitable for publication. He felt obliged however to share this responsibility with one of Middleton's oldest friends, the retired politician and orator Henry Saint-John, Lord Bolingbroke, who lived at his family seat in Battersea. Bolingbroke had had a chequered career; as a young man he had been Secretary-at-War and Secretary of State, but his attachment to the Jacobite cause led to his impeachment and flight to France, where he lived until pardoned nine years later. He was an author of some distinction and a friend of Swift and Pope. In the early summer of 1751 William visited him on at least four occasions and it was agreed that one of Middleton's tracts—On the Inefficacy of Prayer—should be suppressed, to avoid stirring up controversy injurious to its author's memory. Cole retails an anecdote to the effect that William, on hearing that a bookseller had offered the widow £50 for the work, called on her, threw it into the fire 'and with the other hand gave her a £50 note'.[10] Even if the event was accurately reported, it is hard to believe that William was compensating her for the burnt manuscript; more probably he was simply paying a sum due to her from a bookseller which he, as Middleton's literary executor, had received on her behalf.

William's conversations with Bolingbroke were of considerable interest (as sources of literary material) to Dr Birch who noted down in his spidery handwriting the gist of what William reported to him.[11] Both of them were no doubt aware that Bolingbroke was by now a sick man; before the end of the year he had died.

By now, the pattern of William's life was made up of several separate (though interlocking) strands: he was taking an active part in the affairs of the Royal College of Physicians; he was meeting many of London's brightest intellects at the Royal Society, of which he had recently been elected Fellow; he was building up his practice; he was entertaining his friends at Cecil Street—but he was 40 and still unmarried. According to Cole,

> Dr Heberden before he left Cambridge was very desirous of marrying a daughter of Dr Clark, Dean of Salisbury, who lived in a house opposite St Clement's Church; but she did not accord and married a physician of Salisbury . . . a younger man and better person;[12] although Dr Heberden, a tall, thin, spare man was perfectly well made, and of a florid, good countenance, short-sighted.

But if William was rebuffed by Miss Clark, another introduction was soon to follow. At the small village of Quy, between Cambridge and Newmarket, William had become acquainted with the brother of John Martin, Banker of Overbury in Worcestershire and MP for Tewkesbury. The banker had a daughter named Elizabeth, born in 1728; William was introduced to her and in due course a marriage was arranged.

While the preparations were going forward, William applied for and received—on 24 April 1752—a Grant of Arms. It would be interesting to know whether it was William himself who took the initiative in applying for this symbol of distinction, or whether he was prompted by his future father-in-law; in any case, the Grant enhanced his position on the social ladder.

As William would have been consulted by the College of Arms on the most appropriate symbols to be displayed on the escutcheon, it seems reasonable to suppose that they referred in some way to his profession or family connections. The most prominent feature was a fesse (or row) of four lozenges—a clear reference to 'physic'; above these were two suns, which could be interpreted either as emblems of health and light or as a punning reference to Brightling, the home of William's maternal grandfather, William Cooper. Sandwiched between the two suns was an annulet or ring, the significance of which may be revealed by its inclusion (because of its barrel-hoop shape) on the arms of the Coopers' Company of London.

While the coat of arms was being prepared, two other matters—both concerning St John's—required William's attention: the first was his Fellow's stipend, to which he continued to be entitled while he remained a bachelor. Instead of waiting for the wedding day, he relinquished his Fellowship in March[13], thus enabling some needier graduate to be elected in his place. It was customary also for former Fellows of St John's to make some gift to the College when they married; to meet this obligation William combined with his friend the Revd John Green (who had been a sizar at St John's and a contributor to the *Athenian Letters*) in jointly presenting a silver inkstand.[14]

The wedding was held on 1 June in the church of St Martin-in-the-Fields, and we can be sure that Elizabeth did not come empty-handed.

But whatever the terms of the marriage settlement, William soon benefited in other ways from the Martins' liberality; first, his brother-in-law Joseph transferred to him the lease of the manor of Abingdon Court in Cricklade,[15] Wiltshire, thus making him the landlord of thirteen properties—mainly farms—from which he drew the rents; and some time later William acquired from his father-in-law the tithes of Bevington and Blisbury, two hamlets in the parish of Berkeley, Gloucestershire, by the assignment of a lease granted by the Dean and Chapter of Bristol Cathedral.[16]

William was now able to visit his patients in his own coach, its doors emblazoned with his coat of arms, and on one of his longer drives he offered his friend Dr Birch a lift:[17]

10 June 1754

Dear Sir,

The Chariot does not take me up at my own house but meets me in another part of the town. If it will be any convenience to you to go in it, I shall be extremely glad of your company, but must beg of you to let me take you up at Mount Coffee house in lower Grosvenor street where I shall call for you at a quarter past Ten, if you do not forbid it.

Your most humble servt W Heberden

But although the outlook seemed set fair, William had already received two reminders that affluence offered no guarantee against natural hazards. In spite of his own sound and healthy constitution, he was attacked within a few months after his marriage by some obscure complaint which involved, amongst other symptoms an unsightly swelling of the limbs, followed by a fit of the gout.[18] By the following March he had made a full recovery and Elizabeth was looking forward to the birth of their first child. A boy, named John, was born in May, but failed to survive. Early next year Elizabeth was again pregnant and it was agreed that she should go for her confinement to her parents' stately mansion at Overbury, where the purer air and more peaceful surroundings would provide the most favourable conditions for a happy outcome. The child (a boy) was born on 28 September 1754 and was baptised Thomas in the village church adjoining the house. But for Elizabeth, his birth was the beginning of the end. Probably an infection had led to puerperal fever and William was powerless to save her. Towards the end of November she died.

William returned to London leaving the infant in the Martins' care and at once began to compose a lengthy letter[19]—or homily—addressed to Elizabeth's two younger sisters Anna and Margaret and this provides the fullest account we have of his religious beliefs and his essentially practical attitude towards suffering and bereavement. He begins:

I hope you both stand in much less need of comfort in our present affliction than I do; but I have in other cases found that the best way to learn anything was to undertake the teaching it to others. Imagin therefore that I am here endeavouring to relieve your minds in order more effectually to relieve my own; & that I suggest the following considerations to you, that they may make the deeper impression on myself.

Pain, losses, diseases, disappointments & innumerable calamities are distributed thro' every age and condition of men; how unreasonable therefore is it for anyone to behave in such a manner, when any misfortune befalls him, as if he expected that providence should be partial in his favour & exempt him from the common lot of mortals?

A Christian should not repine and be discontented at any thing that happens 'when he knows that such a state of things has been ordained us, no doubt for good & even kind reasons, by that gracious Being who cannot wantonly or maliciously afflict his creatures.' One of the most important lessons to be learned from calamities is 'a proper indifference to the things of this life' and a readiness to 'aspire after a happiness more properly adapted to our nature, which is intended for us in another life'. A special problem arises from our love for our friends and relations:

They are apt to engage our affections too strongly while they are with us; & their loss is the most difficult trial of our patience & resignation. And yet . . . if our love was as disinterested as it should be in true friendship, & aim'd as much as it ought at the happiness of the beloved object, we should soon be at least easy & contented that our friends were removed from trouble to joy, from earth to heaven . . .

At every stage of our lives the pursuit of happiness proves vain and empty and we should despair of finding it any where 'unless reason or revelation has taught us to look for it in another state'.

It is in that state only, that the human mind shall enjoy sincere & lasting pleasures; for that we were originally intended by our gracious Creator, there is our proper country & until we arrive at it, we are but strangers & travellers, expos'd to perpetual inconveniences & injuries. From all these the righteous are delivered on the day of their death . . .

In leading up to his conclusion William asks whom we should desire to imitate when we lose a friend or relation:

One that is wild and fantastical in his grief, forgetting his duty to God, his friends & himself; or one who . . . thinks with himself in the following manner:

'It has pleased God to take to himself the dear companion of my life, for whom I had the highest esteem & the tenderest affection; but I will not be so selfish & impious as to murmur at it . . . I will not not be so unreasonable as to indulge my sorrow & fondly think it a duty that I owe to the dear friend, whom I have lov'd & lost; for what good or pleasure will it do anyone? or who expects it of me? . . . My departed friend would have been displeased with the thoughts of my giving way to sorrow: & my duty to my living friends & relations & to the station of life in which I am plac'd, calls upon me to support my health & spirits, that I may not be disabled by a fruitless grief from being a comfort to them & useful in the world . . .'

The scepticism so often evident in William's medical writings has no place here and we may hope that the blend of faith and reason with which the letter is infused succeeded in bringing some consolation both to William himself and to his two young readers. If we are surprised that Elizabeth is not directly mentioned, this is surely because William's 'considerations' were not intended to apply exclusively to the tragedy of her death, but had a universal application.

The welcome that William had received from his friends when he migrated to London speedily led to new contacts with potential patients. Several of them (as was to be expected) had literary interests and among these was the printer and novelist Samuel Richardson, now famous as the author of *Pamela* and *Clarissa*. He had suffered for some years from nervous tremors which sometimes made it difficult for him to hold a pen, and had evidently consulted William some time in 1750. In February of the following year a friend wrote to enquire after his health and ended his letter thus:[20]

... but I must dismiss you or I shall bring Dr Heberden upon my back. Yet he does not say that you must not read letters? No—but he will say that I write with a wicked Design to provoke you to write again.

Presumably William had advised his patient to employ an amanuensis; but whether or not this advice had any effect, the two men soon became friends, often visiting each other's houses.

It was through Richardson's recommendation that William acquired another literary patient—the Revd Edward Young, rector of Welwyn in Hertfordshire, whose poem *The Complaint or Night-Thoughts on Life, Death and Immortality* had won him European fame. In November 1753 Young wrote to Richardson (his Printer):[21]

... I have been for two or three weeks under a painful lowness of spirits. I have often a sort of moving pain on my left side, and near my heart; and am pretty much troubled with wind and frequent indigestions. Pardon the great liberty I take in requesting you to give, in my name, two guineas to Dr Heberden, and to desire his advice. Mr Gosling [Young's banker] on sight of this letter, will repay the doctor's fee . . . As I am scarce known to the doctor myself, I am almost forced to give you this trouble.

Four days later (26 November) Richardson replied:

My dear Dr Young, You will before now have heard from Dr Heberden; God give success to his advice! I sent him your letter the moment it came to my hand; with two guineas inclosed, as you directed. Last night he sent me back your letter, with a few lines, signifying he had written, and with them inclosed the returned fee. He is a fine-spirited man . . .

William's advice (which he dispensed free of charge to the clergy) evidently had some effect and after a fortnight Young wrote to Richardson: 'I bless God I am better; and by no means despair, through his mercy and blessing, on my good friend Dr Heberden's assistance, of a perfect cure.'

One of Richardson's numerous female admirers was Susannah Highmore, daughter of the artist who had done illustrations for *Pamela* and had later painted the author's portrait. In August 1756 he wrote to her:[22]

. . . Good Doctor Heberden has made me within a week two friendly visits; and yesterday (Friday) I had the pleasure of dining with him and six other learned gentlemen at his house by particular invitation. I mention this with an intention of making an observation on the conversation of learned gossips. But I will let it alone—being not myself a learned man, I ought to forbear and revere in humble silence. What makes me think there is nothing either improving or delightful out of the company of intelligent women? They soften and harmonize every conversation where men, however learned, are admitted a share in it.

Richardson was again at William's table in December 1756, when one of the guests was the physician-poet Mark Akenside. To everyone's irritation he virtually monopolised the conversation.[23] Meanwhile Richardson's tremors and 'convulsive startings' were as troublesome as ever and in July 1757 he wrote:

I have left off Physic. Good Dr Heberden . . . told me that I must not expect relief from it. And I am got deep into Tar-Water. Three or four times a day, by Entreaty of an experienced, tho' not medical Friend.

Tar-water had been popularised by the philosopher Bishop Berkeley, who had learned about its virtues from the Indians during his visit to America;[24] Gray and Walpole both drank it—so Richardson was in good company. William continued to visit him and when he died of a stroke, he left William a ring as a token of their friendship.[25]

One of Richardson's aristocratic admirers was Mary Delany (née Granville), wife of the scholar, preacher and former friend of Dean Swift, a member of the Blue Stocking circle and a tireless letter-writer. She first mentions William in a letter dated January 1754, when he attended her husband for what she describes as a slight attack of the palsy.[26] Early in December (writing again to her sister Mrs Dewes) she comments on William's bereavement and gives us our first glimpse of his personality as perceived from a female viewpoint:

> I am sure you are much concerned for Dr Heberden on the death of his wife; his gentle and affectionate disposition will make him for some time very miserable.

Although Mrs Delany's sympathy was genuinely felt, her attitude was practical and realistic: life must go on and William would soon recover his natural buoyancy if he kept himself fully occupied. Within a month she is describing his attendance on the schoolboy son of the Duchess of Portland at her Buckinghamshire mansion, Bulstrode Park, some eight miles to the north of Windsor, following a Christmas dance:

> The next morning Lord Edward complained of excessive weariness, and had no appetite; at night the Duchess ordered him some Gascoign's powder and small negus, but it would not stay on his stomach; he fell asleep and the next morning was a little feverish, the apothecary sat up with him. Doctor Hays from Windsor was sent for, and all symptoms made them suspect it would prove the small-pox. We were yesterday greatly alarmed; the child was excessively ill, Dr Heberden is here; he finds the child in as good a way as can be expected in the beginning of such a disorder, for it proves the small-pox. The doctor seems to think it will be a middling sort, neither the best nor the worst.

Gascoign's powder was one among hundreds of patent medicines to which the inventors (sometimes reputable physicians, sometimes quacks) had given their names, thus benefiting directly from the sales and indirectly from the publicity. The advertisers' claims were often wildly exaggerated, but as the public's level of credulity was high, it is not surprising that the Duchess was prepared to prescribe the powder, without waiting for advice. Her employment of the apothecary as a nurse is a reminder that these very important members of the medical fraternity were not limited to their primary function of pharmacy. As for William's assessment of the severity of the boy's illness, he classified each case of smallpox as mild, middling or severe in the light of the early symptoms.[27]

On this occasion (as on many others) more than one doctor was called in. There is no evidence that this caused resentment; it was generally accepted that the powers of even the most respected physicians were very limited, that most illnesses were dangerous and that the effects of any course of treatment were very uncertain. The most sensible thing to do if you could afford it, was to take at least two opinions from the best qualified physicians within reach. From the physician's viewpoint, this was an entirely satisfactory arrangement: he got his fee, while sharing the load of responsibility.

William in fact was no stranger to this kind of multiple attendance. Soon after arriving in London he had been called in to attend the Duke of Leeds in the company of the ageing Dr Mead:[28] and when the Archbishop of Canterbury Dr Herring was ill with 'pleuritic fever' in 1753, William was at his bedside with Sir Edward Wilmot and Dr Peter Shaw.[29] Two years later, in a note to the Duke of Newcastle, he makes it clear that once again the patient had the benefit of two physicians:[30]

My Lord, Your Grace's message in relation to Mr Fuller was not received by me, till it was too late to send an answer last night.

A case of multiple attendance. 'The Doctors Puzzled' by Rowlandson.

He was so much better yesterday that the other physician and myself took our leave of him; and if he has no relapse today, he will probably in a few days be perfectly recovered.

By this time Mrs Delany had become one of William's patients and was prepared to accept his advice even against her own inclinations:[31]

. . . I hope it will not be thought necessary for me to go to Cheltenham till the middle of August. I pleaded hard for drinking the waters at home, but Dr Heberden will not hear of it.

Cheltenham's claim to be called a spa was comparatively recent; the mineral springs had been discovered in 1716 and a pump-room was erected twenty years later. Mrs Delany could (if she had chosen to flout William's advice) have drunk the waters at home, as Cheltenham, in common with other spas, bottled its waters for distribution to other parts of the country.

Spas were in fact an important feature of the eighteenth century medical scene and William frequently recommended his patients to visit them. There were two reasons why this advice could have beneficial results: much of the water available to Londoners was (as we shall see later) heavily polluted and even those who drank only beer or wine were still at some risk from the water used for washing dishes or food; by comparison, spa water was pure and wholesome. No less important was the fact that a visit to a spa involved a change of routine and a respite from business, domestic worries or over-indulgence. But was there any special virtue—apart from purity—in these so-called medicinal waters?

Most of them contained mineral salts of various kinds and had been frequently analysed; at Scarborough, for instance, Dr Peter Shaw and later William carried out tests,[32] but the techniques of chemical analysis were not sufficiently refined to give accurate results. It was, however, generally agreed that most waters could be classed as chalybeate (containing iron), saline or—like the 'stinking well' at Harrogate—sulphurous. But as for the therapeutic value of these constituents, William remained unconvinced.

The most celebrated of all English spas was Bath, where visitors could drink the waters, bathe in them and enjoy the social pleasures of a fashionable resort. In his chapter on 'The Bath Waters' in the *Commentaries* William admits that immersion appears to be serviceable 'against contractions and other spasmodic affections of the muscles', but suggests that a warm bath at home would have the same effect. Drinking the waters is 'of singular use' in remedying such troubles as 'pains of the stomach and other ill effects of hard drinking'—but once again we are left with the impression that in William's opinion any pure clean water would have been equally beneficial.

One of the killer diseases for which no remedy existed was diphtheria or 'malignant sore-throat' and in the summer of 1759 two of William's patients—Mrs Charles Yorke and one of her children—caught the infection and died.[33]

A number of different theories were current on the best ways of nursing patients through the 'distemper' and very recently an anonymous pamphlet had been printed entitled *A Letter from a Physician at Bath to Dr Heberden . . . Wherein are set forth the Nature, Symptoms and Cure of the Malignant Sore-Throat; with a Hint or Two concerning the Efficacy of the Bark on some Important Occasions.*[34] One of the factors that had prompted the letter was a monograph on the subject by William's friend and colleague John Fothergill.[35] The author begins rather turgidly:

> Sir, Notwithstanding the Reluctance you are not insensible I naturally labour under, in regard of putting pen to paper, yet to so great a degree am I affected by the calamitous Situation I lately beheld a Young Lady in at this place, from her being seized with a highly malignant Sore-Throat, which carried her off in four days, that I look upon it as a Duty incumbent on me in point of Humanity to communicate to the Public my Thoughts and Reflections concerning that terrible Distemper. I shall make no apology for my conduct in performing this Task under the Sanction of an Address to your Name, it being very natural for a Person of my Obscurity, in order to raise a suitable attention to the Matter he is treating of, to recur to an Expedient of this Sort, and to introduce another as interested in his Subject, whose Parts, Education, and distinguished Character are the Object of a general Esteem and Respect.
>
> The Application of this to yourself is very easy, whose early and rapid Progress in Literary Studies at Cambridge was a sure Prognostic of the Applause, which at present attends you in London, and is every day more and more diffusing itself, so that e'er long no Part of this Kingdom can be unacquainted with your Merit . . .

Although all this was highly complimentary to William, the letter had nothing of value to communicate on possible therapeutic measures; after referring to other varieties of sore throat which can always be cured 'by Bleeding, Physic and a common Gargle', the writer has to confess:

> But alas! the Sore-Throat I am now giving my Thoughts upon is quite of another Class, and seldom, very seldom, yields to that mild Treatment, or, in reality, to any Treatment at all . . . These Cases are very distressful, and ever carry with them an ominous Prognostic . . .

I assure you, Sir, and Practitioners in general, that the few Instances I have seen of Recovery in regard of this severe Disorder, have been intirely owing to repeated Bleedings, Blistering, and Keeping the Body constantly open, the Throat the meanwhile being scarified deep, and dressed with warm tincture of Myrrh . . .

The treatment suggested by William in his *Commentaries*[36] was equally ineffective—as it was bound to be, as the bacillus that caused the disease was not discovered until 1883; he disapproved of bleeding and scarifying and recommended gargles and drinks; but if his measures had little or no effect on the progress of the illness, his patients (many of them children) were at least spared the tormenting régime of the physician from Bath.

At the moment when the letter from Bath appeared, William was conducting a correspondence with the Revd Stephen Hales, whom we have already met in the diaries of William Stukeley. On leaving Cambridge, Hales was appointed Perpetual Curate at Teddington, Middlesex and continued to pursue his scientific interests, while combining them happily with his duties to his parishioners. He made notable contributions to the understanding of vegetable and animal physiology and was elected FRS in 1718. Of special relevance to medicine were his experiments on blood pressure and the vascular system and his invention of a special catheter for the relief of 'the stone'. Throughout his life he used his talents for philanthropic purposes: he designed 'ventilators' to remove the foul air in prisons and the holds of ships; and he invented an improved still, which could distil liquid three times faster (he claimed) than the conventional model and thereby produce pure water on ships more cheaply—a boon for seamen when water kept in casks became undrinkable. The still, he realised, could equally well be used for producing strong liquor, but this disadvantage was balanced by the fact that the speedier process would produce a purer and therefore less injurious spirit. Nevertheless it was ironic that it was these spirituous liquors that were the target of his fiercest denunciations.

Now, at the age of eighty, still alert and enthusiastic, he sought William's advice on some problem connected with counterfeit drugs, which were occasionally used by unscrupulous apothecaries to cut the cost of making up the medicines prescribed by the physician. In his reply William took the opportunity to ask for his friend's help on two subjects that he was researching: the first was the purification of contaminated water, to render it fit to drink—a problem to which the improved still seemed the perfect answer. The other subject— on which Hales had written some unpublished observations—was concerned with the so-called Bills of Mortality, the annual summaries, compiled from parish registers, showing the total number of deaths from each supposed cause. In the following acknowledgement Hales, having provided the requested information, gives a memorable description of some of the effects he had achieved by tirelessly campaigning for his favourite good causes:[37]

Teddington 31 Aug 1758

Dear Sir, . . . As to the stills with improved heads[38] which you inquire after, they are made by Mr Durand a Pewterer in St Martins Lane, where you may see them . . . You may see an account of these stills in my Book on the uses of ventilators, the first part which is just reprinted, (by Manly in the Old Bailey) one third abridged, so that both parts can well be bound up in one Book.[39]

I have lately given him orders to send . . . 400 of them to all our colonies in America from Barbados to Hudson's Bay. My principal and indeed only motive for it is to endeavour thereby to rouse the caution & indignation of Mankind against those great Decolonizers, those mighty destroyers and debasers of the human species, distilled spirituous Liquors, those worse than infernal spirits, which bewitch the infatuated Nations . . . And with the same view I have already sent the book to the Principal Nations of Europe, especially the more Northern as far as Petersburgh. It is a matter of the greatest satisfaction to me to have been instrumental in getting Strong Drams out of the Royal Navy. For Admiral Vernon[40] acknowledged he took the Hint to mix three parts of water with one of Dram, from a Book of mine in which I took occasion to mention their noxiousness in the year 1739, when he went to take Porto Bello, and from the apparent good effects of this practice, it is made a general Rule in our whole Fleet. And Admiral Boscawen[41] told me little before he went on his present Expedition, that he did not suffer a Dram to be in his whole Squadron, but procured Mountain and Madeira wine, so that there is great encouragement, resolutely to persevere in warning mankind against these mighty destroyers.

Mr Boscawen told me just before he went to Lewisburgh, that he ordered the ventilators to be provided incessantly night & day which had the desired effect of preserving his men in Health, for Mrs Boscawen told me that he wrote her word from Madeira, that on mustering his numerous crew of about 800 there, there was but one so ill as not to be able to come up on Deck to answer to his name . . .

This remarkable letter illustrates several of Hales's most important qualities: his enthusiasm, his disinterested benevolence and generosity, his missionary zeal against the drinking of spirits and his practical inventiveness. The letter is also a useful reminder of some of the events taking place at the international level, events which were symptomatic of England's steadily increasing wealth and influence and which were reflected in William's personal rise to fame and fortune; the *annus mirabilis* of 1759 in which England won resounding victories in Africa, India, Canada and the Caribbean can be counted as a significant year of achievement for William also.

During his correspondence with Hales, he had been busy making a collection of the yearly Bills of Mortality for the London parishes and had amassed an unbroken sequence running 1657 to 1758, with

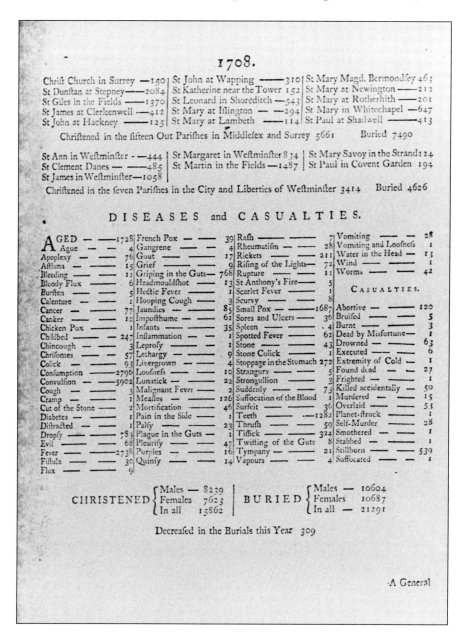

A page from A Collection of the Yearly Bills of Mortality.

some earlier bills dating back to 1593. These formed the core of a substantial volume which William published anonymously in January.[42] In his 'Preface' he explains his intentions and makes due acknowledgement to other writers past and present, whose work is included in the volume to supplement his own contribution:

A Register of the births, diseases, and deaths among any considerable number of people will easily afford much useful information to philosophers in general, as well as to the statesmen and physicians of the particular country, in which it is kept. For their sakes, therefore, and by their means for the sake of the public, some pains have been taken to make as perfect a collection, as was possible, of all the London bills of mortality, from their beginning to this present year 1758. It can only be from a long series of such registers, that we are enabled to make any near approaches to truth, in the calculations founded upon them; and the longer the series is, the nearer will our approaches be. But as these bills are published in loose leaves, and very little care has hitherto been taken to preserve them, it is evident that the keeping of this register has lost a great part of its use. For it is become a matter of great trouble to find any number of bills together, greater perhaps than many of those would chuse to take, who are able, and might be willing, to draw out several important conclusions from them, when thrown in their way, as by the present publication . . .

As a specimen of the use, which may be made of them, there are subjoined to this collection: Capt Graunt's[43] *Natural and Political Observations on the Bills of Mortality*; Sir William Petty's[44] *Essay concerning the Growth of the City of London*; the very judicious performance of Corbyn Morris, Esq[45] entitled *Observations on the past Growth and present State of the City of London*; and lastly, *A comparative view of the diseases and ages, for the last thirty years, drawn from the bills of mortality, with their proportions to a thousand; and also a table of the probabilities of life, for the last thirty years . . .*

William then proceeds to give the reasons why 'these bills are very far from being so accurate, as they might have been'. The registers of births and deaths cover only baptisms and burials performed according to the ceremonies of the church of England; many who die in London are carried out to be buried in the country, and are therefore not recorded in the London bills. Another 'material defect' arises 'from the neglect of parish clerks and their deputies, in not making exact returns'. And the records of deaths are very defective for a further reason—that only those buried in parochial cemeteries are recorded, and no account is taken of those buried in other burial grounds belonging to the church of England 'such as St Paul's cathedral, Westminster abbey, the Temple church St Peter's ad

Vincula, the Rolls, and Lincoln's-Inn chapels, the Charter-house, and divers others belonging to hospitals'.

As to the causes of death:

> Every parish appoints a searcher, whose business it is to examine the corpse, and to report the distemper. The low capacity of the person usually chosen into this office has been made an objection to the truth and justness of the bills. But with regard to natural deaths, there seems no other capacity necessary in these searchers, than that of relating what they hear. For the wisest person in the parish would be able to find out very few distempers from a bare inspection of the dead body, and could only bring back such an account, as the family and friends of the deceased would be pleased to give. And it should indeed be always remembered from whom this account comes, that proper allowances may be made for mistakes, or misrepresentations, in those distempers, which they might not be very able to know, or not very willing to own.

Although the Bills collected by William referred only to parishes in London, the very first sentence of his 'Preface' suggests that a 'register' on a national scale could be valuable for a whole range of medical, actuarial and demographical purposes. Since the time of Petty and Graunt, the search for improved methods of estimating the population (both of London and of the whole country) had often been discussed—not least by members of the Royal Society. The most recent controversy had begun with a paper published in the Society's *Philosophical Transactions* by the Rector of a London parish, the Revd William Brackenridge, who argued that since the earlier part of the century the population of London had fallen. He was in due course attacked by the Rector of a parish in Berkshire for his pessimism and bad arithmetic; but the arguments on both sides were bound in the end to be somewhat inconclusive as the statistics which underpinned them were hopelessly inadequate.

The many defects in the London Bills which William describes were widely recognised and his friend Dr Fothergill was among those who proposed improvements. Thomas Birch, who was by now Secretary to the Royal Society, also interested himself in the discussions and it was no doubt for this reason that William's (anonymous) volume was for a time erroneously believed to be his. Serious attempts to improve the accuracy and comprehensiveness of the Bills were made by the Company of Parish Clerks in London who were responsible for publishing them; in the 1730s they petitioned Parliament for authority to register deaths instead of burials, but their plea was rejected. In 1751 they drafted a Bill seeking to make it compulsory to notify births and deaths (instead of baptisms and burials); this, after objections from some of the clergy was withdrawn in favour of a National Registration Bill, introduced by a Mr Potter in 1753. But this effort and another Bill introduced five years later were both thrown out. It was in this context that William's volume appeared.[46]

In the remaining pages of his 'Preface' William summarises the history and development of parish registers and the Bills that were based on them. Referring to the Bills for the Plague years, he speculates on the reasons why London had been free from this scourge for nearly a century:

. . . One of the causes of this happy event seems to be the greater freshness and purity of the air of London, since the rebuilding of it after the great fire; the streets being made wider, and the inhabitants not crowded so closely together . . . Another, and probably the most effectual preservative has been the great quantity of water from the Thames and the New River,[47] which, for the last century, has washed the houses so plentifully, and afterwards running down into the kennels and common sewers, constantly hinders, or weakens the tendency to putrefaction . . .

The mortality figures for measles next come under scrutiny, and William suggests that many of these deaths should have been attributed to scarlet fever or malignant sore throat. Almost the whole number of deaths by convulsions[48] are suffered, William argues, by children under two years of age.

The yearly sum of the deaths ranged under the heads of apoplexies, suddenly, planet-struck, lethargies, and palsies, fluctuates without any constant increase or decrease, till the beginning of the present century: from which time this sum has been perpetually increasing . . . In the last ten years this increase has been the greatest of all . . . Is this difference only an apparent one, arising from the placing of some deaths under these in the later bills, which formerly came under other articles? There seems no reason for such a suspicion . . . If the increase be real, is it owing to any alteration in our manners or diet? And what is that alteration? The practice of drinking spirituous liquors must, probably, answer for some part of this; and it might be of public use, if some attention were paid to the finding out of the other causes.

Other factors which in William's view 'restrain the natural fertility of mankind in Great Britain' are:

. . . pride, poverty, the crowded manner of living in our cities, the unhealthfulness of many occupations, and the false ridicule thrown upon marriage, particularly by those great patrons of debauchery, who wrote for the stage towards the end of the last century and in the beginning of the present.

There were many besides William who recognised the appalling wastage of life during the first half of the century, and who were capable of making intelligent guesses regarding the main causes. William's special contribution was to draw attention to the importance of statistical evidence as raw material from which plans for future improvements could be evolved. Whatever we may think of his views on the influence of the stage, there can be no doubt that 'the abuse of spirituous liquors' had had a devastating effect particularly between 1720 and 1751—when the Government was at last forced to increase the duty on spirits and to forbid distillers, chandlers and grocers to retail them. Among the stream of petitions to the House of Commons urging the absolute necessity of curbing the consumption of spirits, was one from the Ministers, Church-wardens, Vestrymen and Inhabitants of William's own parish—St Martin-in-the-Fields,[49] dated 26 February 1750/1, which stated:

> . . . that by the frequent and excessive use of spirituous liquors religion is scandalously prophaned, the health of the people destroyed, their strength and substance wasted, their lives shortened and the human species lessened and decreased; and that idleness and disorder take the place of industry and morality amongst the labouring and common people; and that numberless robberies in the streets and elsewhere, and even murders are committed by the common use of low-priced spirituous liquors; and that if an immediate restraint is not put to this pernicious vice, it will not only increase the above-mentioned evils, but also tend to the destruction of the trade and power of the kingdom . . .

By the time William published his *Collection of Bills*, the tide was beginning to turn; the mortality rate had passed its peak and would thereafter slowly decline. Several different causes contributed to this improvement: gin consumption was falling; better administration at local level was providing more sanitary conditions in the streets and more enlightened care for parish children; standards of personal cleanliness were rising; and gradually a new spirit of humanity was emerging, the tangible results of which could be seen in the foundation of lying-in hospitals, isolation hospitals and free medical dispensaries.

There was one more factor of crucial importance—the growing practice of inoculation against smallpox, which William actively encouraged. This had been a subject of lively controversy since 1717, when the adventurous Lady Mary Wortley Montagu, wife of the English Ambassador in Constantinople, wrote a letter to a friend in England describing how in Turkey the smallpox had been rendered 'entirely harmless by the invention of ingrafting, which is the name they give it'.[50] On her return to England, Lady Mary's attempts to promote this novelty met with a frosty reception from some of the doctors and clergy; Sir Hans Sloane however endorsed the practice and when the children of George I were inoculated, the Royal initiative was widely followed. A vocal minority, however, continued to oppose it, among them a Dr Cantwell, who had set up a practice in Paris. In 1755 he published a dissertation attacking inoculation and this stimulated the Royal College of Physicians to take concerted action.[51] On 22 December nineteen of the Fellows (William among them) unanimously approved a resolution[52] 'that in their opinion the objections made at first to it have been refuted by experience and that it is at present more generally esteemed and practised in England than ever and that they judge it to be a practice of the utmost benefit to mankind'.

William at once agreed to translate the resolution into French and to communicate it to the editor of the *Journal Britannique*[53]—a pocket-sized bi-monthly published at The Hague, which disseminated English literary and scientific ideas in several countries on the Continent.

Although he was totally convinced that inoculation was the best safeguard against smallpox that had yet been discovered, William was aware that recently inoculated persons had sometimes passed on the disease to others. When he came to write his Preface to the *Bills* two years later he referred to this risk, which he felt would be steadily reduced as inoculation became 'more general'; in other words, the dangers were minimal when every member of a community could be inoculated—a fairly simple matter in a small country village; but in large cities it was impossible to inoculate everybody, and the risk of spreading the infection could not be lightly dismissed.

Among the most ardent supporters of inoculation was Benjamin Franklin, who came to London in 1757 to represent the Pennsylvania legislature; when William asked him for details of its success in America, Franklin sent him a paper[54] showing that during an outbreak of smallpox in Boston, the operation had saved many lives. The paper continued:

Notwithstanding the now uncontroverted success of Inoculation it does not seem to make that progress among the common people in America, which at first was expected. Scruples of conscience weigh with many concerning the lawfulness of the practice . . . The expense of having the operation performed by a surgeon weighs with others . . . Many of these, rather than own the true motive for declining Inoculation, join with the scrupulous in the cry against it, and influence others. A small pamphlet wrote in plain language by some skilful Physician, and publish'd, directing what preparations of the body should be used before the Inoculation of children, what precautions to avoid giving the infection at the same time in the common way, and how the operation is to be performed, the incisions dressed, the patient treated, and on the appearance of what symptoms a Physician is to be called, &c, might, by encouraging parents to inoculate their own children, be a means of removing that objection of the expense, render the practice much more general, and thereby save the lives of thousands.

William readily agreed to write a pamphlet on the lines suggested and the result of this collaboration was published in 1759 under the title *Some account of the success of inoculation . . . in America together with Plain Instructions by which any person may be enabled to perform the operation and conduct the Patient through the Distemper.* In the first part Franklin follows his Account (from which we have already quoted) by informing the reader that William, having written the *Plain Instructions*, had

... generously at his own private expense, printed a very large impression of them, which was put into my hands to be distributed gratis in America. Not aiming at the prize which however is justly due to such disinterested benevolence, he has omitted his name;[55] but as I thought the advice of a nameless Physician might possibly on that account be less regarded I have, without his knowledge, here divulged it . . .

B Franklin of Philadelphia

William begins his *Plain Instructions* with some observations on the age and state of health of the persons to be inoculated. Under the next heading 'Of Preparation', children under two years, he writes, require none; everyone else, for a fortnight before they are inoculated, should take laxatives, drink nothing stronger than water and reduce their intake of meat. 'All great fatigue and violent exercise should be forborn, together with all intense thinking and application to perplexing business.'

Then comes the crucial section 'Of the Manner of Inoculating', in which William makes the tacit assumption that 'matter' can be readily obtained from someone already in the throes of smallpox:

The proper time for taking the matter is just before it would have dried up. In order to take it, any sort of thread must be had ready about the thickness of a common pin. The head of one of the small-pox may be opened with a needle, or pin, and then the thread is to be drawn along this, and other pocks, if it be necessary, till it is thoroughly wetted. The thread thus wetted may be put into a common pill-box, into which the air can easily get, and here it will soon become dry: you may either inoculate with it as soon as ever it is dry (and I advise it not to be used while it is wet) or you may then put into a close box or vial, (for it will keep without spoiling after it has been dried) and use it some days after. It has been known to keep its power of communicating the infection for many months. Half an inch of that part of this thread which had been well soaked in the matter, (and this will be known by its stiffness) must be cut off at the time of use. The person who is to be inoculated, must have the fine edge of a penknife or lancet drawn along that part of the arm where issues are usually made; and it must go deep enough to make the blood just begin to appear; that is to say, the slightest incision which can be made is sufficient: this small wound should be a little more than half and inch long. In, or rather upon, this the bit of thread must be put, and a small plaister of what is called the Ladies black sticking plaister, or plaister of simple diachylon, is all which need be put over it to keep it on . . .

The final section of the *Instructions* deals, as we would expect, with the management of the patient after the operation, and the reader is assured that if the inoculation fails to 'take', 'it may safely be repeated after waiting one month; for if it does not succeed, it does no harm, and the patient is just in the same state with those on whom it had never been attempted . . .'

Franklin's recommendation virtually guaranteed that the *Plain Instructions* would be widely read, and before long they were receiving favourable publicity in the American newspapers. In April 1760 the *Pennsylvania Gazette* published a letter[56] from a physician signing himself Americanus in which he wrote:

I think it [the pamphlet] is a very Useful performance, not only as it tends to promote the Practice of Inoculation in general, but as containing some of the best general Rules for the Preservation of our fellow creatures from the dismal and fatal Effects of that Frightful Distemper.

The letter, reprinted three months later in Weyman's *New York Gazette*, significantly increased the public's awareness of the pamphlet both in the towns and the countryside.

Records of inoculations performed according to William's instructions are sparse, but one account has survived in letters written by Charles Carroll,[57] the proprietor of a plantation in Maryland, to his son and namesake in the spring of 1770. In April he writes:

Dr Charley . . . The Small Pox is all Round us, which Has determined me to Innoculate all our young negroes there will be about 120 send the medicines mentioned in the Inclosed to prepare them for Innoculation, the Quantity of Plaster must be proportioned to the number, Rather more than less . . .

The medicines separately listed were those that William had recommended—rhubarb, jalap, ipecacuanha and a lenitive electuary. Mr Carroll was already familiar with the routine, which had been followed on an earlier occasion 'According to Do[r] Heberdens Directions'. The inoculator had been a certain Mr Ireland, 'who succeeded very well Heretofore & I doubt not will do so again'. Although the Rhubarb was unobtainable, the inoculations were performed on 26 April; the patients included 110 negroes, 'the Eldest not Exceeding 10 yrs' and by 24 May Mr Carroll was able to inform his son that 'all the People innoculated are well, it was very favourable to all . . .'

Having briefly enjoyed the married state, William could not have been expected to remain a widower indefinitely. In September 1758 Daniel Wray, apparently a confirmed bachelor, had married a lady from Richmond-on-Thames[58] and this event may have focused William's thoughts on a daughter of the Wollaston family to whom Wray had introduced him some ten years before. The Revd William Wollaston who had died in 1724 was the author of the widely read *Religion of Nature Delineated*; one of his sons, Francis, studied law at Cambridge and was elected FRS. In 1728 he married Mary Fauquier, whose father was Deputy Master of the Mint and a Governor of the Bank of England, and a daughter, Mary, was born in January 1729/30. According to Gray,[59] William had formerly courted her, but could not at that time afford to marry her 'for she has (they say) but 2000£ fortune'. By the late 1750s, however, William's financial position was secure and Mary's comparatively modest fortune was no longer an impediment. He proposed and was accepted, and in January 1760 the couple were married at St Botolph's, Aldersgate. Thomas, who until now had been in the care of the Martins, came to join his father's household and over the years the size of the family gradually increased. Of Mary's seven children three died in infancy; the others were Mary, born in 1761, William (the future Royal Physician) in 1767, George in 1770 and Charles in 1772. We shall meet them again at a later stage in the story.

In the meantime, any attempt to draw a picture of William's private domestic life would be largely a matter of guess-work. He lived in a world dominated by men and for the most part recorded by men, from the man's point of view. Wives (with rare exceptions) took a back seat, and it is therefore not surprising that as William's first marriage was so brief, we know nothing of Elizabeth's personality. Even Mary (who outlived her husband) is a somewhat shadowy figure; Cole reported that she was considered 'learned' and as she came from an intellectual family, her education was probably more thorough than was usual among young ladies of her generation.

Her presence enabled William once more to entertain mixed company instead of the all-male gatherings which Richardson had found boring. The list of guests included Gray, who had temporarily forsaken Cambridge for London, in order to study in the British Museum; and he closes one of his letters to Wharton[60] with the words 'Dr Heberden enquires kindly after you, & has his good dinners as usual'. Daniel Wray and his wife would also have been on the list and would in turn have entertained Mary and William at their Richmond home 'Mount Ararat Lodge'. But the formal dinner parties at Cecil Street could only have been held at well-spaced intervals; apart from his daily visits to patients and the many other activities that took him out of the house, William had to find time for his correspondence, for reviewing and indexing his case-notes and for keeping himself properly informed by regular reading. Besides his well-stocked library of printed books, he had amassed hundreds of letters, including a voluminous correspondence between Conyers Middleton and his literary patron Lord Hervey who had died in 1743. Soon after his marriage, William decided (no doubt with Mary's approval) that these loose papers should be tidied up, and in the following note[61] he takes the first step towards providing them with suitable protection:

> Dr Heberden sends his compls to Dr Birch & if he happens to go near his Bookbinder, begs him to order four quarto gard-books (of the same size with the inclosed paper or rather of a size fit to receive letters of this bigness) as handsome as he can make them of calves leather; gilt on the back and letter'd
> Letters of Ld Hervey
& Dr Middleton

31 July 1760

Three months later George II died of an apoplexy. As the new King, his grandson, was unmarried, the immediate problem was to find him a wife. Matters were duly arranged and on 7 September 1761 the future Queen, Princess Charlotte of Mecklenburg-Strelitz, aged sixteen, landed at Harwich; next day she set eyes on the King for the first time and the same evening was married to him in the chapel of St James's Palace. The Coronation followed a fortnight later.

It is not known whether William had by now been introduced to the King, but certainly the latter knew of his reputation and almost immediately offered him the appointment of Physician to the Queen. As the King was the ultimate fount of patronage, such an offer was not to be lightly dismissed. Nevertheless William refused it on the grounds that 'it might interfere with those connexions in life that he had now formed'.[62] In his place he recommended

Dr Joseph Letherland,[63] whereupon it was proposed that the two physicians should hold the appointment jointly. The formal proposal came from Lord Bute,[64] to whom William replied:[65]

I waited upon your Lordship this morning to return my thanks for the honor of your letter which I received last night. His Majesty's goodness in appointing me as well as Dr Letherland is what I did not expect when I took the liberty of mentioning Dr Letherland. It is a concern to me to think that I have hurt somebody's fortune whom your Lordship had intended to nominate with me; and I should be much better pleased if this person was still to be made physician instead of me. Your Lordship imputes more dis-interestedness to me than I have any right to for I should accept this charge out of duty rather than as what suits my inclination. There is indeed nothing in it which gives me any pleasure, but his Majesty's favourable opinion of me and the most obliging manner in which your Lordship received me; and if it would not be too late, I would rather decline this honour in favor of the person for whom it was at first intended. I have written to Dr Letherland but was obliged to go out before I could hear from him.

William's refusal, though couched in respectful phrases, is quite blunt, and is based on thoroughly practical considerations: his services were already in continuous demand and his 'connexions' included not only his many patients, but the Royal Society and the Royal College of Physicians, in whose affairs he was actively involved. Thus his days were fully occupied and although he must often have been prepared to accept new cases (replacing those who had died or moved away), the young Queen was no ordinary patient; acceptance of the royal appointment would have involved a long-term commitment and the time-wasting frustrations of Court formalities and protocol. Moreover, William was aware that the Queen would probably spend part of each year at Kew—the King's favourite rural retreat, roughly six miles away—and that each visit to the palace there could occupy the best part of a day. As for the financial rewards and the cachet of 'royal physician', he could afford to be indifferent to these attractions, as his income was already very substantial and his reputation assured.

In 1763 William was briefly involved in the actions of a fellow-member of the Royal Society, the notorious 'Champion of Liberty', John Wilkes, MP for Aylesbury. Following the Treaty of Paris, Wilkes had made a virulent attack in his journal *The North Briton* on the King's speech to Parliament; for this he was arrested and briefly confined in the Tower for seditious libel. Soon after his release, one MP was so affronted by his behaviour that he challenged him to a duel in the course of which Wilkes received a pistol bullet in the groin. His wound made it impossible for him to attend the House of Commons to answer the charges of libel, and after some delay the Government, suspecting that he might be malingering, ordered William and a surgeon named Hawkins to visit him and report on his progress. Next day (17 December) William wrote[66] to Wilkes's physician, Dr Brocklesby:[67]

> Dear Sir, An order of the house of commons is come to Mr Hawkins and me, to attend Mr Wilkes from time to time, in order to observe the progress of the cure, and to make a report to the house together with you and Mr Graves. You will oblige me by acquainting Mr Wilkes with this; and if you will let us know at what time you intend to see Mr Wilkes on Monday, we will be ready to meet you there. Mr Hawkins desires that the appointment may be for some hour after twelve. I am yours, W Heberden.

Brocklesby forwarded William's letter to Wilkes, enclosing the order of the House and a covering letter asking him 'to fix the hour for our attendance at your house'; Wilkes sent William a prompt— and ironic—acknowledgment:

> Mr Wilkes presents his compliments to Dr Heberden, and is duly sensible of the kind care and concern of the house of commons, not only for his health, but for his speedy recovery. He is attended by Dr Brocklesby, of whose integrity and ability he has had the experience of many years, and on whose skill he has the most perfect reliance. Mr Wilkes cannot but still be of opinion, that there is a peculiar propriety in the choice he at first made of Dr Brocklesby, for the cure of what is called a gunshot wound, from the circumstance of the doctor's having been several years physician to the army; but at the same time entertains a real esteem for Dr Heberden's great merit; and tho' he cannot say that he wishes to see the doctor at present, he hopes in a few weeks he will be well enough to beg that honour to eat a bit of mutton in Great George-Street.

Before the month was out—and before the wound had healed— Wilkes had crossed the Channel into voluntary exile and his hope of inviting William to share his mutton remained for the time being unfulfilled. Nevertheless, the closing phrases of his note confirm that William was no stranger to him and it would indeed be surprising if they had not already made each other's acquaintance at the meetings of the Royal Society or of the dinner club. In what sense William was a 'Wilkite', as Cole alleges, we can only guess; he would surely have agreed with the campaign that Wilkes waged against corruption and with his support for religious toleration; and even if he disapproved of his outrageous behaviour, he would still have appreciated his wit and cheerful resilience.

While the furore over Wilkes was at its height, William was attending the poet William Cowper at his rooms in the Inner Temple. Cowper (1731-1800) had trained for a legal career and been called to the Bar; but his prospects of success in his profession were blighted by mental instability, and when he was given the opportunity of applying for a salaried position as a clerk in the House of Lords, he became overwhelmed by a sense of his unworthiness and attempted to commit suicide. In his memoir of his early life[68] he gives the reader a glimpse of his state of mind:

> I saw plainly that God alone could deliver me; but was firmly persuaded that he would not, and therefore omitted to ask it. Ask it indeed at *his* hands, I would not; but as Saul sought to the witch, so did I to the physician Dr Heberden; and was as diligent in the use of drugs, as if they would have healed my wounded spirit, or have made the rough places plain before me.

The drugs were presumably opiates and the passage seems to imply that William's attempts at therapy were a failure; but twenty years later in his poem *Retirement*, the poet pays his physician a handsome tribute, as if wishing to make amends for the somewhat slighting reference to him in the *Memoir*:

> Virtuous and faithful HEBERDEN! whose skill
> Attempts no task it cannot well fulfil,
> Gives Melancholy up to nature's care,
> And sends the patient into purer air . . .

Even allowing for some poetic licence these lines make it clear that William's visits had not after all been wasted; true, it was beyond William's powers to provide a permanent cure; but the verses certainly imply that he was successful in relieving the poet's depression at least for a while. The last two lines accurately summarise William's faith in the healing powers of nature and in the value of a change of surroundings. As Cowper went to Margate during the summer, we can assume that the trip was taken on William's advice.

One of William's most valuable attributes as a physician was his empathy with his patients' anxieties and his ability to alleviate them with appropriate advice; in his conversations with Cowper he would no doubt have sought to overcome the poet's feelings of despair by trying to inculcate a more optimistic brand of Christian belief than the gloomy Calvinistic creed by which he was engulfed. If this theory is correct, it gives added point to Cowper's choice of the epithets 'virtuous' and 'faithful'.

In the following two letters we see William's reactions to the demands of clients with different social backgrounds. The first[69] is addressed to Philip Yorke, who had recently succeeded to his father's title, Earl of Hardwicke. He now had two enormous country estates—Wrest Park in Bedfordshire, which he had acquired at the age of twenty by his marriage to an heiress; the other, Wimpole Hall near Cambridge, which had passed to him on his father's death. He had two daughters, and it is to the younger one, Lady Mary Jemima, (as yet unmarried) to whom William refers:

> 1 Oct 1765
>
> My Lord, As I know nothing of Lady Mary's disorder but from one conversation with Sir W Duncan,[70] I can hardly imagin that I have anything to say about it more than your Lordsp must have already heard. As far as I am able to judge, nothing has yet happened to make us despair that her health may be perfectly restored. But if I had been longer acquainted with the case, it is such an one which so seldom happens, that I am sensible it would not be in my power to judge with certainty of the event. When Lady Mary returns to town, I shall be ready to wait upon her Ladyship, as soon as I receive your commands. I am, my Lord, your Lordship's most humble servant   W Heberden Cecil St.

In spite of the courteous tone of the letter, William barely disguises his feelings of impatience at being asked for advice without being given enough information on which to form a judgement. Whatever the nature of Lady Mary's complaint, she must have made a good recovery: in due course she married, produced a family and survived well into the next century.

William's second letter[71] is addressed to the Revd Philip Morant, author and antiquarian, who had written a history of Essex and held several livings in and around Colchester; evidently he had travelled to London in the hope of seeing William personally and on finding that he was away, had written a note describing his symptoms. William replied:

> Cecil St 16 May 1767
>
> Sir, I am extremely concerned that a sudden call out of town hindered me from seeing you on Thursday. But your case appears so clear to me that I think you could not have given a better account of it if I had seen you, than you gave in your letter. The Bark is in my judgment the proper remedy for your disorder and if you will be pleased to take half a quarter of an ounce every three hours for 24 hours and then four times a day for a week, you are not likely to have it return any more. Nothing need be added to the Bark and it may be taken in a glass of water alone or of milk and water. If after the fever is cured, the faintings should continue, be pleased to

acquaint me with it and I shall with great pleasure endeavor to find out the proper means of removing them. I am, Sir . . . W Heberden

The 'sudden call out of town' was an inescapable feature of William's practice; his wealthy clients often had houses in the country as well as in London and as they paid the piper (handsomely) they expected to call the tune.

In commending the thoroughness with which Morant had described his condition, William touches on a crucial feature of eighteenth century practice: the physician had no diagnostic aids, such as the thermometer or stethoscope and to arrive at a correct assessment of a patient's condition he had to rely on his own five senses and on his experience in interpreting the signals. If a patient was able (like Morant) to give a clear and accurate account of his own case including the pains and sensations which could be known only to himself, then his physician had as good a basis for a diagnosis as he could hope for.

As Peruvian Bark (from the cinchona tree) was so efficacious in controlling certain fevers, William began to use it as one of the ingredients in a medicine formulated by himself under the title Mistura Ferri Aromatica (Aromatic Mixture of Iron). It was made up as follows:

> Take a lance-leaved cinchona, reduce to coarse powder, 1 ounce; colomba root, sliced, 3 drachms; cloves bruised, 2 drachms; iron filings, ½ oz. Digest for 3 days in a closed vessel, shaking occasionally, with as much peppermint water as will be sufficient to afford 12 oz of strained liquor; then add compound tincture of cardamon, 3 oz; tincture of orange peel, 3 drachms.

In 1826 the formula won a measure of official recognition by its inclusion in the *Dublin Pharmacopoeia,* and when four years later an English version appeared,[72] the editors remarked:

> This is a very old preparation, now for the first time introduced into this *Pharmacopoeia,* and not ordered by other Colleges. It was formerly much extolled, and known in practice by the name of Heberden's Ink from its colour, which is black, owing to the chemical action of the bark on the iron.
>
> Medical properties and uses: It is a most valuable tonic medicine in weak states of the stomach arising from dyspepsia and in various states of debility.
>
> Dose: ½ an ounce to 2 ounces.

The mixture was held in high repute for many years on both sides of the Atlantic; its last appearance was in 1910 when it was listed in Lippincott's *New Medical Dictionary*, published in Philadelphia.

According to Cole, William 'took no fees of the clergy'—though no doubt the more prosperous members of the 'sacred profession' found other ways of showing their appreciation of his services. Sometimes however his rule could cause a measure of embarrassment. Thus Dr John Taylor one day mentioned rather peevishly to a friend that he was costive; when asked why he would not consult Dr Heberden, he said 'How can I do so? He will not take anything.'[73]

Jeremiah Markland,[74] who exchanged numerous letters with William on matters of classical scholarship, also received free advice, as the following extracts from his correspondence make plain:

30 May 1762

Dear Sir, Before I wrote to you I was willing to see what effect the physic would have upon my eyes. I have taken three doses, all which have performed their parts very well, except in the cheif article, in which I find no alteration either from physic or from the water you prescribed, as it is one eye cheifly (the right) which is bad, and affects the other, tho not much; I am advised to shut up that eye from the light, which however it can bear without much pain: tho the light causes it now and then to drop a tear, and it is blood-shot. In these circumstances it is impossible to do anything that requires much use of the eyes; nor do I think of it, but as I fancy Mr Bowyer will be here this day 7night, I will write to you again after I have seen him . . .

12 Oct 1762

Dear Sir, I did not mention to you my Ague, because I did not intend you should know any thing of it, unless there had been some difficulty in the case: imagining that an ordinary country Apothecary could remove that Distemper as well as the best Physician. But I shall very readily and thankfully follow your prescription of taking more Bark than might be thought necessary, especially since I have seen in my News-paper (the *St James's Chronicle* from Thursd Oct 7 to Sat Oct 9) an account from an Officer at Chester of the Gouts being kept off by him in the same method as Ague is cured: which agreed with my own experience and observation that there is something Aguish in the Gout . . .

29 July 1763

Dear Sir, I am greatly obliged to you for your kind enquiry after my health. It has been bad enough since the last Fitt of the Gout in the Spring, which has left behind it a weakness and swelling about my Ancles, which hinder my walking, and I find are not to be removed by warm weather, not to mention seventy years, which I suppose are the foundation of those and many other almost daily complaints . . .

When Markland wrote again on 9 June 1771, he had moved to a smaller house, where there was no room for his library of books; he begged William to accept them as a gift 'because it is the only way I have of showing my thankfulness to you'. He ends with a PS:

I chew a bit of rhubarb every other night, which does its business very well; but my legs continue obstinate and will not suffer me to walk as I us'd to do. Can any thing more be done by, or to, a person who is near 78 years old?

One of William's more colourful patients was Philip Thicknesse, traveller, soldier, amateur physician and writer. In 1780 he published his *Valetudinarian's Guide to Bath* and revealed that he had for many years suffered from gall-stones.[75]

The last violent fit I had was ten or twelve years ago, when I passed the largest, and as Dr Heberden *then* assured me, the only one that was in the gall bladder, and which is now in his possession; he knew it to be the only one, because it was not (like the others I passed) burnished in any part, as it would have been had other gall stones lay in contact with it . . .

The account does not make it clear whether William retained the stone in lieu of fee, but he was sufficiently intrigued by the stories he had heard of his patient's adventurous life to subscribe to the *Memoirs* which Thicknesse eventually published in 1788.

William's interest in scientific matters had been greatly stimulated by his membership of the Royal Society. During the first hundred years of its existence the papers published in the *Philosophical Transactions* had made important contributions to many different areas of enquiry, and of these Astronomy had received its full share of attention. Apart from the enormous interest in the subject which had been generated by Newton, recent improvements in the quality of telescopes held the promise of further exciting discoveries. In this field, as in many others, the Royal Society had acted as a pace-setter and in 1758 had awarded the Copley Medal to the optician John Dollond for his work on achromatic lenses. William had a personal interest in these developments: during the 1760s his brother Thomas was scanning the heavens with his telescope in Madeira,[76] and even if William did not as yet have an instrument of his own, this omission was certainly rectified some years later.[77]

In 1765 St John's decided to erect an observatory on the West tower of the second court—a project that attracted William's enthusiastic support. When the building was completed in 1767, he presented the college with a valuable set of astronomical instruments and received in return an elaborate letter of thanks in Latin, a translation of which appeared in the *St James's Chronicle*;[78] the opening sentence sets the tone:

> Sir, The favours we have received from you are so numerous and signal, that if Justice did not call upon us to acknowledge our obligations, the satisfaction we feel on this Recital of them would not suffer us to be silent.

After a further shower of compliments the writer continues:

> Your removal into the Polite world and uncommon eminence in your profession have not induced you to forget the place of your former residence. Time and absence have not lessened your regard for it. No one of our numerous body, on any occasion of illness, has known the want of advice; the best the greatest could desire. And to these private acts of kindness so often shewn to each of us in particular, you have now added the most public and permanent memorials of your friendship for us all. The only thing wanting to the completion of our plan, and the cultivation of science in its noblest branch, is given to us by you . . . And thus, by supplying in your favourite College a defect lamented in all, you have conferred on us the peculiar distinction of pursuing philosophy by the sure road of EXPERIMENT and OBSERVATION . . .

Although the items in William's presentation package are not specified, the letter clearly indicates that the gift provided the basic equipment required to make the observatory fully operational. Four items are listed in a hand-written inventory of the observatory's contents made in 1838;[79] these are the only ones in the catalogue unaccompanied by any explanation of how the college acquired them, and perhaps we may assume from this that they are the items that William presented.

Not the least significant part of the letter is its preamble; the writer postpones any mention of the recent gift until he has laid proper emphasis on the medical advice which William had continued to dispense long after his migration to London.[80] As the Fellows would usually have been capable (like Morant) of giving a coherent account of their own or their colleagues' ailments in writing, we may suppose that most of William's advice was conveyed to them by letter; but if there was a serious emergency, he was prepared (subject to his many other commitments) to make the journey to Cambridge and attend the patient in person. An instance of this was to occur some years later— but before describing it, we must give some account of William's activities in the two institutions which played a leading part in his life—The Royal Society and the Royal College of Physicians.

Chapter 5

The Royal Society ·

The dinner club to which William had been welcomed on his arrival in London had close ties with the Royal Society, and it was predictable that his name would soon be proposed for membership of the more august body. He was elected FRS on 25 January 1749/50; four of his sponsors—Wray, Birch, Mead and Wilmot—are already familiar to us; the fifth was Lord Charles Cavendish, father of the distinguished scientist, Henry.

The Royal Society for the Promotion of Natural Knowledge (to give its full title) had been founded in 1660 with the blessing of Charles II and had been incorporated by Royal Charter two years later. The membership included many gentlemen of private means who could afford to pursue scientific researches at their own expense; there was also a good proportion of physicians and clerics and of men with practical skills and experience such as engineers and instrument makers. Under the terms of the charter, no art or craft was to be unworthy of consideration.[1]

Although each individual member might have some special interest, specialisation in the modern sense hardly existed; and as the language of science was un-specialised, ideas could be easily discussed with the minimum of technical jargon. The Society was international in its outlook and in the year of William's election it had roughly 350 British and 150 foreign members. Members met once a week to listen to papers which, if approved, would later appear in the volumes entitled *Philosophical Transactions*, published each year. Papers by authors who could not attend the meetings were usually read by the Secretary—an office filled by Thomas Birch from 1752 until his death thirteen years later. Fellows could if they wished, present their own papers and were sometimes permitted to read communications addressed to them personally by others—a procedure followed on several occasions by William. The administration of the Society's business was handled (not always very efficiently) by a Council of twenty-one members, elected annually, who met about six times a year and shared out the work by appointing committees. Besides keeping an eye on such routine matters as the collection of subscriptions and payment of servants, they had to select the winner of the Society's annual award—the Copley medal—for the most distinguished contribution to scientific knowledge. Although the Society received no subsidy and was financed by the contributions of its own members, the Government looked to it for advice on a variety

Sir Isaac Newton, President of the Royal Society, from the portrait by Charles Jervas, 1703, (The Royal Society.)

of scientific matters and on these occasions it was the Council that responded.

Soon after William's election, the Council took over the responsibility (which had hitherto been the Secretary's) for editing and publishing the papers in the *Transactions*. No other society in England published scientific papers and it was not until 1767 that the Royal College of Physicians adopted William's proposal that they should publish *Medical Transactions*. Thus, for the first hundred years of its existence papers on medical topics were accepted by the Society as readily as papers on any other branch of enquiry.

In 1710 the Society had acquired its own premises in Crane Court off Fleet Street (an easy stroll from Cecil Street) and it was there that William attended many meetings and discussions until the Society moved in 1780 to its splendid rooms in the newly built Somerset House.

The meeting room of the Royal Society in Crane Court, from 1710 to 1780, (The Royal Society.)

William read his first paper in the December following his election; it required very little preparation, as he had collected all the relevant facts nine years earlier. His subject was an outsize human calculus which had been on view in the library of Trinity College since the reign of Queen Anne. The explanatory note, originally displayed with it, had been lost and in order to discover its history William had written to a knowledgeable friend Cox Macro, antiquary and Doctor of Divinity who lived in considerable affluence on his estate near Bury St Edmunds. Macro obligingly supplied the details and William, having weighed and measured the stone, had all the material he needed for the following brief discourse:[2]

There is preserved in the Library of Trinity College in Cambridge, a Stone taken from a human Bladder, which, for its uncommon Size, may deserve the Notice of this Society. It is of an oval Shape, flatted on one Side and its Surface is smooth. The specific Gravity plainly shows, that it is of an animal Origin; for its weight is to that of Water only as 1,75 to 1.

The sufferer, the wife of a locksmith in Bury, had felt much less Pain than might have been expected from so large a Stone; and might probably have lived much longer with it, if she had not thought herself well enough to attempt a Journey on Horseback; for while she was riding, she was suddenly seized with violent pains, that obliged her to be taken off the Horse immediately: After which she could never make water, unless the Stone was first moved, and she continued in great Agonies till she died.

This happened in the Reign of King Charles II, who being then at Newmarket, had the Stone brought to him; some Part of which was chipp'd off from one of its Ends, to shew the King that it consisted of various Coats formed one over another, as animal Stones usually do.

Mr Samuel Battely, who was Member of Parliament for Bury, had Possession of this Stone, either immediately, or very soon after the Woman's Death, and kept it till it was presented to Trinity College, which was about the Middle of Queen Anne's Reign.

This monstrous Stone weighs 33 Ounces 3 Drachms and 36 Grains, Troy Weight. There appears to have been at least half and ounce broken off on the Occasion before related; not to mention what it must have lost by mere Wear in fourscore Years . . .

This History may confirm to us the Usefulness of endeavouring to relieve the Violence of Pain in this Distemper, by altering the Position of the Stone in the Bladder, either with the Help of the Catheter, or by some proper Alteration in the Posture of the Patient; since, with respect to the Pain which it occasions, the Situation of the Stone appears to be of far greater Consequence than its Size.

'Stones'—of whatever size—were objects that aroused great curiosity; how could the human body produce such things; what were they made of? could they be dissolved? As no one could answer any of these questions, William limited himself in his concluding paragraph to a simple statement of what he had observed in the course of his own practice. The catheter to which he refers had been invented by Stephen Hales[3] and had apparently been used with some success.

It was Hales who had also made the first serious attempt to discover the chemical composition of calculi and in his book *Vegetable Staticks*[4] he describes how he heated a number of them in an iron retort and measured the amount of air given off. He concluded that 'we may well look upon the calculus and the Stone in the Gall Bladder, as true animal Tartar'. If this conclusion was unhelpful, he was no more successful in his efforts to find a suitable dissolvent.

A less scientific approach had been adopted a few years earlier by Mrs Joanna Stephens[5] who (with an eye to the main chance) had published a book of medicines against the stone. Her sound judgement in matters of business was vindicated when a grateful but gullible Parliament rewarded her efforts with a grant of £5,000 in return for her recipe. Unfortunately her medicines were so bulky and nauseous that some patients preferred the hazards of surgery.

During the next few years William read several papers on behalf of authors who for various reasons could not attend the Society's meetings in person, and it was not until 1764 that he presented a second paper of his own composition. In this he describes the damage caused by lightning to a church at South Weald, a village standing on high ground in Essex, about eighteen miles from London:[6]

> . . . On 18 June 1764, between twelve and one . . . there was a storm at South-Weald, attended with uncommonly loud thunder. The lightening struck the weather-cock, and passing along the iron bars, upon which it stands, rushed against the wall of the turret, and has broken a space from the top of the turret to the leads of the tower, about four feet wide being about one third of the circumference of the turret and facing the North. The weather-cock and irons that support it seem to be unhurt . . .
> The whole appearance of the damage done to this church very much favours the conjecture of that sagacious observer of nature, Dr Franklin, who thinks it probable that, by means of metallic rods or wires reaching from the roofs to the ground, any buildings may be secured from the terrible effects of lightening.

Franklin had begun his investigations into electrical phenomena in 1746 and sent regular reports of his work to England; his ideas on lightning conductors would thus have been already familiar to William's audience. In one of his experiments Franklin flew a kite in a thunderstorm to prove the identity of lightning and electricity and described the 'electrical fire discharged when a body with an over-quantity approached one with an under-quantity'.

Interest in the study of meteorology (which was at least as old as Aristotle) had received a new impetus in the seventeenth century from the invention of the thermometer and barometer and the researches of the physicist Robert Boyle. The importance of keeping regular records of variations in the weather had long been recognised by the Royal Society as a means of improving man's ability to make forecasts. William's contribution to the subject concerned rainfall, and in a paper presented in December 1769[7] he described a series of experiments which had led to a minor but significant discovery. In the first trial . . .

> A comparison having been made between the quantity of rain which fell in two places in London, about a mile distant from one

another, it was found that the rain in one of them constantly exceeded that in the other, not only every month, but almost every time that it rained.

Care was taken to eliminate any sources of error by using two rain-gauges 'very exact, both being made by the same artist'—probably Mr Durand who had made the stills for Stephen Hales. Speculating on the cause of this 'unexpected variation' William concluded that it must be connected with the fact that one of the gauges 'was fixed so high, as to rise above all the neighbouring chimnies', whereas 'the other was considerably below them'. To test his theory he next set up a gauge above the chimnies of a house (presumably his own home in Cecil Street) with a second gauge on the ground in his garden; over a period of several months, the readings showed the same variation as in the earlier trial. But would the variation be greater if one of the gauges were to be placed on the top of some very high building? To answer this question William got permission from the authorities to place a rain-gauge 'upon the square part of the roof of Westminster Abbey . . . being much higher than any other neighbouring buildings'. For a whole year, beginning in July 1766, William took monthly readings of the two gauges at Cecil Street and of the third on the Abbey roof; precautions had been taken to prevent any of the rain from evaporating, and when, near the end of his paper, William disclosed his results, his audience, even if surprised, could hardly question their validity: in the course of the year only 12 inches of rain had been collected on the Abbey roof, nearly twice that amount (22½ inches) in the gauge at ground level, and an intermediate amount (18 inches) at the level of the Cecil Street chimnies.

William cannot explain 'this extraordinary difference'; it is probable (he suggests) that some hitherto unknown property of electricity is concerned in this phenomenon . . .

More than a century later his paper was reprinted in *British Rainfall*[8] and the editor gives William the credit of being 'as far as we are aware, the first person to notice that the amount of rain collected by a rain gauge placed at a height above the ground was less than in one on the ground'.

Most of the other papers read by William were extracts of letters from his brother Thomas, whose career had taken an unexpected turn. From the records of the Barber-Surgeons' Guild,[9] to which he paid an annual subscription, we know that he practised in Rotherhithe until 1739; the subscriptions then ceased, and by the beginning of 1741 we find him living in the village of Orotava in Tenerife. Why he decided to emigrate is not recorded; perhaps he was suffering from some complaint such as bronchitis or consumption; if so, this could explain why he chose to settle in an obscure village on a small Spanish island, where he could live quietly in a climate more genial than the fogs and damp of the Thames water-side.

Happily there is no hint of ill-health in the published extracts of his letters in the *Philosophical Transactions*. The first of these,[10] which William read in 1752, is a lively and observant account of a leisurely ascent of the island's volcanic mountain, the Pic (Mt Teide). The first part of the ascent was made on horseback; then after spending the night under the shelter of some rocks, the party resumed their climb on foot. From the crater at the summit Thomas collected some salt, which he despatched to William for analysis. The nature of the salt was the subject of a much later paper which William presented in 1764:[11]

> ... It is not so easy to understand how a salt of so fixed a nature, as this is, should be sublimed to such a height without being cooled and fixed long before it arrives at the surface of the earth, where no sensible heat is perceived. Neither am I able to explain how it happens that a substance, so easily melted in water, is not dissolved and washed away, as fast as it can be produced. by the dews, and rains, and melted snow ... It appears to be the natron or nitrum of the antients or, as it is sometimes called, the fossil alkali, which is the basis of sea-salt ...

For much of the information contained in the rest of the paper William gives the credit to two of his distinguished contemporaries: the first of these was Joseph Black, a Fellow of the College of Physicians in Edinburgh who, in his *Essays and Observations*, described his experiments on crystals; the second was Henry Cavendish who had carried out three experiments on the salt at William's request. Cavendish stands near the top of any roll-call of outstanding scientists and is remembered particularly for his investigations into the nature of gases and the constituents of air and water. At forty he inherited an enormous fortune which made him in the opinion of the French scientist Biot 'the richest of all learned men and very likely the most learned of all the rich'. Yet his personality was eccentric and unsociable. He was morbidly shy, disliked women, spoke very seldom, and then only hesitantly in a shrill voice. Science was his only interest, but he was so uncommunicative that although some of his papers were read to the Society, much of his work remained unknown until his unpublished manuscripts were discovered after his death.

After remarking that the natives of the Canary Islands use natron for making matches, William concludes his paper by observing:

> ... The natron must be in great abundance in the air or earth, as it is the base of that salt, which is the commonest of all in almost every part of the world; but though it be everywhere found, when

united to the acid of sea-salt, yet there are but very few places, where we have been able to procure it by itself.

In or about 1747 Thomas said goodbye to his friends on the island and sailed on to Madeira, where he remained for the rest of his life. Having established himself in a house on the hills about two miles from Funchal, he divided his time between practising medicine and pursuing his other scientific interests. He observed the island's weather patterns and kept regular records of temperature, barometric pressure and rainfall. 'The Leste, Levant or hot winds', he notes, 'are very troublesome; the remedy is to keep ourselves within doors.'[12] With his reflecting telescope he observed 'the immersions and emersions of Jupiter's first satellite' over a five years period[13] — a task probably undertaken to determine the longitude of Funchal. In other papers he gives eye-witness accounts of two earthquakes, the first in 1755 being part of the seismic disturbance that devastated Lisbon;[14] and six years later a second 'quake was strong enough to damage Thomas's house, splitting the walls in several places, although they were built of stone and two feet thick.[15]

Inspired perhaps by his brother's work on the London *Bills of Mortality*, Thomas conducted an enquiry into The Increase and Mortality of the Inhabitants of Madeira:[16]

> This has excited my curiosity; and, by my interest with the vicar-general of this diocese, I have procured a survey from house to house in each of the respective parishes; from which, and the parish registers, I have deduced the adjoined account.

The survey was made in 1767 and Thomas reported the total number of inhabitants as 64 614.

In the three traditional branches of the medical profession Thomas, as a qualified surgeon, was firmly in the second division — higher in status than the Apothecary, but far below the Physician. Although he would have been forbidden to act as an unqualified physician so long as he remained at Rotherhithe, he would have been under no such restriction after leaving England; and his desire to master the physician's skills may have been implanted — or increased — by the demands of the local population in Tenerife. In Madeira his status as a doctor is referred to in the Portuguese directory *Elucidario Madeirense*: 'Dr Thomas Heberden . . . exercised the medical profession in Funchal, having fulfilled excellent services on the occasion of a measles epidemic in 1751.'

In view of his accumulating experience, backed up by the knowledge gained from his contacts with William, he was naturally interested in gaining formal recognition as a physician by the degree of MD. For Thomas, the only way of attaining this ambition was to apply to a University which conferred degrees by recommendation.

Understandably, this procedure was frowned upon, as there was no guarantee that the doctors who sponsored a recommendation were either competent or conscientious. Nevertheless he had good reasons for believing that he was as well equipped as the majority of physicians who had gained their MD by examination; accordingly, in 1759, sponsored by William and Dr Munckley,[17] Thomas made his application to King's College, Aberdeen. On 10 July he was entitled for the first time to style himself MD.[18]

Two years later he was recommended as 'a proper candidate' for admission to the Royal Society; his papers had already paved the way, and in December 1761 he was elected FRS. His sponsors were William, Thomas Birch, Francis Wollaston (William's father-in-law) and Charles Morton, the Society's President.

Two more papers read by William on their authors' behalf remain to be mentioned. One was by Daniel Peter Layard,[19] FRCP, FRS who had developed a spa at Somersham in Huntingdonshire and had written a book extolling its virtues. The purpose of the paper was to describe the exhaustive tests he had carried out over a period of fourteen years to determine the spa-water's constituents and he prefaces his account with a letter to William acknowledging that these tests had been 'undertaken with your approbation and pursued through your encouragement'. Layard's work established that the water was 'chalybeate'—or impregnated with iron—and that traces of alum were also present.

The other paper[20] was by Benjamin Wilson who had made a successful living as a portrait painter before becoming involved in scientific research; for his Treatise on Electricity he had been elected FRS. His paper concerning 'positive and negative electricity' was in the form of a letter addressed personally to William who had lent him, from his collection of scientific curiosities, a piece of 'tourmaline'—a mineral with crystalline formations which displayed some unexpected electrical properties. In the course of his paper Wilson refers to no less than fifty-three experiments on various substances; in some of these the tourmaline was subjected to heat and in others to friction and Wilson, who believed that electricity was identical with the aether which according to Newton permeated space, concluded that 'the tourmaline suffers electrical fluid to pass through it in only one direction'. Two remarks in the paper show that William's interest in the subject was both practical and of long standing; in one passage Wilson refers to 'the trials you made with the same stone before I had it'; and elsewhere he mentions 'the tourmaline belonging to our friend Dr Sharp which you recollected to have seen in his possession many years ago at Cambridge.'

Another electrical theorist was John Canton, a schoolmaster, who had been elected FRS in 1749 and had been awarded the Copley medal for making artificial magnets. He too borrowed William's 'largest tourmaline' and recorded an experiment in which he placed it 'edgeways on a heated poker' and noticed that one side developed a positive electrical charge and the other a negative.[21]

In a separate series of experiments carried out in the same year, Canton demonstrated before the Council of the Society that water was compressible. The Council was not entirely convinced and decided to appoint a committee to carry out further trials. William was one of the five members selected for this task; the others were Lord Charles Cavendish, Benjamin Franklin (who could now style himself 'Doctor', having received an honorary LLD from St Andrew's University), Dr William Watson, who had read papers on electricity, and Mr John Ellicot. The last named was well known as a clock-maker and was a frequent attender at the dinner club. The trials took place in July 1765 and were reported to the President by the Secretary Mr Da Costa.[22] The members of the committee, he wrote,

> . . . have measured and weighed the balls, tubes &c and made all other preparatory experiments and seem convinced of the truth of the proposition; but, as the gentlemen who have hitherto met, appear all friends to the experiments, I much doubt whether there will not arise some contest, especially as these experiments are of too great a nicety to be immediately conclusive.

After further consideration, the Council accepted Canton's conclusions and awarded him the honour of the Society's Copley Medal. William was the first to give him the good news in a hasty note: 'Dr H sends his compl'. The medal was unanimously adjudged last night to Mr Canton Nov 29.'

Canton died in March 1772 and the following month William received from his son John some token of remembrance which he at once acknowledged:[23]

> Sir, I return you many thanks, & am much obliged to you for the favor, which I have received in memory of my late worthy friend. His death will be a great loss not only to his private acquaintance, but to the whole Royal Society, of which he was a very valuable member: his many ingenious papers inserted in the *Philosophical Transactions* will be a lasting monument of his abilities.

Elections to the Council were held annually and William was elected on several occasions between 1760 and 1779. During his term of office in 1765 he became involved in the problems of the Royal Observatory at Greenwich, for which the Society had certain responsibilities as 'Visitors' under a Royal Warrant granted in the reign of Queen Anne.[24] The Astronomer Royal had recently died and the Visitors on making their inspection found the observatory building in a state of disrepair; a more serious matter was the neglect of the instruments and the disappearance of many important records;

but when the Council was informed of the situation, it was discovered that the Warrant had lapsed and the Society no longer had any authority to act. Accordingly a letter was despatched to the King requesting a new Warrant, which he readily authorised. The Council then drew up a set of regulations to which the newly appointed Astronomer Royal, The Revd Dr Nevil Maskelyne, and his successors would be bound to adhere, and when this document had received the King's approval, the members of the Council took a boat down to Greenwich to carry out a survey of the building and make an inventory. Having completed its task, the Council applied to the Board of Ordnance 'for the repair of the house and instruments' and in due course the necessary works were carried out.

During the 1760s the Society elected two men who not only became William's friends but were for a few days the companions of his brother Thomas in Madeira. The elder of the two, Daniel Solander was born in Sweden in 1736 and became the pupil of the great botanist Linnaeus. From the age of twenty-four he made his home in England and was engaged to catalogue the natural history collections in the recently opened British Museum. In 1764, having successfully introduced the Linnaean system of classification, he was elected FRS. Two years later the Society elected a young man of twenty-two—their future President Joseph Banks.[25]

Banks had been an ardent botanist from the age of fourteen, when he was a schoolboy at Eton. On the death of his father he inherited a large fortune with landed estates in Lincolnshire; as soon as he came of age, he took a house in London, met other men who shared his enthusiasms and through his friendship with Lord Sandwich (First Lord of the Admiralty) was allowed to sail as a guest on HMS Niger to Newfoundland and Labrador, where he collected and made exact records of 340 plants and numerous birds, fishes and mammals. When he reached home, he found he had already been elected FRS.

During the next eighteen months he engaged artists to paint his collection of flora and fauna, moved to a house in New Burlington Street, which he shared with his sister, went on botanical trips to Wales and the south-west and formed a lasting friendship with Solander. Meanwhile the Government, in consultation with the Royal Society were making plans to observe the rare phenomenon of the passage of Venus across the face of the sun; if this 'transit' could be viewed from different parts of the earth, the knowledge gained could be of great value to navigation. The place selected as the observational base in the southern hemisphere was the recently discovered island of Tahiti. The original (astronomical) purpose of the expedition was soon extended to include exploration and the 'advancement of useful knowledge'; the vessel chosen was the Endeavour, under the command of James Cook and at the Society's request it was agreed that Joseph Banks should be accommodated

on board as chief naturalist, together with his suite of seven (including Solander) and their baggage.

The historic voyage began on 25 August 1768 and on 12 September they anchored off Funchal. During their five-day visit the two naturalists stayed at the house of the English consul Mr Cheap—but it was Thomas who acted as their guide to the island's flora. 'While we were here', wrote Banks in his Journal,[26] 'we were much indebted to Dr Heberden, the chief physician of the island' who had written a description of the trees that grew there. 'Of this work he immediately gave us a copy, together with such specimens as he had in his possession, and indeed spared no pains to get for us living specimens of such as could be procured in flower.'

They climbed up to Thomas's house (noting the drop in temperature during the ascent) and observed the different woods used in the construction of his bookcase and the healthy cinnamon plants growing on the roof. From Thomas they also received 'among many other favours' samples of the salt and sulphur which he had collected when he ascended the Pic in Tenerife. Solander[27] sent a report of the visit to the President of the Royal Society, supplementing Banks's account with the words: 'At Madeira met Dr Thomas Heberden . . . who is greatly respected in the island and obtained access everywhere, including the nunnery.' The following year Thomas died and when the two naturalists eventually returned to England—laden with botanical specimens—Banks named a tree of the family Myrsinaceae 'Heberdenia' in Thomas's memory.

The Endeavour having circumnavigated the world arrived back in England in July 1771. Banks and Solander received a rapturous welcome, were given honorary degrees at Oxford, were fêted by everyone and received by the King. Cook too was presented to the King and promoted to the rank of Master and Commander—but his tremendous achievement in navigation did not receive the ecstatic acclaim bestowed on the naturalists. The effect of all this adulation on Banks (who was still only twenty-nine) was unfortunate: he forgot his own limitations and when he was invited to sail with Cook on a second voyage of exploration in the Resolution, he insisted on having the ship 'improved'; but the improvements made the ship unstable and it had to be restored to its original state. Banks, feeling very foolish, withdrew from the venture and Resolution sailed without him. To restore his self-esteem, he chartered a brig and accompanied by Solander set sail in July 1772 on a botanical expedition to Iceland. He returned home in the late autumn and the next few years were spent bringing order to his enormous collection of plants, preparing an account of his voyages, looking after his estates, advising the King on developing his gardens at Kew, socialising, writing letters and having some amorous adventures. During this period William had many opportunities for getting to know Banks at the meetings of the Royal Society, at the dinner club and at the Society of Antiquaries[28] of which both by now were Fellows. He was also on friendly terms with Solander who was still at work at the British Museum as keeper of the natural history collections.

In 1772 the Royal Society had elected as their President Sir John Pringle MD, who had served as Physician-General to the forces in Flanders and had later won wide respect in scientific circles. In 1778 ill-health obliged him to resign and the Society was faced with the task of choosing a worthy successor. Few if any of the members possessed all the attributes—such as wealth, nobility and intellectual distinction—that might have made the choice a simple one, and it was only after lengthy discussion in the Council that two candidates emerged as front-runners: Alexander Aubert, wealthy head of the London Assurance Company, was a talented astronomer and linguist who understood business methods and was supported by Pringle. Banks, the alternative choice, had comparatively few qualifications; at 35, he was very young to hold such an exalted office; he spoke no foreign language and in the years that had elapsed since his voyage on the Endeavour he had still failed to complete his official account of his discoveries. On the other hand he was business-like, sociable and energetic, he was internationally famous and was highly regarded by the King. In November 1778 the Council decided the issue in Banks's favour and a few days later their recommendation was approved at the Society's anniversary meeting.

Although Banks was to remain President for the next forty-two years, there were some awkward moments during the early stages of his régime. Shortly before his election the Council had asked the Government to find the Society more spacious accommodation: when offered rooms in the new Somerset House, the Council accepted the offer before giving sufficient thought to the size, layout and general suitability of their new premises. On moving from Crane Court in November 1780, they found that there was no room for their collections—which therefore had to be given to the British Museum; this lack of planning and foresight also caused an interruption in the meteorological observations that had been regularly made in the old building. After three years' delay a committee (which included William) was appointed to consult with the architect of Somerset House, Sir William Chambers, to decide on a proper place for making observations in the future.[29]

The mismanagement of the move was a sign that the Society's administration needed overhauling, but to carry out any reforms without causing resentment required extreme tact and it was unfortunate that this quality was missing from Banks's handling of the problem. The Society had two secretaries—Mr Maty and Mr Planta—and a foreign correspondent, Dr Charles Hutton,[30] who besides dealing with the letters was expected to translate foreign papers and make extracts from foreign books. In 1782 the Council was informed that he had fallen behind with his work, whereupon his duties were redefined and limited to dealing with the correspondence. With his work-load thus reduced he continued for some months to carry out his duties from his home in Kent, until late in 1783 the Council informed him that in future the foreign correspondent must live in London. Hutton understandably resigned and when at the next meeting one of the Fellows proposed a vote of thanks to him for his past services, Banks opposed the motion on the grounds that Hutton had not performed his duties efficiently. Despite this intervention, which to many seemed both offensive and unjustified, the motion, to Banks's embarrassment, was carried.

When the Society held a further meeting the Revd Dr Horsley (a mathematician) made a violent attack on Banks, using the Hutton affair as a pretext for giving vent to a whole range of pent-up grievances, based on his belief that Banks had interfered in the process of electing Fellows and in the appointment of members to the Council and to its various committees. More generally, Horsley and his supporters felt that Banks was overbearing and autocratic and that he was favouring botanists and natural historians at the expense of mathematicians, astronomers and chemists. Banks very properly asked for a formal vote of confidence and this was carried by 119 votes to 42. After this defeat the number of Horsley's supporters steadily dwindled, but by now Banks had also antagonised the Secretary Mr Maty, who soon found his position untenable and in March 1784 resigned.

Among the candidates for this new vacancy was Dr (later Sir) Charles Blagden—MD of Edinburgh and a promising scientist—who had been elected FRS twelve years earlier at the age of twenty-four and had been a friend of Banks ever since. Having decided on a career as an Army physician he had been posted to America in the early stages of the War of Independence, but was back in England again in 1780, when he accepted an appointment as physician to a military hospital in Plymouth.[31] Within two years he had returned to London and when Banks proposed him for the Secretaryship, he was elected by a large majority. William had known him almost as long as Banks and their exchange of letters (from which some extracts are quoted in a later chapter) demonstrate Blagden's respect for his older colleague. One of Blagden's first acts as Secretary was to ask William to serve on a committee, whose task was 'to prevent a few turbulent individuals from continuing to interrupt the peace of the Society'.[32] The committee evidently did its job tactfully and effectively and thereafter Banks (who had learned some lessons from his past mistakes) met no further opposition. Nor did he again attempt to introduce reforms, and it was only after his death in 1820 that the much-needed changes were carried through which enabled the Society to achieve its later pre-eminence as a scientific institution.[33]

There was one other member of the Society for whom William had a special respect: Joseph Priestley had two consuming interests that competed for his time and energies; as a young man he had studied theology and become a Presbyterian minister. As his ideas developed, he adopted Unitarianism and expounded his views in a periodical called *The Theological Repository*. Meanwhile he pursued his scientific enquiries into the nature of gases, but his non-conformist beliefs and independent attitude prevented him from rising very far above the poverty line. In 1772 he accepted a generous offer from the Earl of Shelburne to act as his librarian at Bowood in Wiltshire; but although this provided him with a house and a small salary, he was still unable to afford the scientific equipment, books and other items that he needed, if he were to pursue his researches effectively. For some reason, he was reluctant to apply for a pension from the state, but let it be known that he was willing to accept help from his wealthy friends. Accordingly, Fothergill[34] opened a fund to provide enough income to meet his needs. In his memoirs[35] Priestley mentions his chief benefactors by name; some, he says, subscribed to defray the expenses of the experiments only, but the majority 'were equally friends to my theological studies', and amongst these was William, 'equally distinguished for his love of religious truth and his zeal to promote science'.

William remained keenly interested in the outcome of the experiments, which he realised could have far-reaching implications for medicine. On 30 December 1784 Priestley wrote to Henry Cavendish on the subject they were both investigating—the properties and composition of air; the letter ends:[36]

> I will be obliged if you will show this letter to Dr Heberden who is pleased to interest himself in my experiments and to whom I have not written lately, tho he is already acquainted with many particulars of this letter.

And nearly four years later the potter Josiah Wedgwood,[37] acknowledging a letter from Priestley in defence of the 'phlogiston theory' of combustion,[38] writes: 'I shall be in London in about ten days and the copy intended for the Society may then pass through my hands, as you propose, to Dr Heberden.'

This is the last significant reference to William's involvement in the concerns of the Royal Society, where for so many years he had enjoyed the company of men whose talents and interests ranged over many different fields of knowledge. We must now describe his role as a Fellow of that other body—smaller in numbers, more restricted in its interests and often slow to accept new ideas—on which he exercised a decisive influence: the Royal College of Physicians.

Chapter 6

The Royal College of Physicians

Soon after his arrival in London, William was nominated by the Royal College of Physicians as Gulstonian Lecturer[1] for 1749. He chose as his subject 'The History, Nature and Cure of Poisons', which he defines in his first discourse as 'what do more hurt than good to the generality of men in all the known ways of using them'. Fortunately these 'known ways' may be extended:

> Use & observation have taught us to make remedies of many of these substances & still more of them will be improved into such by posterity. Whatever yet remains in the class of poisons, we should consider as the particular objects of our attention & observation as things capable of doing us great service ... There is the highest probability (to argue only from what we have experienced) that there is nothing but what upon the whole does or is capable of doing us more benefit than mischief . . .[2]

As we might expect, William takes a sceptical view of many alleged cases of poisoning; many accounts arise from mankind's love of prodigies, or from ignorance or misunderstanding—and he gives several examples to illustrate his point.

In the second lecture William divides poisons into two classes— acrimonious (i.e. corrosive) and intoxicating. After giving numerous examples of the first category, he remarks:

> It is observable that the effects of acrimonious poisons on different animals of the same species, or on animals of different species, vary much less than those of the intoxicating ones; almost all are affected by the former in the same manner, though there are a few remarkable exceptions, as for instance the juice of the Tithymali,[3] which is so caustic to the firmest human skin, yet affords an innocent nourishment to a tender caterpillar, whose consistence is hardly firmer than a gelly.
>
> Among the intoxicating poisons, the inebriating power of Tobacco is universally known; the nerves of all animals on which it has been tried are strongly affected by it, though use, as in all other nervous poisons, greatly weakens its effects ... But above all the oil which arises from it while it is burning is equal I think to any & superior to most nervous poisons for strength & quickness of operation, either externally or internally. It is this oil which makes the custom of smoking so agreeable by that calm & indolence

& slight degree of inebriation which it diffuses over the nerves, which has made this as necessary to many as opium is to the Turks. Thus we see the strongest of all our poisons played with every day & become the most general amusement & delight of almost every nation upon earth. This may encourage us to hope that a better acquaintance with those that are weaker might in like manner make all their qualities subservient to our use and pleasure.

Was William himself a snuff-taker or smoker? We have no evidence on the subject, but the above passage suggests that even if he did not habitually indulge, he had occasionally experienced the pleasures of tobacco at first hand.

Next in his list of intoxicating poisons comes opium[4] — almost the only one that had been used for centuries as a soporific medicine.

It might be wished perhaps that the experience of mankind had rather been employed on some of the weaker nervous simples, for it is reasonable to expect that we might have had all the good effect of opium from any one of these & possibly without running the risk of those troublesome symptoms which opium often occasions; at least there would have been less danger from a slight overdose, whereby much mischief would have been prevented & many lives saved, that I fear are every year destroyed by a rash & ignorant use of this powerful drug. It must be owned that after all our long experience, we are not yet masters of opium nor sufficiently secure of its effects; its violence is such that many little circumstances make us unwilling to give it in cases where it would be of the utmost importance to make the patient sleep.

Many of William's most original and penetrating observations are contained in the third and final lecture, where he describes the effects of intoxicating (or 'nervous') poisons. He begins by giving his reasons for believing that these effects are exerted on the nerves:

. . . they are frequently too sudden to arise from any disorder of the blood & sensible humours, no disorders of these parts are to be found by dissection & animals killed with nervous poisons are safely eaten without any of those ill consequences that might be expected to arise from their juices if they were at all vitiated. The symptoms too are all of them merely disturbances or interruptions of the known offices of the nerves: they are unquestionably the chief causes of motion throughout the body, whether known by the name of animal or vital, as is evident from the decay or total loss of motion in proportion as the nerves of any part are compressed. The vigor of the external & internal senses are found in like manner to be wholly owing to the vigorous state of the nerves, & to decay as these languish & are disordered. The secretions likewise are greatly dependent on the nerves, as may be inferred from the great number of them which go to all the glands where they neither serve as instruments of motion nor of sense; which is further confirmed from what we daily observe, that affections confessedly of the nerves have the greatest influence in stopping or quickening the secretions, or in altering the qualities of the liquor secreted. Hence therefore all convulsions, tremblings, palsies of all the muscles animal & vital, swoonings, apoplexies, madness, stupidity, sleep, epilepsies with all their species & degrees, together with several alterations in the colour & consistence of the secretions are disorders of these important parts of the animal body, & these are precisely the symptoms from these poisons which are therefore properly stiled nervous.

William admits that the operation of the nerves is a mystery:

. . . the immediate sympathy frequently observable through the nerves of the whole body shows that they are endowed with properties & governed by laws very different from anything of which we have had any experience in the grosser vessels & fibres of the body.

He illustrates the point by referring to children who have been

. . . tickled to death by imprudent nurses; this gentle impression throws the nerves into extasies & convulsions which are propagated throughout the whole nervous system, & so become fatal. On the contrary, the most violent attacks of the colic are almost constantly relieved by putting the patient into a warm bath: this soothing of the nerves on the surface of the body diffuses an indolence over the whole system, the nerves of the intestines are lulled into inaction & the spasm ceases. The mere vibration of the air on the auditory nerves will throw persons almost out of themselves by the agony of the pleasure or pain communicated from these nerves to those over the whole body. Some animals, it is said, may be killed by an ungrateful sound. The exquisitely small tremor on the optic nerve made by a wheel running rapidly round makes some people sick, giddy, vomit & fall into a sort of epilepsy & changes the colour of the bile immediately into a porraceous green . . .

After observing that the nerves of the stomach 'yield to none for the quickness of their sensibility & their strong sympathy with every other in the whole body', William considers whether particular nerves can be rendered inactive by intoxicating poisons while the rest of the nervous system remains unaffected. As 'palsies, convulsions & torpors' often affect only small parts of the body, he concludes that the answer is 'yes' and points to the fact that tinctures of opium are often applied locally to relieve toothache, earache and pains in the eyes. But the general rule concerning narcotics is that

> ... they are equally capable of affecting all the nerves, & whenever their action is determined to a few or those only of one kind, it is wholly owing to some peculiarity in the constitution of the person who takes them, & not to any in the nature of the drugs themselves. For a drug will at one time only affect the nerves of motion & bring on trembling, spasms & palsies; the same drug is at another time attended with such symptoms as belong only to the external senses, as vertigos, mists, noises in the head, insensibility of pain & strong impressions on every nerve of imaginary objects; & the same dose of it is sometimes found to pour all its force on the nerves which actuate the internal senses, as they are called, that is, the passions, attention, imagination & memory, the symptoms of which are strong, unusual starts of various passions, all sorts of visionary scenes represented by the imagination as actually existing or by the memory as having once, & such a fixedness of attention as is not to be moved by common objects. All this is frequently exemplified in the effects of opium & still more frequently in those of wine & other vinous spirits. These various effects are experienced not only by various persons, but also by the same at different times, for men vary from themselves as well as from others in the irritability & tender mobility of their nerves ...

William concludes his lecture with some advice on the best procedures for saving a patient who has relapsed into a stupor:

> It will be necessary to use the most expeditious & powerful remedies without the least delay. Everything that strongly irritates & keeps the nerves awake is a proper remedy for this stage of the disorder. Many of the acrimonious poisons will be useful for this intention; the patient should be placed in a room with a very strong light; he should be perpetually called to by a loud voice & teazed with every kind of disturbance ... & though all these and the like remedies should seem to have no effect, yet they should not be given over too soon, for in people seemingly dead with narcotics, the wheels & springs of life are only stopped, not broken or hurt, so that strong agitations & stimulating will often recover them, as they do those that are drowned ...

Amongst many memorable passages the comments on tobacco and on the uses and dangers of opium have interesting echoes in today's world; but perhaps the most remarkable sections are those concerning the nervous system. When William delivered the lectures, the mechanisms by which the nerves conveyed their messages were—as he readily admits—a mystery. He therefore concentrated his attention on the observable effects of the messages and on how these could be altered or interrupted by poisons or other influences; his marshalling of the available facts and the conclusions he draws from them are hardly less impressive than his classic description of angina later in his career.

The following year the College invited him to deliver the annual Harveian Oration.[5] Although the text has not survived, the elderly William Stukeley (FRCP and an ordained minister of the Church) was present as chaplain and noted in his diary for 18 October 1750, 'Dr Heberden gave us an excellent oration.'[6] Ten years later William delivered the Croonian Lectures, but the text of these too is lost.[7]

The College *Annals* reveal that on two occasions William was recommended to fill a vacancy at St Bartholomew's Hospital, the venerable foundation which still occupied its original mediaeval site at Smithfield in the City. Early in the century the ancient wards had become badly delapidated and overcrowded; in 1729 plans for new buildings, designed by James Gibbs, were approved and work began the following year. Despite the gradual increase in the number of beds, there was no corresponding increase in the number of physicians, which remained at two until 1750, when the Governors appointed a third; but their choice was unfortunate, as their new recruit died the following year. This was the background of the letter addressed to them by the Royal College of Physicians on 13 January 1752 recommending two names as candidates for the vacancy: Dr William Heberden and Dr Thomas Lawrence.[8] Barts had its own ideas and appointed an MD from Aberdeen. Two years later another vacancy occurred and the College put forward William's name for the second time—but once again Barts appointed someone else.[9]

There was considerable competition for hospital appointments; some physicians were attracted by the opportunity to widen their experience through contact with large numbers of the sick poor; others more by the knowledge that the prestige enjoyed by the holder of such a post would improve his prospects in the more lucrative sphere of private practice. William's own motives in offering himself as a candidate are obscure; perhaps he welcomed the chance of returning to a hospital where he had worked happily during some of his Cambridge vacations; more probably—in January 1752—he felt that by seeking to attach himself to a respected charitable institution, he would win the approbation of John Martin, his prospective father-in-law.

Fellows were expected to play their part in the administrative affairs of the College; the Censors, elected to serve on an annual basis had the sometimes awkward task of deciding who should be admitted to Fellowship and who should be given the status of Licentiate—essential for anyone desiring to practise as a Physician in the London area. Under the statutes, Fellowship was restricted to graduates with an MD from Oxford or Cambridge. Licentiateships might be awarded to holders of medical degrees from other Universities, but the decision to grant or withhold the award rested with the Censors.

These restrictions, which had been in force since the time of Henry VIII, had been imposed for sound reasons. There were four criteria by which candidates were judged: birth, education, religion and type of practice. As for the first, a College founded on English soil could have no truck with a candidate whose culture and language might be foreign; still less could it tolerate any Roman Catholic, inevitably associated with treason and plot. Education should be of the kind obtainable at an English University, embodying an admixture of classics and sound Protestant theology. Finally, with regard to the candidate's type of practice, he was expected to adhere to the traditional three-tier system and not soil his hands by meddling in matters that were the legally recognised sphere of the surgeon or the apothecary.

These attitudes were scarcely challenged for two centuries, but a foretaste of the battles to come occurred during William's first stint as a Censor in 1750. A Leyden doctor, Isaac Schomberg,[10] had begun to practise in London, and when summoned before the Censors for his Licentiate examination, he sent a letter asking to be 'indulged in practice as others had been' until he had taken a Cambridge doctorate. Foolishly he added that he would have made his request in person but that he did not choose to meet a man who was disagreeable to the whole profession. The Censors adjudged this remark groundless and improper and Schomberg was inhibited from practice. He then went to Cambridge and was in due course created MD by royal mandate. When he applied again to the College for permission to practise, a majority of the committee, consisting of the President and four Censors including William, accepted his request and the College removed its veto. But when Dr Schomberg appeared before the board to be examined, he demanded that as he was now a Doctor of Cambridge University, he should be admitted a candidate for Fellowship as a matter of right. Once again, his application was unsuccessful and it was not until 1771 that his ambition to be elected FRCP was realised.

The pressure for reform intensified in 1765, when the College revised its statutes and had copies printed and circulated both to Fellows and Licentiates. As the statutes had previously been regarded as private and confidential, Licentiates had hitherto had no opportunity to study them; but if they were expecting that the revisions would make it easier for them to achieve Fellowship, they were disappointed. No concessions were made on this crucial issue; indeed a new restriction was added by a rule that Licentiate examinations must be conducted in the Latin language.

The next stage in the controversy was sparked off by the case of an obstetrician, Dr Letch, who had, like Schomberg, been summoned before the Censors to be examined as a prospective Licentiate. Due to a muddle in counting the votes, he was told first he had passed and then that he had failed, and it was this second decision that was upheld at the next meeting of the general comitia. Letch was understandably incensed and went to law. Other Licentiates rallied round him and formed themselves into 'The Society of Collegiate Physicians', their aim being to campaign for amendments to the College's constitution. When subscriptions were invited to support Dr Letch's cause, two of William's friends, the Quaker Dr Fothergill[11] and the anatomist William Hunter[12] each gave £500.

The case came to court before Lord Mansfield in May 1767, Charles Yorke appearing on behalf of the College. The question to be decided was whether the College was under a legal obligation to admit Dr Letch to membership (i.e. to Fellowship) of the College and after lengthy arguments from both sides, Lord Mansfield rejected Dr Letch's plea, though he advised the College that their statutes were in need of amendment.

The question of whether Licentiates were or were not members of the College, with the right to attend meetings and have votes was left open and in order to bring this issue to a definite conclusion, twenty-three of the Licentiates applied in writing to the College to be admitted as Fellows. The applications were refused. The next act in the drama occurred at the quarterly meeting of the College comitia held in June 1768, when ten of the Licentiates entered the room unbidden and sat down among the Fellows, thus claiming the right to take part in College business. After the Licentiates had claimed the right to speak, the President told them that unless they withdrew quietly, he would send for constables and have them removed; whereupon William Hunter declared that 'if any man or constable offered to lay hands upon him to turn him out of their House (adding for this is our House) he would run him through the body'. Finding it impossible to transact any business, the President brought the meeting to a close.

The Licentiates were now ready to use more violent tactics and when they heard that another meeting of the comitia had been arranged for 24 September, they engaged a gang of hirelings and arrived with them at the College gates at the time appointed for the meeting. As the gate had been locked, they broke it open and for good measure smashed several windows; then with the help of sledgehammers and crowbars they broke the Hall door, forced their way into the meeting-room and sat down among the Fellows. As on the previous occasion, the President dissolved the comitia.

The regular quarterly meeting of the comitia was due to be held the following week; to avoid the risk of a second invasion the College had the gates repaired and provided with a stronger lock and for further protection hired a body of constables. The Licentiates meanwhile hired a gang of forty ruffians to mount a more formidable attack, but abandoned their plan when they failed to find a blacksmith who would be prepared to break open the now strengthened gate. Instead they wrote to the President demanding admittance to vote in the election of officers. The College replied in writing that they apprehended the gentlemen who had signed the letter had no right to vote.

The invasion of the College premises in Warwick Lane (near St Paul's Cathedral) was a prime subject for cartoonists and the playwright Samuel Foote satirised the affair in *The Devil upon Two Sticks*.[13] It did little to enhance the image of physicians in the eyes of the public and the Licentiates wisely refrained from attempting a repeat performance. Nevertheless, there were more lawsuits still to come (brought against the College by individual Licentiates) and these dragged on into the next century.

Although the College continued to insist that Licentiates were not automatically entitled to become members, certain limited concessions were made; the first of these provided that any Fellow could propose a Licentiate of seven years' standing and not less than 36 years of age as a candidate; after the usual examination, the Fellows would ballot on his election. The second concession at least had the merit of simplicity: the President could propose one Licentiate in each year for immediate election.

Before considering William's involvement in these events, we must try to explain why the controversy had reached boiling point in 1767; the answer is closely bound up with the steady increase in the total number of Licentiates and in the proportion of them who had trained at Scottish Universities.[14]

When William was elected in 1746, there were 54 Fellows and a mere 24 Licentiates; but in 1765 the picture had changed dramatically. Fellows now numbered only 46, whereas the body of Licentiates had swollen to 63, a number reflecting the increasing demand for trained physicians in London's new hospitals. If some of the Fellows began to feel threatened by their own numerical inferiority, they were still more perturbed by the intake of Scottish graduates to the Licentiate ranks: from 1741-50, an insignificant total of three; from 1751-55, a total of seven; in the next five-year period, eleven; and then, in 1761-65 an explosion of 25.

What set the alarm bells ringing loudly in the College was the contrasting attitudes to medical training north and south of the Border. In England the medical profession was, as we have mentioned earlier, stratified in three distinct tiers—physicians, surgeons and apothecaries—each having its separate and legally defined privileges. As the physicians were at the top of the heap, both socially and professionally, they were understandably reluctant to permit this comfortable arrangement to be disturbed.

Scottish doctors however had long been trained as general practitioners and as far back as 1599 physicians and surgeons had been united in one Faculty. By the middle of the eighteenth century Edinburgh's medical school was one of Europe's best. Thus the Scottish Licentiates had good reasons for believing that they were at least as well qualified as their English counterparts and that their training had been more broadly based and comprehensive. To be debarred from taking part in College affairs seemed to them an inexcusable affront and it is not surprising that they were well represented among the militants.

Evidence of William's personal attitude towards the problem of the Licentiates comes from a letter written by Dr William Watson FRS[15] (an Edinburgh graduate) to Dr Fothergill, describing a meeting of the comitia in 1771. After four Licentiates, including Schomberg, had been elected members 'by special grace', the former President Sir William Browne rose and, to everyone's surprise, proposed the 'arch-rebel' Fothergill. 'After a considerable pause, both Dr Heberden and Sir John Pringle rose and seconded Sir William's motion.' The proposal was rejected by 13 votes to 9. Watson added that if Fothergill had been elected 'Dr Heberden told me that he intended then to have proposed me . . . but, upon seeing the sense of the Fellows towards rebels, he declined it.'

William was sympathetic to the Licentiates' case for two reasons: he knew several of them personally through their membership of the Royal Society, and considered that their exclusion from the College deprived it of some of the most talented physicians of the day. In the second place, William was a vigorous supporter of the rights of Dissenters[16] and would have considered that to exclude physicians from English universities (and thus from the Royal College of Physicians) on purely religious grounds was scandalous.

If the history of the Royal College of Physicians at this period had contained nothing but the disputes described above, it would make melancholy reading. Fortunately a far more productive development, in which William played a leading role, began shortly before the muddle over Dr Letch's votes. In 1764 the College decided to honour the memory of the illustrious William Harvey by publishing a collected edition of his works. A committee was appointed to undertake the task; William was one of the members; another, Akenside, wrote a preface and a third—Lawrence—contributed a 'Life'. The project was completed in less than two years to everyone's satisfaction; free copies were presented to Fellows on the best paper, and to Licentiates on paper of a somewhat less excellent quality.[17]

After this success William felt the time was ripe to initiate a more ambitious project and in 1767 he proposed, with the support of his former pupil Sir George Baker, that the College should hold meetings for the reading and discussion of papers which, subject to the College's

William Harvey, the frontispiece to his Collected Works, *after the painting by Cornelius Jonson.*

approval, would then be published in a series of *Medical Transactions*, modelled on the *Transactions* of the Royal Society. The project was not in fact the first of its kind; in 1757 a group calling itself A Society of Physicians had published the first of a series entitled *Medical Observations and Enquiries*. Although the series enjoyed considerable success, the College felt confident that its own prestige would attract the most highly qualified contributors and thus ensure a wide readership for a new series published under its authority.

Having given the proposal its blessing, the College appointed a committee, of which William was again a member, to put the plan into effect. Contributions were solicited and the College took the opportunity to offer an olive branch to the Society of Collegiate Physicians by sending out the beadle to invite them to submit articles.[18] The invitation was considered at their first meeting and was—predictably—refused. In spite of this, the College had no difficulty in collecting enough papers of an acceptable standard to fill the first volume, which made its appearance in 1768. William contributed six papers as well as writing the preface, and seven more of his papers appeared in the second volume, published four years later. After this, there was a pause, due no doubt to the difficulty of stimulating a regular flow of contributions after the first flush of enthusiasm had waned. However, the College managed to produce a third volume in 1785, to which William once again contributed. Thereafter the project lapsed, until it was briefly revived in the next century.

William's first draft of the 'Preface' was considered to be too lengthy; the final version which won the committee's approval begins:

> The experience of many ages hath more than sufficiently shewn that mere abstract reasonings have tended very little to the promoting of natural knowledge. By laying these aside, and attending carefully to what nature hath either by chance or upon experiment offered to our observation, a greater progress hath been made in this part of Philosophy since the beginning of the last Century, than had been till that time from the days of Aristotle.
>
> This advancement hath been greatly owing to those learned societies in Europe who, by collecting papers relating to this branch of knowledge, have preserved many useful observations which would otherwise have been lost.[19]

The reader is then informed that the College is ready to receive papers on medical subjects and to publish the most useful:

> Single cases which occur every day in common distempers, and accounts of the ordinary effects of medicines, must be endless. Whatever important additions or exceptions to the general practice may be contained in those cases, would much better be drawn out by the author himself, and presented without giving along with them a tiresome account of common appearance, with which every one is supposed to be well acquainted.
>
> It is to be wished that writers would not confine themselves to relate only their successful practice. A Physician of great experience might write a very useful paper, if he would have the courage to give an account of such methods of cure only as he had found to be ineffectual or hurtful.[20]

The abandoned prefatory address was later printed in the appendix to the *Commentaries*;[21] in one of the many interesting passages William warns against the danger of facts and observations being misrepresented, in order to make them fit into some preconceived system:

> The Jews were commanded to build their altar with stones unhewn and untouched by any tool; and, in like manner, the best materials of natural knowledge are the plain facts themselves, just as they come from nature; he who pretends to new model and polish them, in order to their being adapted more perfectly to his

system, has utterly polluted them, and made them unfit for the altar of truth.

Of William's sixteen papers, the majority appear again, in modified form, in the *Commentaries*. These include 'Observations on the Ascarides'[22] (intestinal worms), 'Of the Nightblindness or Nyctalopia',[23] 'Of the Hectic Fever'[24] and 'Of the Measles'.[25] The longest paper is concerned with diseases of the liver and includes a discussion of gall-stones and jaundice.[26] Another is on Essera[27]—the ancient name for Nettlerash, a condition which in William's opinion had hitherto received too little attention, in view of 'the intolerable anguish arising from the itching'. Two more papers under the general title of Queries[28] dealt with questions on smallpox, gout, palsies, hernia and other matters.

The first paper in volume 1 of the *Transactions* is not, as we might have expected, an account of some disease, but deals with a matter related to public health; it was entitled 'Remarks on the Pump Water of London and on the methods of procuring the purest Water'. Very recently Henry Cavendish had analysed the water from a pump in Rathbone Place and his paper had been published in the *Philosophical Transactions*; he was not however concerned with the hygienic implications of his findings, and it was left to William to underline the dangers of pollution.

> Several pump-waters of London which I have examined, and probably most of them [he begins] contain powder of lime-stone and the three mineral acids of vitriol, nitre and sea-salt;[29] besides which there is an oiliness which discolours these waters, giving them a remarkably yellowish cast, when compared with pure distilled water . . . It might be expected that all these disagreeable substances should remarkably taint the water; and yet the London pump-water is by many esteemed for its goodness and purity . . .
>
> It must, I believe, wholly be resolved into the power of custom, that the inhabitants of London are so satisfied with this peculiar taste of their water, which is, as I have often been a witness, much complained of by those who come hither from foreign countries, as very disagreeable to their palates, and sometimes as offensive to their stomachs. Custom makes the Greenlander fond of the taste of train-oil;[30] and its power is no doubt as great in reconciling the drinkers of bad water to its ill taste . . .

With a rather excessive air of caution William goes on to suggest that perhaps custom may not be able to confer immunity from the possible ill-effects of the 'rough and by no means unactive substances' with which the water is contaminated.[31] Indeed 'the uninterrupted drinking of such waters for a long time, may probably be the cause of many . . . disorders, especially to the infirm and to children.

Hence a change of place may often be of as much use to weak persons from the change of water, as of air.' However, William correctly points out that the 'fossil' lime deposits in water cannot, as was commonly believed, be a cause of kidney or bladder stones, which are 'of animal origin'.

Many people who suspect that pump-water may be unwholesome, boil it and let it stand to grow cold; but this does little or nothing to improve its quality.

The best way of avoiding the bad effects of pump-water would be not to make a constant use of it; and in a place so well supplied with river water as London, there is very little necessity to drink of the springs which, in so large a city, besides their natural contents, must collect many additional impurities from cellars, burying grounds, common sewers and many other offensive places, with which they undoubtedly often communicate; so that it is indeed a wonder that we find this water at all tolerable . . .

The Thames water has a share of all these impure ingredients: but as it is a much larger body of water, it is proportionately less infected by them.

There is an inconvenience attending the use of Thames and New River water,[32] that they often are very muddy, or taste strongly of the weeds and leaves. The latter fault is not easily remedied; but they would soon be freed from their muddiness, if kept some time in an earthen jar. If the water given to very young children were all of this kind, it might perhaps prevent some of their bowel disorders, and so contribute a little to lessen that amazing mortality among the children which are attempted to be brought up in London . . .

Alum is very successfully used by the common people in England for the purifying of muddy water. Two or three grains of it, dissolved in a quart of thick river water, makes the dirt very soon collect into flocks, and slowly precipitate. Filtering would immediately make the water so prepared fit for use . . .

Rain or snow-water is much preferable to river, or to any other natural water; but there are almost insuperable difficulties in collecting large quantities for common use, without its being as much altered and defiled by the manner of saving it, as it is when found in rivers . . .

The purest of all waters might be obtained by distillation . . . This method would be particularly useful in some English settlements in foreign countries, where the waters are so bad that, while our countrymen are making their fortunes, they are ruining their health . . . It is a very desirable thing to have pure distilled water kept in the apothecaries shops for the purpose of making up those medicines which cannot be made up with any other. The simple waters of the shops add much to the nauseous taste of many draughts, without at all improving their virtues . . .

Unfortunately distilled water often has 'a disagreeable empyreumatic or burnt taste'—a problem that can be overcome 'by ventilating it in the manner described by Dr Hales'.[33] In many cases of chronical pains in the stomach and bowels 'a course of distilled water might be as beneficial as the most celebrated mineral waters are in any other disorders, and might prove no inconsiderable addition to the Materia Medica'.

As to the wholesomeness of distilled water for general use, there can hardly be any doubt of it, if we recollect that all the fresh water in the world has been distilled.[34] But if any one think there may be a difference between natural and artificial distillation, I need only quote the example mentioned, I think, by Tournefort of one Francis Secardi Hongo, who made distilled water his constant drink, without the addition of wine or any strong liquor, to the last, and lived with remarkably good health to the age of 115 years.

This excursion into the realm of Public Health displays William's talents at their best: he analyses the water; he specifies the dangers of drinking it; he lists the ways by which the dangers can be minimised—and ends his discussion with a humorous and highly improbable anecdote.

'An account of the noxious effects of some Fungi'[35] shows that some of these effects were distinctly psychedelic:

A middle aged man having gathered what he called champignons; they were stewed and eaten by himself and his wife; their child also, about four years old, eat a little of them and the sippets of bread, which were put into the liquor. Within five minutes after eating them, the man began to stare in an unusual manner, and was unable to shut his eyes. All objects appeared to him coloured with a variety of colours. He felt a palpitation in what he called his stomach; and was so giddy that he could hardly stand. He seemed to himself swelled all over his body. He hardly knew what he did or said; and sometimes was unable to speak at all. These symptoms continued in a greater or less degree for twenty-four hours; after which he felt little or no disorder. Soon after he perceived himself ill, one scruple of white vitriol was given him, and repeated two or three times, with which he vomited plentifully.

The woman, aged thirty-nine, felt all the same symptoms, but in a higher degree. She totally lost her voice and her senses, and was either stupid or so furious that it was necessary she should be held. The white vitriol was offered to her, but she was capable of taking very little of it; however after four or five hours she was much recovered: but she continued many days far from being well and from enjoying her former health and strength. She frequently fainted for the first week after, and there was, during a month longer, an uneasy sense of heat and weight in her breast and stomach and bowels, with great flatulence. Her head was at first waking much confused; and she often experienced palpitations, tremblings and other hysteric affections to all which she had ever before been a stranger. Her appetite and stools continued in a natural state.

The child had some convulsive agitations of his arms, but was otherwise little affected. He was capable of taking half a scruple of ipecacuanha, with which he vomited, and was soon perfectly recovered.

In his paper on chickenpox[36] 'the sagacity of Dr Heberden enabled him to give to us the first scientific account' of the illness 'and to mark the differences between this eruption and that of the Small-Pox'.

William's opening sentences explain the importance of being able to distinguish between the two diseases:

The chicken-pox and swine-pox differ, I believe, only in name; they occasion so little danger or trouble to the patients, that physicians are seldom sent for to them, and have therefore very few opportunities of seeing this distemper. Hence it happens that the name of it is met with in very few books, and hardly any pretend to say a word of its history. But though it be so insignificant an illness, that an acquaintance with it is not of much use for its own sake, yet it is of importance on account of the small-pox, with which it may otherwise be confounded, and so deceive the persons, who have had it, into a false security, which may prevent them either from keeping out of the way of the small-pox, or from being inoculated. For this reason I have judged it might be useful to contribute, what I have learned from experience, towards its description.

William made another notable contribution in his 'Remarks on the Pulse',[37] which he read in July 1768. Although Harvey had announced his discovery of the circulation of the blood as long ago as 1616, many physicians were still interpreting the pulse according to doctrines derived from Galen; William seems to have been the first to have rejected these out-dated theories and to give a detailed account of the significance of the pulse based firmly on the new understanding that Harvey had revealed. He begins:

I have more than once observed old and eminent practitioners make such different judgements of hard and full and weak and small pulses, that I was sure they did not call the same sensations by the same names. It is to be wished therefore that physicians in their doctrine of pulses and descriptions of cases had attended more to such circumstances of the pulse, in which they could neither mistake nor be misunderstood. Fortunately there is one of this sort, which not only on this account but likewise for its importance, deserves all our attention. What I mean is, the frequency or quickness of the pulse . . . This is generally the same in all parts of the body, and cannot be affected by the constitutional firmness or flaccidity, or smallness or largeness of the artery, or by its lying deeper or more superficially; and is capable of being numbered, and consequently of being most perfectly described and communicated to others.

The degrees of quickness of the pulse belonging to the several ages and distempers have been taken notice of by few physicians in their writings; and, as many observations are necessary to settle this doctrine, what I have made and am going to relate, may be of use towards confirming, correcting or enlarging those which have been made by others . . .

The pulse of children under two years old should be felt while they are asleep; for their pulses are greatly quickened by every new sensation, and the occasions of these are perpetually happening to them while they are awake.

After giving average pulse rates for children and adults in good health, William considers the significance of pulses that are much faster or slower than normal; but he reminds his audience that although the pulse is in many cases 'an useful index of the state of the health', it can mislead us if we fail to have due regard for other signs. Towards the end of his paper he observes . . .

Some books speak of intermitting pulses[38] as dangerous signs, but I think without reason; for such trivial causes will occasion them, that they are not worth regarding in any illness, unless joined with other bad signs of more moment. They are not uncommon in health, and are perceived by a peculiar feel at the heart by the persons themselves every time the pulse intermits.

But of all William's contributions, none made such a lasting impact as the paper he read at the College on 21 July 1768 and which was published in the second volume of the *Transactions*; it was entitled 'Some Account of a Disorder of the Breast':[39]

There is a disorder of the breast, marked with strong and peculiar symptoms, considerable for the kind of danger belonging to it, and not extremely rare, of which I do not recollect any mention among medical authors. The seat of it, and sense of strangling and anxiety with which it is attended, may make it not improperly be called Angina pectoris.

Those who are afflicted with it are seized, while they are walking, and more particularly when they walk soon after eating, with a painful and most disagreeable sensation in the breast, which seems as if it would take their life away, if it were to increase or to continue: the moment they stand still, all this uneasiness vanishes. In all other respects the patients are at the beginning of this disorder perfectly well, and in particular have no shortness of breath, from which it is totally different.

After it has continued some months, it will not cease so instantaneously upon standing still; and it will come on not only when the persons are walking, but when they are lying down and oblige them to rise up out of their beds every night for many months together . . .

In the course of his practice William had seen hardly more than twenty cases and nearly all of them, he remarks, were men over fifty. On one occasion he was able to take the pulse of a patient in a paroxysm and found that it was not disturbed by the pain. He continues:

The os sterni is usually pointed to as the seat of this malady, but it seems sometimes as if it was under the lower part of it, and at other times under the middle or upper part, but always inclining more to the left side, and sometimes there is joined with it a pain about the middle of the left arm. What the particular mischief is, which is referred to these different parts of the sternum, it is not easy to guess . . .

The opinion of its being a convulsion of the part affected will readily present itself to anyone who considers the sudden manner of its coming on and off; the long intervals of perfect ease; the relief afforded by wine and spirituous cordials; the influence which passionate affections of the mind have over it; the ease which comes from varying the posture of the head and shoulders, by straitening the vertebrae of the thorax, or by bending them a little backwards or forwards; the number of years which it will continue without otherwise disordering the health; its generally bearing so well the motion of a horse or carriage, which circumstance often distinguishes spasmodic pains from those which arise from ulcers; and lastly its coming on in certain patients at night just after the first sleep, at which time the incubus, convulsive asthmas, numbnesses, epilepsies, hypocondriac languors, and other ills justly attributed to the disturbed functions of the nerves, are peculiarly apt either to return or to be aggravated.

Bleeding, vomits and other evacuations have not appeared to me to do any good. Wine and cordials taken at going to bed will prevent or weaken the night fits; but nothing does this so effectually as opiates. Ten, fifteen or twenty drops of Tinctura

Thebaica taken at lying down will enable those to keep their beds till morning, who had been forced to rise and sit up two or three hours every night, for many months.

William regrets that he has never had an opportunity to witness an autopsy on a victim of angina, 'the sudden death of the patients adding so much to the common difficulties of making such an enquiry, that most of those with whose cases I had been acquainted, were buried before I had heard that they were dead' . . . Time and attention, he concludes . . .

. . . will undoubtedly discover more helps against this teizing and dangerous ailment; but it is not to be expected that much can have been done towards establishing the method of cure for a distemper hitherto so unnoticed that it has not yet, as far as I know, found a place or a name in the history of diseases.

The element that qualifies this paper for a permanent place in medical history is (to quote one modern authority)[40] its 'unsurpassed outline of the clinical data'; and Dr D Evan Bedford[41] comments:

Today, when coronary disease is recognised in all civilised countries as a main cause of death, we should not forget that it was Heberden's original description of the symptoms of coronary disease that set in motion the vast researches now in progress to discover its causes and prevention. Looked at in perspective, we may well regard his paper of 1768 as one of the greatest mile-stones in the history of cardiology after Harvey's discovery . . .

In view of such tributes it is not surprising that in later years the disease was often referred to as 'Heberden's angina', or alternatively ·as 'Heberden's asthma'.

When the paper was published, an abstract of it was printed in the *Critical Review*[42] and was read by a doctor who realised that the account accurately described his own symptoms. Accordingly he wrote to William—without disclosing his identity—and this remarkable letter provided the starting-point for a further paper which William read at the College soon afterwards.[43]

After giving a detailed account of some of his experiences the anonymous doctor goes on to describe certain sensations which 'have frequently led me to think that I should meet with a sudden death':

I have often felt, when sitting, standing, and at times in my bed, what I can best express by calling it an universal pause within me of the operations of nature for perhaps three or four seconds; and when she has resumed her functions, I felt a shock at the

John Hunter by Robert Home, c 1768.

heart, like that which one would feel from a small weight being fastened to a string to some part of the body, and falling from the table to within a few inches of the floor ... If it please God to take me away suddenly, I have left directions on my will to send an account of my death to you, with a permission for you to order such an examination of my body, as will shew the cause of it; and perhaps tend at the same time to a discovery of the origin of that disorder, which is the subject of this letter, and be productive of means to counteract and remove it.

I am, Sir, Yours, UNKNOWN

In less than three weeks after sending the letter, the writer was dead; in accordance with the directions he had left in his will, William was immediately informed and asked John Hunter[44] to carry out an autopsy, which was done within 48 hours of the death. But, in spite of the most careful examination,

... no manifest cause of his death could be discovered; the seat of the disease having been, as we may suppose, in some of those parts, the functions of which not being well understood in life, we can find no traces of their disorders after death.

This anatomical examination, for which I acknowledge myself much indebted to the manly sense and benevolent spirit of this worthy man, though it do not inform us what the cause of the disease was, will however have its use by informing us what it was not. For since it was not owing to any mal-conformation, or morbid destruction of parts necessary to life, we need not despair of finding a cure; and as there were no appearances of inflammation or scirrhus or abscess, which in the former volume I mention as possible causes; we must not seek the remedy in bleeding and purging, and lowering the strength, but rather in the opposite class of medicines, which are usually called nervous and cordial, such as relieve and quiet convulsive motions, and invigorate the languishing principle of life.

The reprint of William's earlier paper which had appeared in the *Critical Review* had also been read by John Wesley, who was concerned with the bodily as well as the spiritual health of his followers and had written a handbook (first published in 1747) entitled *Primitive Medicine*, which contained definitions of diseases and prescriptions for their cure. In his Journal[45] for April 1774, when he was in the West Riding, he noted:

Tues 19. I found Mr Greenwood (with whom I lodged) dying (as was supposed) of the gout in the stomach; but on observing the symptoms, I was convinced it was not the gout but the angina pectoris (well described by Dr Heberden . . .)

On one occasion William asked his brother to submit a paper on leprosy[46] — or, to use Thomas's term, elephantiasis. This was a disease 'almost unknown in this country; and in order to form an idea of it, we must necessarily apply to those, who practise physic in foreign nations'. In the paper that follows William's introductory remarks, Thomas once again displays his talent for vivid reporting, but he readily admits that of all the patients he had treated, only one appeared to be cured.

One more example of a paper read — but not composed — by William takes us to the Orient:[47]

The following account was communicated to John Burrow Esq by a Mandarin, who had presided by the Emperor of China's order in that part of Tartary where the Ginseng is gathered and cured. He allowed ours to be the same with theirs,[48] and that they differed only in the curing, which, in the opinion of the Chinese, makes a very great difference to the virtue of this root. They suppose it to be a sovereign analeptic, and useful in almost all disorders. Their manner of infusing it is, to slice it into a vessel of cold water, which vessel is covered, and put into boiling water, where it soon becomes fit for use . . .

William's work was occasionally acknowledged by other contributors to the *Transactions* and Sir George Baker (who established the fact that Colica Pictonum (or 'Devonshire colic') was a form of lead poisoning, refers to one of his cases as follows:[49]

> Dr Heberden had a patient, who became paralytic, in consequence of frequent attacks of colic. How the disease had been excited, it did not immediately appear; but an enquiry being made into all this gentleman's habits, it was discovered that it had long been his custom every day to drink a pint of Lisbon wine. Dr Heberden having before had reason to suspect Lisbon wine of being sometimes corrected by lead, desired him to drink no more of that liquor. His advice was complied with; after which the patient was very soon freed from the disorder, of which he has had no return.

Fothergill also referred to William's work, twice in connexion with angina and on another occasion in the course of an article about the colic suffered 'by Painters in water colours prepared from white and red lead:'[50]

> Many diseases affecting young children may be ascribed to a cause which I am obliged to Dr Heberden for suggesting to me; many of their playthings are coated with paint, a great part whereof is white lead . . .

William in his turn referred to the experiences of his friends and colleagues to illuminate his own discourses; and to his paper on Essera (or nettlerash) he appends a letter from Messenger Monsey,[51] from which a few sentences deserve to be quoted:

> About the year 1752, WA aged near 30, of a thin, spare habit, was seized with a disorder attended with symptoms of a very uncommon kind. Whenever he went into the air, especially if the sun shined bright, he was seized with a tickling of his flesh on those parts exposed to the sun; this tickling by his continuing in the air increased to a violent itching attended with great heat and pain: the skin would be as red, nearly, as vermilion, and thicken like leather; and this remained till he got out of the air, and then in ten, fifteen or twenty minutes abated . . .

After suffering without relief for several years, he came to Monsey, who asked him

. . . if he could in the least guess at the cause or causes or his complaint: he told me, that being very poor, he and a comrade lived all one winter upon bullock's liver and porter. How far this method might go in bringing on his disorder, I leave to the researches of others . . .

A variety of remedies were then tried, without any beneficial effect, until finally Monsey

. . . not knowing what to do in so anomalous a disorder, in which I had no guide, determined at last to give him mercury, and he accordingly took five grains of calomel for three nights together and a purge the next morning . . .

This treatment did the trick and in less than six weeks the patient was entirely cured and could enjoy the sunshine with impunity.

In two papers which appeared under the general title of 'Queries',[52] William invites his readers to consider whether certain items of received wisdom are validated by experience; is gout (for example) a remedy for other complaints 'as it is generally supposed?' Or again, may not mischief be done, he asks, by an indiscriminate use of large bleedings in cases of palsies and apoplexies? And what information does the colour or texture of the blood provide that can be of use to the practitioner? Perhaps the most controversial, and therefore the most widely discussed, of all the 'Queries' was the one that William read to the College in August 1770:[53]

In England few make any doubt of the great danger attending wet rooms, and damp cloaths, or beds: Is this opinion founded upon experience, or is it a prejudice, which has been suffered to grow up and get strength merely for want of being examined?

If we enquire into the arguments in favor of this notion, we shall hardly find any other, than the random conjectures of the sick about the cause of their illness; or than their artfully substituting this origin of it instead of some other, which they are unwilling to own. A sick man is the best judge of what he feels; but is seldom more able than any bystander to find out the immediate occasion of his illness; and is much less able than those whose business it is to attend to facts of this nature, and who, from a great variety of instances, can most justly decide which among many pretended ones is the real cause of a disorder. I hardly know a distemper of which at different times I have not been told that it was occasioned by lying in a damp bed, or by sitting in a wet room; and yet I do not know any one which will certainly be produced by these causes: and people frequently expose themselves to such causes without suffering any ill effects.

After admitting the dangers of vapours arising from 'putrid

moisture' such as the bilge-water of ships, he gives reasons for his belief in 'the inoffensiveness of mere wetness', and refers to the moist air near rivers and at the sea-side, which is recommended for its 'peculiar healthiness'. He continues:

> Those who are much disposed to sweat, lie many hours in bed-cloaths, impregnated probably with a less wholesome moisture than would have been left in the sheets half dried after washing . . .
>
> Yet they apparently suffer no injury and the same seems to be true of children, and such as are troubled with the stone, and those who from other infirmities, or age, constantly wet their beds with their urine . . .
>
> It is a common practice in certain disorders to go to bed at night with the legs or arms wrapped in linen cloths thoroughly soaked in Malvern water, so that the sheets will be in many places as wet as they can be; and I have known these patients and their bedfellows receive no harm from a continuance of this practice for many months . . .

More surprisingly, William seems to discount the dangers to health arising from perpetual exposure to wet floors or pavements or from clothes 'often wet for many hours together'. He ends with some more questions:

> Is it the coldness of wet linen which is feared? But shirts and sheets, colder than any unfrozen water can be, are safely worn and lain in by many persons, who, during a hard frost, neither warm their beds nor their shirts. Or does the danger lie in the dampness? But then how comes it to pass, that a warm or cold bath, and long-continued fomentations can be used, without the destruction of those who use them? Or is it from both together? Yet we have long heard of the thickness and continuance of the cold fogs in the seas north-west of England; but have never yet been told of any certain ill effect, which they have upon those who live in them.

No doubt this 'Query' stirred up some lively discussion, particularly after its publication in the second volume of the *Medical Transactions*. Walpole[54] was not at all impressed by William's reasoning; but however controversial the arguments may have appeared, the paper exemplifies William's talent for asking searching questions about popular entrenched assumptions—the first essential step towards the discovery of correct answers.

In June and July 1767 there had been an outbreak of influenza; William kept notes on its progress and when it had subsided in August, he described it in a paper entitled 'The Epidemical Cold'.[55] When the next epidemic arrived in London in the autumn of 1775,

Fothergill decided to draw up 'A Sketch of the Epidemic Cold' and to invite his friends to comment on it. It was his intention to publish the symposium in the sixth volume of his *Medical Observations and Enquiries* and in spite of his uneasy relations with the College, Heberden, Baker and Pringle were among the Fellows who responded with contributions. Fothergill did not live to see the symposium in print and it was not until 1784 that it appeared in the sixth (and final) volume of the series which he had done so much to sustain.[56]

In the meantime, a third epidemic had arrived and the College decided to carry out an enquiry into its causes and effects, but on a wider scale than Fothergill had attempted. In 1782 the Registrar was instructed to place advertisements in the press asking for information on 'the late prevailing disease commonly called the Influenza'. No doubt many of the replies were of little or no value and the registrar had the task of sifting the wheat from the chaff before passing on the more promising contributions to the committee (to which William had been elected) for further consideration. Three meetings were needed before a final selection was agreed and these were eventually published in the third volume of the *Transactions* a year after the appearance of Fothergill's symposium. If the College's project fell far short of a scientifically conducted survey, it was at the least a creditable pioneering venture.

Meanwhile the Licentiates' animosity against the College was fading. Many of them had built up reputations—and fortunes—as substantial as those achieved by the Fellows, and the importance of Fellowship as a symbol of status was no longer perceived as a burning issue. Goodwill between the two parties was formally re-established when the Society of Collegiate Physicians invited the College President Sir George Baker to dine with them in November 1786; and the Society's minute book records that at another dinner held at the Crown & Anchor five months later Dr William Heberden and two other Fellows 'honoured the Society with their company'.

Our account of William's activities in the Royal College of Physicians provides ample evidence that his colleagues held him in considerable esteem; why, then, was he never President? From 1762 he had been one of the 'elects' who had the privilege of choosing the President from among their number; yet whenever the highest office fell vacant, William's name was passed over. It is hard to believe that he was unwilling to serve—at least for a short period—however numerous his other commitments. Had he disqualified himself by appearing too sympathetic to the cause of the rebel Licentiates? Was his refusal of a Court appointment held against him? We can speculate, but all we know for certain is what we can read in the College Annals—that in June 1781 he resigned from the body of Elects, thus indicating that any ambitions he might have had to fill the Presidential chair were now finally put aside.

Chapter 7

The Church, Literature, Correspondence

The twin pillars of William's early education—the Classics and the Established Religion of the Church of England—remained potent influences throughout his life. The Classics provided much of the mental furniture shared by many of his educated friends, while his scholarly understanding of religious matters could well have led (if the notion had attracted him) to some high position in the Church. Indeed the possibility of ordination must surely have been in his mind during his undergraduate years; why else should he have postponed the start of his medical studies until he had received his Fellowship?

His decision to reject a clerical career may have been influenced by the attitude of the many Fellows and tutors who, though in Holy Orders, showed no sign of any serious religious commitment. If their spirituality seemed to be in short supply, this was partly due, as William was well aware, to events in the previous century, when bigots and fanatics of varying hues had caused considerable misery and destruction. No wonder that by the time William came on the scene, 'enthusiasm' had come to be regarded as 'a horrid thing' and 'toleration'—even though of a limited kind—was the order of the day. This toleration, though desirable when directed towards dissenters, had its negative side when applied to the shortcomings of the bishops, priests and deacons of the Established Church, who often pursued their private interests to the detriment of their ecclesiastical duties; and as the laity expected little more from their parsons than the performance of the mandatory services, such as baptisms, marriages and funerals, criticisms were generally muted. Despite the many individual parsons who brought honour to their profession, the Church of England as a whole contributed too little either by precept or example to the development of the nation's moral awareness.

The Dissenters, on the other hand, tended to have a more serious vision of Man's place in the divine scheme of things; the Quakers, for example, though rejecting Creeds and Articles combined prudence and thrift with imaginative benevolence and a sense of social responsibility—and Dr Fothergill was a worthy representative of this persuasion. The subtle variety of beliefs among other dissenting sects were numerous and confusing, but all of them rejected at least some of the Thirty-nine Articles, either from disbelief or from sheer incomprehension. Being debarred from higher education at the English Universities, they set up their own Academies at

Warrington, Manchester, Hackney and elsewhere and it was from this atmosphere of independent enquiry that Priestley formulated his Unitarian theology.

William's friendships with dissenters in no way undermined his own Anglican convictions; he was an active member of the congregation at his parish church of St Martin-in-the-Fields and his staunch support was recognised in 1765 by his election as a Gentleman of the Vestry.[1]

His earliest surviving letter on a religious topic was addressed to his Cambridge contemporary, the former St John's sizar Thomas Rutherforth, who was by now Regius Professor of Divinity and FRS. Rutherforth had delivered a sermon (which he then published) entitled *The Credibility of Miracles defended against the author of Philosophical Essays*—the author being David Hume, whose sceptical views had disturbing implications for the Church. On receiving a complimentary copy of the sermon William wrote:[2]

> Cecil Street 4 Oct 1751
>
> Your principles seem to me to be just, & your application of them is fair and convincing, & fully exposes the fallacy of the argument, which you examin. What you have so well considered, & so clearly drawn up on this important subject lets in a great deal of light on the question of miracles, &, I dare say, will do you as much credit with your readers, as I am sure it must have done with your hearers. The only objection that I could make to what you have written is, that the doctrine advanced by Hume is in itself so paradoxical at first sight, & on examination seems so destitute of any solid foundation, that it hardly deserved the attention of such an able thinker. But he has his admirers I suppose, & it might be proper to shew them with how little reason they admired him, at least in this part of his doctrine.

Hume's Essays, which were in fact the first edition of his *Enquiry Concerning Human Understanding*, were published in 1748—a few months before the appearance of Conyers Middleton's book on the miraculous powers attributed to the early church; insofar as Middleton's arguments against the credibility of miracles were based on the unreliability of the witnesses' testimony, William may have been prepared to give them his cautious assent, as the crucial belief in 'revelation' was not undermined. Hume's arguments however were more radical and appeared to strike at the very foundations of Christian belief. In an ironical passage at the end of his essay 'Of Miracles' he writes:

> Upon the whole, we may conclude that the Christian religion not only was at first attended with miracles, but even at this date cannot be believed by any reasonable person without one.

Mere reason is insufficient to convince us of its veracity: And whoever is moved by Faith to assent to it, is conscious of a continued miracle in his own person, which subverts all the principles of his understanding, and gives him a determination to believe what is most contrary to custom and experience.

This was too much for William to stomach and was certainly a fitting target for a thunderbolt from Rutherforth.

Hume indeed was widely perceived as a threat to stability, a condition prized as much by politicians as by churchmen. But there were many men of liberal views (William among them) who felt this craving for stability stood in the way of certain modest but very desirable reforms. One of these concerned the Thirty-nine Articles, incorporated by Cranmer in the Book of Common Prayer, to which all clergy of the Church of England were obliged to subscribe; a substantial number however refused to do so on grounds of conscience, and no doubt there were many more who subscribed reluctantly from motives of convenience. Matters came to a head when the dissatisfied clergy appointed a committee at the Feathers Tavern to take political action by submitting a Petition to Parliament, urging that 'subscription' be abolished. Cole leaves us in no doubt that William was actively involved:

Dr Heberden, a great and zealous favourer of the petitioners against the Liturgy and Articles of the Church of England . . . has lost himself much in point of character lately in interesting himself so warmly and pertinaciously with the petitioners and factious clergy and laity . . . [an] advocate for the petitioning clergy, unbecoming a man of moderation.

'The Feathers Tavern Petition' was debated in the Commons in February 1772 and Walpole[3] gives us a lively and illuminating account of the arguments put forward by supporters and opponents of the motion:

Lord North[4] was very uneasy at the progress of this controversy, and not being able to prevent it, though resolved not to favour the demand, recommended to his party great decency and moderation in treating it; but the High Church and old Tories, secure of the King's favour, paid little regard to a Minister who, they knew, was but the servant of a junto that really governed; and though all other men allowed the absurdity of the Articles, and agreed that the Bishops themselves could not believe them, but that yet a door was not to be opened to farther innovation and religious disputes which are the most dangerous of factions, the Tories still combated for their old Diana[5] as stiffly as they could have done in the monkish ages.

On the 7th [Feb] Sir William Meredith, seconded by Mr Thomas Pitt, informed the House that he had in his hand a petition, signed by many respectable clergymen, complaining of the subscription to the Thirty-nine Articles: that the grievances which affected the minds of those gentlemen were greater than any that could regard their properties: and that the whole clergy were obliged to sign those Articles, which not three of them had ever defended. The petitioners set forth that they desired to subscribe to no Articles, but to the Holy Scriptures themselves; with many other heads, on which Sir William commented very ably. Sir Roger Newdigate, a hot-headed bigot, and formerly as warm a Jacobite, desired to know how many of the clergy had signed the petition. Sir W Meredith answered, 250, most of them beneficed clergymen. Sir Roger ridiculed them and said, tender-conscienced as they were, they had however signed the Articles. Everything had been overturned in the last age by tender consciences! The walls of religion must not be broken down; Church and State were inseparable. But his great argument was, that it was a breach of the Union with Scotland to alter the Thirty-nine Articles, and that the petition was therefore inadmissible . . .

Lord George Germayne defended the petition, and said most of the clergy in his neighbourhood had signed it . . . He wondered the House did not take some steps on this subject with regard to the Universities, where boys were made to subscribe the Articles without reading them—a scandalous abuse. His son might be obliged to subscribe to what he himself should not be able to explain to him . . .

Edmund Burke made a fine laboured speech against the petition, urging that the civil war began by forcing Episcopacy on Scotland against the bent of the nation: but his chief argument was the necessity of a precise rule of faith. The petitioners declared they would be bound by the Scriptures; but what are the Scriptures? are they a book bound in red morocco with clasps, and printed by Baskett? What was the Bible but a miscellaneous body of writings? Was he to find the Scriptures in the Mosaic Law, in the Psalms, or in the New Testament?

At the conclusion of the debate the majority of Members opted to maintain the status quo and the petition was accordingly rejected by 217 votes to 71.

After three months had gone by, another petition was presented— this time by the Dissenters, who were still treated in certain respects as second-class citizens. Four Acts had been put on the Statute Book in the 1660s, debarring them from all church and municipal appointments and severely curtailing their freedom of worship. Despite the subsequent Toleration Act, the earlier laws had not been repealed, with the result that Dissenters still suffered disabilities which (as the Licentiates had good cause to know) could affect a man's status and career prospects.

The petition (in which the Dissenters sought exemption from the laws which discriminated against them) was allowed to pass through the Commons in May; but when it reached the House of Lords it ran into trouble. Of the twenty-six Bishops who sat there as Lords Spiritual, William was on friendly terms with at least six[6] and would not have been backward in recommending to them the merits of the Petition. One of them—William Warburton[7] the Bishop of Gloucester—had written books which appeared to favour toleration; but now, in his old age, he saw matters in a different light, as Walpole (who heartily disliked him) records:[8]

> Warburton, formerly a heretic, had now driven the Bishops upon this opposition to toleration; then changed his mind and declared he would not attend the Bill. His friend Dr Heberden, the physician, went to him and told him, if he had changed his mind, he ought to declare it like a man, but would lose all character if he absented himself. He went to the House, but did not mend the matter . . .

> The Duke of Richmond supported the Petition and . . .

> warmly attacked the Bishops on the Jesuitic spirit, want of candour and scandalous love of power and money and he read many quotations in favour of toleration from Bishop Warburton's 'Divine Legation' and 'Doctrine of Grace'.

But Warburton made no reply 'but said he scorned to answer or to stay away'. When the debate was finally concluded, the Petition was firmly rejected and a century was to pass before the offending Acts were at last repealed.

Although there were many Bishops who fully deserved the Duke of Richmond's strictures, the abuses were the inevitable result of the system. The Church in Hanoverian England was subordinate to the state and was expected to support the existing order.[9] Appointments to ecclesiastical offices were subject to political considerations and party loyalty was the price expected for preferment. Bishops were expected to attend the House of Lords and to demonstrate their allegiance by their votes. This obligation kept them away from their dioceses for part of each year, and as each diocese covered a wide area and travel was slow, it was difficult for the most conscientious bishop to carry out his duties adequately. But despite the fearsome problems of attempting to serve God and the politicians simultaneously, few clerics near the top of the pyramid had any desire to rock the boat and it was inevitable that the kind of arguments advanced by Edmund Burke appeared persuasive to those in positions of power and influence.

William's involvement in these excitements drew differing reactions from his friends; Cole's disapproval was predictable, as his views were rigidly Tory. Dr Thomas Balguy, William's contemporary at St John's and by now Archdeacon of Winchester had recently defended subscription to the Articles in a published 'charge' or exhortation, but included in it a note supporting the petition of the Dissenters. Hurd felt that as a layman William had trespassed in fields which were the proper preserves of the Bishops and other senior members of the ecclesiastical establishment; in a letter to Balguy written a few months after the debates he gives us a lively picture of one of William's visits in which medical advice is a prelude to theology:[10]

> . . . But apropos to my bilious cholic. The news of it flew to Dr Heberden, who very humanely came to me this morning. As soon as he had heard my history, and prescribed as he thought fit, he passed immediately, and with high approbation, to the mention of that note to your Charge which gives up the cause of the Bishops to the petitioning Dissenters. What followed was so warm on this subject, that we had no time to consider the merits of your Charge itself. He reserves himself, without doubt, for your own ear on that subject. Is it not much to be lamented, that so excellent a man, who might claim respect of all the world in his own department, will strive in another province, where, at most, he can but merit our pardon on the score of his good intentions?

Bishop Law,[11] on the other hand, commended William's efforts to promote a spirit of toleration and described him in a letter written in 1775 as 'a worthy liberal layman, who does more service to the cause than all our bench'.

William's opinions had also been noted by Boswell:[12]

> April 1779: I mentioned my having heard an eminent physician (viz Heberden), who was himself a Christian, argue in favour of universal toleration, and maintain that no man could be hurt by another man's differing from him in opinion.
> JOHNSON. Sir, you are to a certain degree hurt by knowing that even one man does not believe.

William had studied the Bible at least as thoroughly as many of his clerical friends and as he understood Hebrew, he was better qualified than most laymen to make informed comments on passages that were obscure or controversial. In 1785, one of his acquaintances, William Newcome,[13] Bishop of Waterford published a work on the Twelve Minor Prophets of the Old Testament; at the end of a lengthy and erudite note on the prophet Haggai he wrote:

After I had finished these notes as to their scope and substance, I received the following valuable communication from the learned and respectable Dr Heberden; which will give the reader great assistance in determining the sense of the prophesy now under discussion.

The passage concerned the rebuilding of Solomon's temple at Jerusalem in the sixth century BC, and one sentence was supposed by some commentators to refer to Christ. William considered this view to be a mistake which arose from a mistranslation in the Latin Vulgate. His note ends:

The most plausible objections to the christian religion have been made out of the weak arguments which have been advanced in its support: and can there be a weaker argument than that which sets out with doing violence to the original text in order to form a prophesy, and then contradicts the express testimony of the best historian of those times in order to shew that it has been accomplished?

William would have regarded himself as a mere amateur in Hebrew studies, compared with his friend Benjamin Kennicott (1718-83) who spent much of his life collecting Hebrew manuscripts and eventually produced a major work which attempted to establish the authentic Hebrew text of the Old Testament. While the work was in progress he published dissertations on various aspects of the subject and these were read by Thomas Rutherforth, who had earned from the poet Mason the title of 'saintly butcher' for his savage and often niggling criticisms of respected authors. When in November 1761 William received a copy of one of his pamphlets criticising Kennicott's work,[14] he wrote:

I am obliged to you for . . . your pamphlet . . . The objections to it which arose in my own mind, & which I have heard from others, are that several of the points seem such minutiae, that your abilities & learning deserved a better employment: and, that together with shewing Mr K his mistakes you may be likely to hurt his subscription,[15] & so the work may be entirely lost to the public, which would be a loss as it would be better to have it indifferently performed, than not begun upon at all.
   I have just printed a few copies of the hitherto unpublished appendix to Dr Middleton's controversy about the physicians,[16] & beg your acceptance of one of them. Be pleased to present my compl to Mrs Rutherforth.

William's mild reproof suggests that he had a high opinion of Kennicott's work—an opinion shared by many men of learning who subscribed the enormous sum of over £9000 for the completed volumes which appeared between 1776 and 1780.

Another of William's literary friends was the Revd Jonathan Toup (1713-85) who graduated from Oxford and after being ordained, spent the rest of his life in obscure parishes in his native county of Cornwall. He built up an enviable reputation both at home and abroad as an editor of classical texts—though he was criticised for his immoderate language and boorish conduct. Three of William's letters to him are preserved.[17]

In the first of these, dated July 1767, William begins by thanking his friend 'for the very obliging present of *Epistola Critica*';[18] then, in the next paragraph, he refers to a forthcoming book on the Greek particles by a Dutch scholar named Hoogeveen:

> I beg your acceptance of the enclosed receipt (being the full payment) of what the annexed specimen and proposal will give you. The work it seems has been some time prepared for the Press but the author had not encouragement to print it. One of his former scholars brought the specimen to London where a subscription was set on foot and about 100 receipts have been disposed of. His Majesty has honoured the list with his name.

After a delay of two years the book was eventually printed and William writes:

> . . . I will take care to get it for you. Be so good as to tell me . . . by what waggon or other conveyance I can send it you.

Hoogeveen in his Latin preface acknowledged William's generous support in ordering ten copies for himself and encouraging others to buy the book. 'Indeed,' wrote the author, 'I could not sufficiently admire his amazing patronage of literary works and their authors.'

William wrote his third letter to Toup on 15 March 1770:

> Cecil St
> Dear Sir, I was yesterday favoured with your letter informing me of the great honour which I have received by your prefixing my name to your notes on Theocritus.[19] I think myself highly obliged to you for this mark of your esteem, to which I might have some better pretention if my study of the ancient authors were equal to my love of them; but I am well enough acquainted with their merit to know the great service which they have done and would still do to mankind and this makes me honour all those who have shewn us that they can contribute to make the Greek and Latin writers more generally read and more perfectly understood. Among them your name stands very high and I hope your health will long enable you to continue those useful services to the world

and that the world may be so sensible of what it owes you for them as not to let the fame you have acquired be your only reward.

William evidently suspected that his friend's health was at risk. Toup later suffered a mental collapse and spent the final years of his life in a state of senility.

If Toup chose to bury himself in the wilds of Cornwall, Jeremiah Markland had an even more reclusive nature, though geographically he was less remote. He was a Fellow of Peterhouse but was never ordained as he suffered from some weakness of the lungs which made it impossible for him to project his voice with sufficient power to be audible from a pulpit. After earning his keep for some years as a private tutor he finally took a house near Dorking, where he devoted his time to producing works of scholarship. He never married and his only close friends appear to have been William and the printer Bowyer.[20] As old age approached, he lost interest in having his works published and on completing an edition of *The Trojan Women* by Euripides, he seemed content to let the work remain in manuscript. When William discovered this, he offered to print the play at his own expense, and the edition duly appeared in 1763.

William's encouragement seems to have given a boost to the old scholar's flagging energies; in January 1768 he was busily engaged preparing two more plays by Euripides and wrote to Bowyer:[21]

> I am going on apace with the two plays; have finished one, and one-third of the other; heartily wishing that it might be agreeable to Dr Heberden to make it a posthumous work, if he approves of the notes; or to destroy them (it will give me no pain) if he does not; either of which will make it very easy to him, and desirable to me In the meantime he shall have them in less than a month. Please to let him know that I wish this most sincerely, and on that supposition have written a dedication to him, as if I was a dead man.

Markland was not quite as near to the grave as he pretended, and when William had the plays published in 1771, the author was still alive and able to enjoy the knowledge that his labours had not been wasted. On his death he left William all his books and papers, including a *Greek Testament* with his marginal manuscript notes.

Bowyer, who had already published his own edition of the *Greek Testament* with critical notes, was preparing a revised edition, and William, to further the project, lent him the Markland copy. Although Bowyer died before the new edition appeared, he acknowledged William's help in his preface, and as a token of his friendship bequeathed to him 'his little cabinet of coins' and some books.[22]

The achievements of men such as Toup and Markland could only be fully appreciated by other scholars; to the wider public, their names meant very little. But if classical literature remained the preserve of a small minority, classical architecture exerted, in the last third of the century, a pervasive influence throughout the country. The man who was chiefly responsible for stimulating this 'Grecian Gusto' was the painter and architect James Stuart (1713-88). His enthusiasm had been fired when as a young man he worked as a fan-painter, copying pictures of ancient ruins. He arrived in Rome (having travelled most of the way on foot) in 1741, and after some years of study, decided that his ultimate objective must be Greece. With the support of the English Dilletanti, he and another artist Nicholas Revett issued Proposals for publishing an *Accurate Description of the Antiquities of Athens*. They reached their goal in March 1751 and for the next two years Stuart made sheaves of coloured drawings, while Revett made accurate measurements of everything in sight. They were back in London in 1755 and Stuart was in due course elected FRS and FSA. The first volume of their joint work appeared in 1762.

Inevitably Stuart and William became acquainted, and it is clear from the following anecdote (recounted by Macmichael)[23] that a friendship developed:

> Mr Stuart, best known by the name of Athenian Stuart, having presented Dr Heberden with a tea-chest made of olive wood from Athens, Mr Tyrwhitt,[24] who soon after dined with him, inspired by so classical a subject, sent him the next day the following copy of verses.

> In Attic fields, by famed Ilissus' flood,
> The sacred tree of Pallas once I stood.
> Now torn from thence, with graceful emblems drest,
> For Mira's tea I form a polish'd chest.
> Athens, farewell! no longer I repine
> For my Socratic shade and patroness divine.

> Sir William Jones[25] afterwards rendered the same into Greek and Jacob Bryant, Esq,[26] author of the *Ancient Mythology*, into Latin.

The mysterious Mira seems nothing more than a thin disguise for William's wife Mary; Bryant was chivalrous enough to dedicate his version to 'the excellent and learned lady MH', and Jones too, who sent his version with a covering letter from the Temple dated 2 December 1778, refers to 'the pretty epigram on Mrs Heberden's tea chest'. He mentions also 'the owl on the Attick tetradrachm on the side of the chest'—the only clue we have to the nature of the 'graceful emblems'.[27]

Macmichael recorded the episode as an example of the amusements of William's 'literary coterie', of which he names several members. Some (such as Wray and Hurd) have been mentioned already; others were Robert Lowth,[28] Soame Jenyns[29] and John Jortin.[30] One name omitted from the list is Dr John Taylor, the Cambridge University Librarian, who later became a Canon of St Paul's; in a letter[31] to him written in 1770 William refers 'to the instances of very old mistakes in the copies of Homer of which we were talking this afternoon'.

Another friend was George Keate (1729-97), poet, naturalist antiquary and artist; in 1781 he published his *Poetical Works*, dedicating them to William as 'an affectionate homage to that intimacy from which I have for very many years derived so much pleasure and advantage'. A few months before the poems appeared he sent William a copy of one of them with a letter[32] which suggests that the recipient had lost none of his zest for entertaining guests at his dinner-table:

> Monday Morning 26 Feby
> As your Roof, my dear Sir, affords so much pleasure and hospitality to your friends, you must not wonder if a poor Bard wishes to shelter himself in any snug corner beneath it, and intreats that the enclosed little piece may have the sanction of lying on your table before it faces the public eye . . .

William tells us nothing about his tastes in English poetry and the only clue comes from Hurd,[33] who mentions in the course of one of his letters that William was 'a passionate admirer' of Abraham Cowley—a poet whose works Hurd had recently edited.

Among the younger generation of writers who valued William's good opinion was TJ Mathias,[34] who in 1786 sent him a copy of his newly published *Pursuits of Literature*, inscribed with some complimentary message. William sent a courteous though formal acknowledgment[35] to 'this celebrated writer whose decrees of praise and censure have been so readily confirmed by the public voice'.

In his eightieth year William penned yet one more note of acknowledgment:[36]

> Dr Heberden presents his compts & thinks himself much obliged to Mr Burney for the favour of the remarks on Milton's Greek verses, for which he returns his thanks.
> Pall Mall Jan 31

The author of the *Remarks* (printed in 1790) was Charles Burney (1757-1817), son of Dr Burney the music historian and younger brother of Fanny whom we shall meet in the next chapter. After his expulsion from Cambridge for stealing books he managed to redeem himself in the eyes of his family by securing a degree from Aberdeen and thereafter settled down to become a schoolmaster, a classical critic and—finally—a clergyman.

Over the years William had built up a well-stocked library and was for a time a regular patron of a West-End bookshop, which stood near what is now Leicester Square. This was 'the great resort, about one o'clock every day, of men of letters'. It was so small that the proprietor Mr Payne found the literary folk very much in his way; among them were Tyrwhitt, Dr Percy (famous for his *Reliques of Ancient English Poetry*), Dr Heberden and many more.[37]

William's love of the classics made him a natural candidate for membership of the Society of Antiquaries. This, like other similar institutions, had developed from informal meetings in taverns or coffee-houses; groups interested in antiquarian studies had existed since the reign of Elizabeth and under the later Stuarts interest became more widely diffused through the publication of several county histories. Papers on antiquarian subjects had for a time been accepted by the Royal Society, but when Newton became President, these were excluded. Deprived of this platform a group of antiquaries began to hold regular meetings in the early years of the century at the Bear Tavern in the Strand and although these eventually lapsed, they were revived in 1717 at the Mitre Tavern, Fleet Street and it was there that the Society of Antiquaries, with the Revd William Stukeley as Secretary was formally established on the first of January 1717/8.[38]

The main focus of the Society's attention was directed to monuments and artifacts found in Britain—for example the stone circles at Avebury, mapped by Stukeley; smaller objects such as ancient coins and medallions were brought to the meetings and handed round during the discussions. But as the century progressed the more conservative members of the Society found their cherished preoccupations being pushed aside by the new taste for the products of ancient Greece and Italy—a taste stimulated by the fashion of the Grand Tour and more recently by James Stuart's volume on the ruins of Athens. Inevitably the qualifications for membership were gradually modified and when in July 1770 William's name was proposed, his classical expertise proved a satisfactory passport.

Nevertheless, the formalities had to be strictly observed: first a testimonial was presented and read, recommending him for election. There were no less than nine signatories, among them the President (the Revd Dr Milles, Dean of Exeter), Daniel Wray, William Hunter and Josiah Colebrook, the faithful keeper of the Royal Society's dinner-books. The testimonial was 'hung up' for several months, to give members ample time to read it and (if they wished) to register an objection. At the end of the year William was admitted Fellow.[39]

During the first ten years of his membership the Society occupied rooms in Chancery Lane and although he was evidently too busy to play an active role in the Society's affairs, William would certainly have attended the meetings whenever he was free to do so. In 1780 the Society was offered accommodation in Somerset House. Before they arrived there, the Royal Society had moved in, having miscalculated (as we have seen) the amount of space they required.

The rooms allotted to the Antiquaries were on the same floor; both suites were approached by a common staircase and shared the same anteroom and hall; this for a while caused considerable annoyance and some of the Antiquaries were further put out on finding that the porter's lodge had been entirely appropriated by the Royal Society. Those members who, like William, belonged to both institutions must have regarded the displays of bad temper with some amusement, and before long the fuss evaporated.

The path that led to his election had begun many years ago at his Grammar School, and William was acutely aware that without the encouragement of Mr Symes (by whose initiative he had been awarded the small but invaluable Exhibition) his career could well have been blighted. Now he was able to repay his debt in a fitting manner and in 1777 — sixty years after his admission to the school — he donated to the school Governors £500 in 3% Consols, to augment the salary of the Headmaster.[40]

Some of William's other interests emerge from his correspondence with Charles Blagden,[41] both during his absence in America and after his return. The fair copies of Blagden's letters no longer exist, but two of his rough drafts survive, the first, dated 3 May 1777 and written at Newport, Rhode Island. Part of the letter is concerned with medical matters:

> . . . In the account which I sent you formerly of the Dysentery[42] of last autumn, I did not state the proportions of deaths & recoveries with the necessary distinctions. Of all those who were treated in general according to the method I then described, about one out of sixty died . . .

In the next paragraph Blagden describes the climate of Rhode Island and mentions some of his meteorological observations. As for the progress of the war:

> The Troops here were alarmed two or three times in the winter by the appearance of boats in the Bay & the Rebels are said actually to have assembled to attack us; but when it came to the push, their resolution always failed. I hope the late destruction of their magazines, effected at such a critical season, will be attended with the important consequences expected from it & facilitate a restoration of the 'blessings of peace'.

There is no record of William's reply, but after a lapse of eighteen months — on 9 December 1778 — he acknowledges a letter he had just received and also thanks Blagden 'for your former accounts of the Thermometer' — a reference no doubt to one of his friend's research projects which were later reported in the *Philosophical Transactions*.

William then proceeds to inform him of Sir John Pringle's resignation,[43]

> ... for which I am very sorry both on his own account, & that of the Society; for in him we lose a most excellent President, & I think his active mind will want the employment, which the Presidentship afforded him, & that he will miss us as well as we miss him.

We would have expected William to refer at this point to Banks's election—an item of hot news in which Blagden would have been keenly interested; yet surprisingly William makes no mention of it and passes on at once to a different topic:

> The best medical news which I know, is that the King of France has instituted a Society for the reception of medical papers.[44] It consists of Fellows & Correspondents & they choose into it Foreigners as well as natives of France. Such a Society well conducted would do more in one century towards the improvement of our Profession than has been done from the time of Hippocrates to the present age: just as the knowledge of other parts of nature has increased more by means of such societies, within the last hundred years, than it had done from the age of Aristotle to the time of their foundation ... I am too old to be otherwise interested in an institution of this sort, than as a well-wisher to mankind; but you, I hope, will live to be one of their members, & to reap benefit from the papers of others, as well as to contribute to theirs by your own.[45] Dr Fothergill[46] has been ill of a suppression of urine by some disease of the prostate gland; I hear he is better, but cannot yet part with his water without the help of a catheter. The Doctor is, I believe, not above two years younger than I am, & a disorder of this kind at such an advanced age affords no great hopes of a perfect recovery. I please myself with thinking that you are now so seasoned to your employment, that we may be in less pain for you, than we were at first; for yours is by no means the least hazardous post in the Army. This unhappy contest must surely be soon ended one way or another:[47] and I doubt not whenever you return, that your conduct & character will have made you so many friends as to give you a ready introduction to practice in London and ensure your success.

Although the war dragged on until the capitulation of the British at Yorktown towards the end of 1781, Blagden (as we have seen) had returned to England the previous year. William's next—and last—surviving letter to him was written from Windsor in October 1783:

Dear Sir, I have just received a letter from Sir H Oxenden[48] who lives near Canterbury, acquainting me that Dr Lynch,[49] the chief physician there is just dead and that there is a very good opening for any physician who could succeed to his business. You will judge whether your present situation and future views will allow you to think of going thither; & I shall be glad to hear your determination as soon as you have made it. Sir Henry tells me that the remaining physician in Canterbury had but little of the best business; that there are many Gentlemen's families in the neighbourhood & that Dr Lynch is supposed to have got about 1000 guineas annually.

Dr Lynch's reputed earnings (which can be multiplied by at the very least sixty to give a modern equivalent) cast an interesting light on a physician's prospects in a Cathedral city; and if he charged the standard rate of a guinea for each consultation, an average of three such consultations a day would have produced the rumoured yearly total. But Blagden, who had a private income, could afford to reject this tasty financial bait; he replied promptly:

8 Oct 1783

Dear Sir, My views are so little turned towards wealth and so earnestly fixed upon objects which can scarcely be obtained out of the capital, that I feel I could not be happy, for the present at least, in any engagement which should remove me to a distance from London. Yet though I do not avail myself of the proposal, be so good as to accept my warmest acknowledgments of your offer: I have ever considered your recommendation on a former occasion[50] as an highly honourable event of my life; and sense the most heartfelt satisfaction from this fresh testimony, that I still retain the good opinion of a gentleman to whom I look up as one of the first characters of the age.

We can assume from this opening paragraph that Blagden was by now fully aware of the tensions within the Royal Society and of the possibility that he might, with Banks's support, be elected sometime in the near future to become Secretary; and the rest of the letter confirms the supposition that his interest in medicine had been supplanted by his enthusiasm for other branches of scientific enquiry. He refers first to 'a paper of the Abbé Fontana's,[51] where he asserts that certain animals of the lower orders, yield dephlogisticated air [i.e. oxygen] in the same manner as plants . . .'
Then he quotes an account of the movement of a meteor observed from Leyden and goes on to talk about 'the enthusiasm which prevailed in Paris on the night of the flying balloon' constructed by the Montgolfier brothers.[52]

In the closing sentence of his letter Blagden writes:

> After leaving your house on Monday evening, we spent a very
> instructive and entertaining night with Mr Herschel.[53]

It is surely safe to assume that William was already acquainted
with the great astronomer—famous as the discoverer of the planet
Uranus, FRS and Copley medallist—who had recently been created
Court Astronomer and had moved his home and instruments to
Datchet, a mere two or three miles from William's residence.

In view of William's interest in astronomy, it is not surprising that
he fitted up one of the rooms in his Pall Mall house as an observatory.
Evidence for this comes from the clock-maker Thomas Mudge
(1717-94) whose achievements equalled those of John Harrison.[54]
After working for many years in London, he retired to Plymouth
in 1771 to concentrate on making further improvements in marine
chronometers and when Parliament (after grudgingly paying
Harrison the reward that was due to him) decided to offer additional
rewards for instruments of even greater accuracy, Mudge set to work
to meet the challenge. For several years he had been encouraged
by his patron Count Hans Moritz von Bruhl, Envoy Extraordinary
from the Kingdom of Saxony to the English Court, who was an
ardent horologist and a Fellow of the Royal Society. When the
chronometer (or 'watch') was completed, Mudge wrote to him:[55]

> Plymouth 5 October 1775
> . . . would it be amiss, if not too much trouble, if you were to try
> it sometime yourself, and if you have interest enough with
> Dr Heberden (for I am totally unknown to him) to have it tried
> by him also, previous to its going to Greenwich?

Certainly considerable trouble was involved in setting up and
carrying through an adequate trial of such a refined instrument:
the observer selected a fixed star on a night when the sky was clear,
trained his telescope in its direction and waited for the precise
moment for the star's appearance in the lens. On the word 'Now!'
his assistant, with his eye on the 'watch', noted the exact time of
the event—and this routine was repeated as often as atmospheric
conditions permitted, over a period of several weeks.[56]

Mudge's next letter was dated 22 December 1775:

> . . . I have this moment received your Excellency's favour of the
> 19th instant, telling me that there is not the least scrap of wainscot
> in Dr Heberden's observatory and consequently that it could not
> be placed upon its own bracket . . . I suppose Dr Heberden will
> register the height of the thermometer as well as the going of the
> watch . . .

To obtain the best view of the night sky, William would naturally have used one of the attics—a fact confirmed by Mudge's comment on the absence of wainscot (or panelling)—a luxury reserved for the smarter rooms on the lower floors. This was a factor that made no difference to the watch's performance, which proved equally satisfactory when standing on a table. To make sure that variations of temperature would have no adverse effects, Mudge had incorporated compensatory devices; regular thermometer readings would indicate their efficiency.

Mudge's final letter shows that the tests were completed to his satisfaction:

> Plymouth 28 January 1776
>
> Dear Sir, I received both your Excellency's last favours, with the enclosed registers of the going of the watch at Dr Heberden's, for which I would wish him to have my acknowledgments . . .

The Board of Longitude recognised Mudge's achievement with a gift of 500 guineas. Mudge made two more chronometers, but the Astronomer Royal, Nevil Maskelyne, refused to admit that they qualified for a government award. In the end, a committee of the House of Commons voted him the sum of £2500.

Chapter 8

Pall Mall

By 1767 the house in Cecil Street was beginning to lose its attractions; William's eldest son Thomas was by now a teenager; Mary was six and on 23 March the future physician William 'the younger' arrived to swell the numbers. As his mother was still only 37, more children might be hoped for (or at least expected), and more spacious accommodation would soon become essential.

After considering the relative advantages of various locations for a new home, William concentrated his search on the area to the south of Piccadilly and in March 1769 was able to purchase from the Waldegrave family a house on the south side of Pall Mall which had the distinction of being the former home of Nell Gwynn. Some further details of its history were recounted by Dr Ewin,[1] a Fellow of St John's:

> My friend Dr Heberden . . . told me it was the only free-hold house on that side; that it was given by a long lease by Charles II to Nell and upon her discovering it to be *only a lease* under the Crown, she returned him the lease and conveyance saying she had always conveyed free under the Crown and always would; and would not accept it till it was conveyed free to her by an Act of Parliament made on and for the purpose. Upon Nell's death it was sold and has been conveyed free ever since.

Despite the substantial purchase price of £5105, William promptly had the house demolished and engaged James Paine, one of the leading domestic architects of the day, to design a new residence.[2] The site, flanked on the east by the imposing edifice of Schomberg House, was narrow, and Paine—an admirer of Palladio—skilfully exploited its considerable depth so as to admit the maximum of light. The most extensive floor was the basement; here were a powdering room, servants' hall, housekeeper's apartment, butler's pantry, wine vault, kitchen, scullery, vaults for coal and a passage 'fitted up with presses and other conveniences'.

The ground floor was approached from the street by seven steps and the visitor, having passed through a vestibule would have been struck by the elegance of the elliptical staircase. Leading off the hall were the dining room and the library—which presumably served also as a consulting-room. The floor above comprised 'Mrs Heberden's dressing room, drawing room, bedchamber, closet'; the attics had

St James's Palace and Pall Mall, c 1753.

two good apartments, and above these was another storey with 'several good bedrooms for domestics'.

The house was ready for occupation by the end of 1770 and the family lost no time in moving in. Walpole, when writing to Cole some years later,[3] considered the move to have been dangerously premature, and was clearly familiar with William's 'Query' on wet rooms:

> I am extremely concerned, dear Sir, to hear you have been so long confined by the gout. The painting of your house may, from the damp, have given you cold—I don't conceive that paint can affect one otherwise, if it does not make one sick, as it does me of all things. Dr Heberden (as every physician, to make himself talked of, will set up some new hypothesis) pretends that a damp house, and even damp sheets, which have ever been reckoned fatal, are wholesome:[4] to prove his faith he went into his own new house totally unaired, and survived it. At Malvern, they certainly put patients into sheets just dipped in the spring—However, I am glad you have a better proof that dampness is not mortal, and it is better to be too cautious than too rash.

A week or two before leaving Cecil Street, William heard that a rare book *On the Muscles* by an Italian author Canneo might be available for purchase; knowing William Hunter's passion for book-collecting, he passed on the information to him in the following note:[5]

Dr Heberden sends his compliments to Dr Hunter; he has been desired by an acquaintance to inform the Doctor that if he have not *Cananus de musculis*, & be desirous of having it, there is a professor in Italy who is willing to dispose of his copy. This was the business about which Dr Heberden called this morning in Windmill street.

3 November 1770

It is not surprising that when William called at the Anatomy School in Windmill Street Hunter was too busy to see him; at this time of year he would have been in the middle of his autumn course of lectures, which were given daily (Saturdays included) and embraced practical anatomy, physiology, pathology, operative surgery and midwifery. The whole course ran to no less than 112 lectures, for which the charge was a modest seven guineas. Both in presentation and content his lectures were considered outstanding and his obituarist in the *Gentleman's Magazine* wrote that 'of all others, he was most happy in blending the utile with the dulce, by

William Hunter after a painting by Allan Ramsay, c 1758, (Wellcome Institute Library, London).

introducing apposite and pleasing stories, to illustrate and enliven the more abstruse and jejune parts of anatomy; thus fixing the attention of the volatile and the giddy, and enriching the minds of all with useful knowledge'.[6]

Three of his lectures were concerned with the making of preparations and embalming—an essential technique for preserving specimens; a few years later his skill in this field led to a somewhat bizarre spectacle which he invited William to come and see.[7] The wife of an eccentric dentist and trussmaker named van Butchell had recently died aged 36, whereupon the widower decided to have her embalmed. The delicate task was entrusted to Hunter and his assistant William Cruikshank and as soon as their work was completed, van Butchell let it be known that requests to view his late spouse in his home would be favourably considered; but as the news spread, the numbers threatened to become unmanageable and he was obliged to publish an announcement 'acquainting the curious' that only those with a personal introduction would thereafter be admitted. Hunter was evidently pleased with the results of his handiwork and his invitation to William was extended to several other members of the Royal Society.

Hunter's respect for William can be seen in a letter[8] he wrote in 1777 to his revered teacher Cullen, whose book *First Lines of the Practice of Physic* had just been published in Edinburgh:

> I was with your bookseller before your books arrived. He sent them round as you had directed . . . I should have carried one in your name to Dr Heberden, whom we all esteem, but the occasion was lost before I certainly knew that there were none to be had on the best paper . . . I should have given my own copy either to him or to the Royal Society, but I had the very first night I was possessed of it made some marginal notes for myself in the first pages.

The relationship between the two Williams was one of mutual respect rather than affection; Hunter (who never married) seems to have reserved his more tender feelings for inanimate objects, particularly his collections and his school. In everything he did, he had an eye to business; the knowledge and skills he had laboriously acquired were properties to be sold for appropriate fees, and for this reason he never published his lectures, which would then have been pirated and his profits lost. Understandably there were some members of the medical establishment who envied his success, while others found his anatomizing and his man-midwifery both distasteful. It was probably for these reasons that he was denied the accolade of a public funeral when he died in 1783. Only six people, including his assistant Cruikshank, his draughtsman, his nephew and his trustee, Dr Pitcairn, were present at the private burial service; the other two were Sir George Baker and William Heberden.[9]

A significant event at which William had been present some years earlier, was the foundation of what later became known as the Royal Humane Society.[10] This had originated at a meeting held in April 1774 at the Chapter Coffee House in St Paul's Churchyard. The prime movers were two doctors—William Hawes (born 1736) and his contemporary Thomas Cogan; each had invited sixteen friends, of whom William Heberden was one. The purpose of the meeting was to found an institution 'for affording immediate relief to persons apparently dead from drowning'; as accidents on the crowded Thames were an every-day occurrence and few people could swim, the need for such a programme could hardly be disputed. Later in the same year the objectives were widened to include 'diffusing a general knowledge of the manner of treating persons in a similar state from various other causes'; the first of these—'strangulation by the cord'—recognised the prevalence of suicide; the second—'noxious fumes'—points to the many hazardous occupations carried on in poorly ventilated rooms, before the age of health and safety regulations.

Cogan had originally studied for the ministry and had become one of the officiating Ministers at the English Church at Amsterdam; he then changed course, abandoning the ministry for medicine, took his MD at Leyden, married a Dutch heiress and practised his new profession in Amsterdam and other Dutch cities. A society for resuscitating the drowned had been founded in Amsterdam (where the canals were a special hazard) in 1767, and Cogan published a translation of the Society's record of activities up to 1771.

Meanwhile Hawes, who had a medical practice in the area of the Strand, had learned about the methods of the Dutch society and had for a year been rewarding rescuers who had brought ashore bodies recovered from the Thames between Westminster and London Bridges.

Several of William's other friends were actively involved in the Society's work; John Fothergill for example had written a paper published in the *Philosophical Transactions* in 1745 drawing attention to the efficacy of mouth to mouth inflation as a means of resuscitation; John Hunter had also studied the subject and recommended blowing air into the lungs (for which he designed a special set of bellows) and stimulating the action of the heart by electricity.[11]

The Society began by adopting the methods used in Amsterdam, which included (in addition to mouth to mouth inflation) warmth, fumigation with tobacco smoke via the rectum, friction, stimulants, bleeding and the inducement of vomiting. Detailed case records were kept, both of failures and successes, and a medal was designed for presentation to rescuers. The title 'The Humane Society' was adopted in 1776 and in November of the following year John Wesley noted in his Journal:

I preached in Lewisham Church for the benefit of the Humane Society instituted for the sake of those who seem to be drowned, strangled or killed by any sudden stroke. It is a glorious design, in consequence of which many have been recovered that must otherwise have inevitably perished.

In 1787, the year in which the Society was permitted to prefix the word 'Royal' to its name, William was invited to become one of its Vice-Presidents; his reaction to this honour is recorded by an anonymous contributor to the *Gentleman's Magazine* who wrote to the editor in July 1801 after reading William's obituary:

As you have noticed in your excellent account of the late universal philanthropist Dr Heberden, that he was an early encourager of the Humane Society, I send you a copy of a letter which expresses his acceptance of an honourable office which he had been unanimously requested to fill:
To Dr Hawes, Spital-square
Windsor, 18 Sept 1787
Sir, I last night received the favour of your letter, acquainting me with the honour done me by my being chosen a Vice-President of the Humane Society, which owes so much to your distinguished zeal and service for its foundation and support. My advanced age makes it necessary to withdraw myself from my usual business and therefore renders me not very fit for any new employment, so that I am not likely to be at all useful to you; but if you have a sufficient number of active members to admit of an inactive one in me, I will receive the honour intended with thankfulness. I earnestly request that you will not let me keep out anyone who might do some service to the Society; for to every such person I would gladly give place, either now or at any other time.
I am, Sir, your most humble servant, W Heberden

Our account of the patients whom William attended during the later years of his practice begins with some of those who are mentioned by name in the fair copy of his *Index*, which he probably compiled immediately after the completion of the *Commentaries*. Most of the entries tell us nothing apart from the patient's name and the ailment; but even this minimal information enlarges our knowledge of William's clientele and the variety of ailments that he had to deal with. Thus we learn that Lord Irwin and Sir William Molesworth were treated for gout; Sir JM Cope suffered from headaches and Sir Martin Wright was unable to swallow meat. Epilepsy attacked a young man of thirty, who remains anonymous but is described as 'an energetic follower of Bacchus and Venus'. Bowyer (probably the printer) had trouble with his knees; Lady Coventry was ill with jaundice; the Bishop of Limerick's wife had what may have been cancer of the breast, and Lady Harcourt was lucky to have nothing worse than a nose-bleed.

An unexpectedly chatty entry under Oculi (eyes) reads:

The Duchess of Somerset had worn glasses from the age of eighteen, then suddenly without their help she could read small print when nearly eighty. Similarly the widow of the Bishop of Ely—Green. I have also heard that the celebrated astronomer Halley, now an old man, had dispensed with his glasses.

But to continue the catalogue of illnesses—Devonshire colic killed Lady St John in 1773 and about the same time one of the Wollaston boys (perhaps one of William's nephews) came out in purple spots; poor Lord Irwin was in trouble again in 1776 with rheumatism and a man of twenty named Heath caused concern by his habit of walking in his sleep. Vomiting proved fatal for Sir James Pettigrew 'of the 20th Regiment in Jamaica' and the final curtain for Sir Joseph Yates in 1770 is recorded under the heading of Tussis—a cough, perhaps of a tubercular kind.

If these 'indexed' patients or their survivors had left their own records of William's visits—with candid comments on his manner and methods—our picture of events in the sick-room would be much sharper and perhaps more balanced. As for the patients who refer (like Hurd) to his visits in their letters, the amount of detail they provide is usually tantalisingly small—although in Hurd's case it is worth noting that William visited him without waiting to be asked.

The order that William had received some years earlier from the House of Commons to attend John Wilkes suggests that there were several other MPs with whom he had personal contacts. One of them was George Selwyn, member for the City of Gloucester, whose circle of literary acquaintances (including Gray and Walpole) overlapped with William's. Selwyn never married, but had a genuine affection for children and in the course of one of his lengthy letters to his friend the Earl of Carlisle, dated 7 December 1773, he writes:[12]

... The little boy has better symptoms, but preserves still a kind of stupor, so that I believe Dr Heberden does not think him out of danger.

The identity of the little boy is not revealed, but as Selwyn's sister Albinia had married into the politically prominent Townshend family (named in William's *Index*) and had produced five children, the patient was probably Selwyn's youngest nephew.

About the same time, William was consulted by John Scott (the future Lord Chancellor and Earl of Eldon) who was endangering his health by overwork. According to Scott's biographer,[13] William, after waiving his fee, despatched him to Bath, with notice that if in three or four weeks the waters should bring on the gout, all was well; but that if this result was not effected, he must prepare for the worst.

The accuracy of this anecdote is suspect for two reasons: it is unlikely that at this stage of his career William still subscribed to the popular view that gout somehow protected the sufferer from other ailments or 'peccant humours' and was thus a beneficial disorder; certainly by the time he wrote his *Commentaries*, he condemned the belief as fallacious. In any case it is unbelievable that William should have given such an inappropriate warning to a young man in his early twenties who simply needed a holiday.

In January 1775 William once more took the familiar road to Cambridge. On Monday 16th William Powell, the Master of St John's, had been 'seized with a fit of the palsy' following a meeting of the governors of Addenbrooke's hospital. Next day, according to Cole,[14]

> ... Dr Heberden was sent for from London, but did not come, tho' Dr Gisbourne did. They were sent for again on Wednesday; and came to Cambridge next morning: but it was too late to do any service; for his speech was gone; and not being able to lie in his bed, he expired in his chair at 2 o'clock on Thursday afternoon Jan 19.

Another Cambridge patient, the Revd Dr Michael Lort, Regius Professor of Greek, was more fortunate and Cole was able to report in March 1781[15] that although he had been extremely ill, he 'is got well again through the care of Dr Heberden'.

William's contacts with other physicians were not limited to those who practised in London. Wealthy patients who resided there for most of the year often migrated to their own or their friends' houses in the country, or perhaps to a spa; and if they required the services of a doctor on these occasions, the local practitioner might welcome the views of the physician who regularly attended them when in town. In the following letter[16] William's patient, Mrs Frampton had gone to Blandford in Dorset to convalesce after some unspecified illness. The letter is addressed to Dr William Cuming, a life-long friend of John Fothergill, whom he had known since their days as medical students in Edinburgh. Cuming practised in Dorchester.

> Pall Mall 14 June 1777
> Dear Sir, I am much concerned to find that Mrs Frampton has not yet begun to recover her strength so fast as we wish. Bitters & gentle evacuants, which you are using, appear to me the best means for the re-establishment of her health & I own I should have a better opinion of their success, when taken under your care & direction, than from any effects which I can promise from

Bath water. There would surely be a great disadvantage in Mrs F's going from you, who have seen the whole progress of the illness, to a Physician who is a stranger to the case, & may not immediately see the nature of it, & find out what the present state of her bowels may require and bear . . . Ass's milk in a morning, if Mrs F can bear it, may help to nourish her & dispose her bowels to do their duty with the help of clysters only, or of such a small dose of Rhubarb, as would be unlikely to do too much . . .
Be pleased to present my compliments to Mr & Mrs Frampton. I am, Dear Sir, Your most humble servant

W Heberden

The course of treatment prescribed above would have been recommended, with minor variations, for many convalescents; bitters—a decoction of quassia wood—would stimulate the appetite, while gentle laxatives and clysters (enemas) would help to keep the body in balance. As to the supposed virtues of asses' milk, its most obvious attribute was its cost—roughly forty times that of cows' milk.

Another provincial doctor who had read William's published papers—though it is doubtful whether they ever met—was Edward Jenner, later to become a household name as the discoverer of vaccination. Jenner lived in the village of Berkeley, Gloucestershire and was a pupil and friend of John Hunter; when the latter became unwell, Jenner decided to seek William's advice and in 1778 wrote to him:[17]

Sir, When you are acquainted with my motives, I presume you will pardon the liberty I take in addressing you. I am prompted to it from a knowledge of the mutual regard that subsists between you and my worthy friend Mr Hunter. When I had the pleasure of seeing him at Bath last autumn, I thought he was affected with many symptoms of the Angina Pectoris. The dissections (as far as I have seen) of those who have died of it, throw but little light upon the subject . . .

After describing what he had learned about the causes of Angina from post-mortem examinations, Jenner continues:

As I frequently write to Mr H I have been some time in hesitation respecting the propriety of communicating the matter to him, and should be exceedingly thankful to you, Sir, for your advice upon the subject. Should it be admitted that this is the cause of the disease, I fear the medical world may seek in vain for a remedy, and I am fearful, (if Mr H should admit this to be the cause of the disease) that it may deprive him of the hopes of a recovery.

For some unexplained reason the letter was never despatched; all we know for certain is that John Hunter survived for another fifteen years. Jenner's reluctance to tell his patient his suspicions about the nature of the disease was understandable—but perhaps rather pointless. After all, it was John Hunter who had at William's request carried out the post-mortem on 'Doctor Anonymous' in 1772, and we can be confident that he had read and heard enough about the symptoms of angina to recognise the true nature of his own complaint. The causes of the disease, on which Jenner speculates, remained a controversial issue for many years.

The earliest reference to William in the pages of Boswell concerns the brilliant but dissipated Topham Beauclerk, descendant of Charles II and Nell Gwynn and an original member of the Club presided over by Johnson at the Turks Head tavern:[18]

> 21 March 1775: Johnson informed me that though Mr Beauclerk was in great pain, it was hoped he was not in danger, and that he now wished to consult Dr Heberden to try the effect of a new understanding.

Johnson and William must in fact have been already aware of each other's attainments for many years, through the conversation of mutual friends; the Revd Thomas Birch, for instance, who had known William from his earliest days as MD, had also been editorial adviser to the proprietor of the *Gentleman's Magazine*; Johnson's stream of articles to this distinguished monthly had brought the two men together and Birch had entertained him at his house. Johnson was also acquainted with William's friend and patient Samuel Richardson and knew him well enough to borrow from him when short of cash.

One of Johnson's friends whom he had known from his schooldays in Lichfield was the Revd John Taylor, who lived at Ashbourne in Derbyshire and was a Prebendary of Westminster Abbey—an office which gave him an excuse for making occasional trips to London. When on one such occasion he was feeling unwell, he sought William's advice; Johnson was evidently present at the consultation and wrote to Taylor some days later:[19]

> Heberden's talk was rather prudential than medical; you might however perceive from it how much he thought peace of mind necessary to your re-establishment.

Johnson's comment points to an aspect of William's talk which must often have been far more useful to patients (if they listened to it) than doses of physic. Clear and coherent advice on 'how to look after yourself' would on many occasions have speeded a recovery or prevented a condition from deteriorating: There were indeed many conditions from which patients would usually recover spontaneously, if only the *vis medicatrix naturae*—the healing power of nature, in which William so firmly believed—was given a fair chance to operate; and although the mechanisms governing the mysterious interactions between a patient's mental and physical states were as yet unfathomed, William knew from long experience that peace of mind was a positive factor in the restoration of physical health.

When in June 1779 the wealthy brewer Mr Thrale had a stroke, Johnson was staying with Taylor in the country and on receiving one of Mrs Thrale's letters giving him news of her husband's progress replied:[20]

> . . . I am glad that you have Heberden and hope his restoratives and his preservatives will both be effectual.

Four months later, when the patient appeared to be on the road to recovery and had been persuaded to make a trip to Tunbridge Johnson wrote:[21]

> I earnestly wish that before you set out, even though you should lose a day, you would go together to Heberden and see what advice he will give you . . . I wish you would do yet more and propose to Heberden a consultation with some other of the Doctors.

Meanwhile Mrs Thrale was recording the events in her private journal[22] and mentions William several times as one of the three doctors in attendance during her husband's slow recovery. Up to the end of the year her attitude to William appears neutral and impersonal—but then her tone suddenly changes:[23]

> 5 January 1780 . . . Heberden and I do not hit it off at all—he is so cold & so dry, and seems to have no notion of *Who I am* as I say sometimes in Joke, that I can hardly bear him: I am not used to People that do not worship me, & of course grow very fastidious in my desire of Flattery.
>   March Another Stroke of the Apoplexy or Palsy or some dreadful Thing! poor Mr Thrale! and with such a Desire of Life too—how it shocks one! but Sir Richard Jebb[24] has saved his Life; Heberden left us in our Distresses very ungenteely . . .

Mrs Thrale is engagingly frank in describing her antipathy to William;[25] he in turn may well have been offended by her evident desire to hold the centre of the stage, when her husband's life was in the balance. Mr Thrale died the following year and much later his widow referred (in a more dispassionate tone) to another visit that William had made to their Southwark house, which adjoined the brewery, sometime in 1780:

20 Aug 1792 One evening . . . Mr Thrale said on a sudden—'when we see Heberden this eveng—I'll tell him all the truth . . . that I am a ruined man and have undone my family' . . . At these words I ran to the Compting House, called Perkins to his master, bid him bring the ledger, books etc & convince him in good time how well things went . . . so he looked grave & kept silent & saw Heberden & said nothing as usual.[26]

In May 1782 apoplexy also struck down Daniel Solander. For several years he had acted as secretary and librarian to Banks, who had moved to a house in Soho Square large enough to accommodate his herbarium, his sister, his mother and the guests he frequently entertained; it was there that Solander was taken ill. Blagden who was conversing with him at the time, at once sent for William and for two other medical friends; but Solander was beyond help and within a few days was dead.

By now William was nearing the age of seventy-two and had for some time been planning to reduce his workload; with this in mind he purchased a house in Windsor as a summertime retreat—away from the bustle of London, to which he could return each winter to continue his practice on a gradually diminishing scale. His refusal of a royal appointment twenty years earlier had not affected the King's regard for him and as he was on friendly terms with members of the Court, the choice of Windsor as the setting for his second home had many attractions. He was already familiar with the town and had stayed there on several occasions. In August 1764 he had written to Birch:[27]

Dear Sir, You gave me some hope that you would make us a visit at Windsor. My coach is now in town and will set out tomorrow . . . for Windsor. The coachman is directed to call at Rauthmell's coffee house at half an hour past nine & will take you up there if you can come . . .

Other visits are mentioned in Daniel Wray's letters to Philip Yorke,[28] by now Earl of Hardwicke; in 1776 he wrote:

We sojourned several days close by the gates of the turret at Windsor, and of the Little Park. Though my Doctor and I argue upon most of the subjects between us, we are not given to dispute. But we are at no loss for entertainment. He had just got possession of Markland's legacy[29]—of his critical MSS and Classic Authors, with noted margins, in a legible hand; and lest our Greek and Latin should be exhausted, Kennicott[30] came with his auxiliary Hebrew.

And in August of the following year Windsor was once again the setting for their mutual entertainment:

Though so near to Court, we come to no cabinet secrets.
My Doctor and I subsist upon our old stores of Greek and Latin
with now and then a little relish of Hebrew.

William chose a house on a site now occupied by the Royal
Mews.[31] Although no picture of it survives, a plan of the area
was made by the Surveyor General in 1810 and this shows 'the
late Dr Heberden's house and offices' built round a large courtyard,
with its entrance in St Alban's Street. At the rear of the house
was an extensive garden, with a gateway leading out onto Castle
Hill; both the parish church and the Home Park were close by. By
June 1782 the Heberden family and their staff were installed in their
summer home and William was able to settle down to the task of
completing the *Commentaries*—which will be described in the
next chapter.

His health was still sound—a point confirmed by his old friend
Dr John Ross, Fellow of St John's and by now Bishop of Exeter.
In a letter written at his London house in South Audley Street in
December 1783 he says:[32]

Dr Heberden this moment called in upon me whilst I was writing
. . . He seems to be in perfect health and almost free from all the
infirmities of age. Such are the good effects of temperance and
virtue.

Although William was naturally reluctant to accept any new
patient during his summer absences from London, he was prepared
to make occasional exceptions and when he received an appeal from
Dr Johnson, he responded to it without hesitation.

Johnson (born less than a year before William) consulted at least
fifty physicians during the course of his life. As a young man he
had assisted a school friend Robert James in the compilation of a
three-volume *Medicinal Dictionary* and his interest in medical
matters had been further sharpened by the indifferent state of his
own health. He considered with some justification that he knew as
much about medicine as most of his doctors and he could describe
his own symptoms in great detail. For several years his favourite
physician had been Thomas Lawrence, Registrar and later President
of the Royal College of Physicians, who had been involved with
William in the 1760s in publishing the works of Harvey. In January
1783, after some months of declining health, Lawrence died. As
Johnson had already sought the advice of another FRCP, Lucas
Pepys, for his asthma, there seemed no immediate reason to call
in William, despite the high opinion of his abilities that Johnson
had often expressed. But in the early hours of 17 June the situation
changed dramatically when Johnson suffered a stroke that rendered
him speechless, though his other faculties remained virtually intact.

In the following letter[33] to the Revd Dr Taylor, who was on one of his periodic visits to London, Johnson seeks William's advice for the first time:

> 17 June 1783
>
> Dear Sir, It has pleased GOD, by a paralytic stroke in the night to deprive me of speech. I am very desirous of Dr Heberden's assistance, as I think my case is not past remedy. Let me see you as soon as it is possible. Bring Dr Heberden with you if you can . . .
>
> I think that by a speedy application of stimulants much may be done. I question if a vomit, vigorous and rough, would not rouse the organs of speech to action. As it is too early to send, I will try to recollect what I can, that can be suspected to have brought on this dreadful distress.
>
> I have been accustomed to bleed frequently for an asthmatic complaint; but have forborne for some time by Dr Pepys's persuasion, who perceived my legs beginning to swell. I sometimes alleviate a painful, or more properly an oppressive, constriction of my chest by opiates; and have lately taken opium frequently, but the last, or two last times, in smaller quantities. My largest dose is three grains, and last night I took but two. You will suggest these things (and they are all that I can call to mind) to Dr Heberden.

Our first reaction to this letter must surely be one of admiration for Johnson's presence of mind; in spite of the shock of finding himself unable to speak, he knew that his powers of thought were unaffected and that he could hold a pen; and when his servant came to call him in the morning, he lost no time in making him understand his immediate needs. His letter is totally coherent and he is careful to include the maximum amount of information which might be useful to his new physician on his first visit.

William came as soon as possible and Dr Brocklesby[34] (who lived near the patient in Norfolk Street) was also summoned. By 3 July Johnson was able to tell Boswell:[35]

> . . . They came, and gave the directions which the disease required, and from that time I have been continually improving in articulation. I can now speak, but the nerves are weak, and I cannot continue discourse long; but strength, I hope, will return. The physicians consider me as cured. I was last Sunday at church . . .

But after two months' respite, Johnson was again in trouble, this time with a testicular swelling. An operation was carried out, but within a few weeks further pain and swelling developed and Johnson wrote to William, begging him to visit him again. By the time he arrived, the fluid had drained spontaneously 'with relief of all distress'.[36]

However great the physical relief, Johnson still had to contend with problems of another kind. For many years he had so dreaded the onset of depression that, in Sir Joshua Reynolds's words, 'he would never trust himself alone but when employed in writing or reading'. Hence the importance of the Literary Club where he had so often enjoyed himself in the company of his friends. But by now several of the original members of the Club were dead and the loss of Henry Thrale had brought to an end the brief Indian summer of Johnson's life during which he had been treated as an adopted member of the Thrale family. To stave off loneliness he decided to form a new conversation club at the Essex Head ale house in Essex Street,[37] not far from the church of St Clement Danes. William was invited to join and the first meeting was held on 8 December; but within a week Johnson was once more housebound by a combination of asthma, dropsy and arthritis. There were days when he felt well enough to preside at small dinner parties; at other times (inevitably) his spirits sagged and in February he wrote to William:[38]

Dear Sir, When you favoured me with your last visit, you left me full of cheerfulness and hope. But my Distemper prevails, and my hopes sink, and dejection oppresses me. I entreat you to come again to me and tell me if any hope of amendment remains and by what medicines or methods it may be promoted. Let me see you, dear Sir, as soon as you can. I am, Sir, Your most obliged and most humble servant, Sam: Johnson.

A few days later Johnson wrote to Boswell that the dropsy was gaining ground and that his legs and thighs were very much swollen with water;[39] and on the 19th February he discharged 'in about twenty hours full twenty pints of urine'—a remarkable event of which he reports that William 'had seen but four examples'.[40]

It was not until mid-April that Johnson was at last able to go out of doors; but only three days later he insisted on attending a dinner to celebrate an exhibition of pictures at the Royal Academy in the newly built Somerset House. On Tuesday 18 May he dined with William at his house in Pall Mall;[41] in June he visited a friend in Oxford and in July set off on an even longer journey, first to his home town of Lichfield and then on to Ashbourne, where he stayed with Taylor for several weeks. In October he wrote to William to bring him up to date with his progress over the past six months:[42]

Not long after the first great efflux of the water, I attained as much vigour of limbs and freedom of breath, that without rest or intermission, I went with Dr Brocklesby to the top of the painters' Academy. This was the greatest degree of health that I have obtained, and this, if it could continue, were perhaps sufficient; but my breath soon failed, and my body grew weak.

At Oxford (in June) I was much distressed by shortness of breath, so much that I never attempted to scale the library,[43] the water gained upon me, but by the use of squills was in a great measure driven away.

In July I went to Lichfield, and performed the journey with very little fatigue in the common vehicle, but found no help from my native air. I then removed to Ashbourne, in Derbyshire, where for some time I was oppressed very heavily by the asthma; and the dropsy had advanced so far, that I could not without great difficulty button me at my knees.

After detailing the medicines he had taken and the effects they had produced, Johnson concludes:

The summary of my state is this: I am deprived by weakness and the asthma of the power of walking beyond a very short space. I draw my breath with difficulty upon the least effort, but not with suffocation or pain. The dropsy still threatens, but gives way to medicine. The Summer has passed without giving me any strength. My appetite is, I think, less keen than it was, but not so abated as that its decline can be observed by anyone but myself. Be pleased to think on me sometimes.

Johnson arrived back in London in mid-November, his health worse than ever; but his spirit was still indomitable and it was not until the final week of his life that he took to his bed. He made his will and bequeathed to William and to several others 'each a book at their election, to keep as a token of remembrance'.

As his legs continued to swell, he asked his surgeon, Cruikshank to make incisions to drain the fluid; when the latter—with William's full support—refused to cut as deep as his patient demanded, Johnson reproached William with being *timidorum timidissimus*.[44] When the doctors had left him, Johnson took matters into his own hands and stabbed his legs with a pair of scissors.

The end came on 13 December and a fortnight later Brocklesby, in the course of a lengthy letter to Boswell in Edinburgh, described the scene at the bedside, when the doctors consulted together for the last time.[45] Johnson knew that he had been a difficult patient and humorously predicted how his doctors would excuse themselves for his death: 'Brocklesby will lay my death to disobedience . . . and Dr Heberden will say, I disturbed Nature's operation . . .'

At some moment during his final illness Johnson (according to Boswell) had referred to William as 'ultimus Romanorum, the last of our learned physicians'.[46] The description was not strictly accurate, as there were many physicians of a younger generation who were good classical scholars; but the days when physicians wrote their major works in Latin were coming to an end. Had William perhaps told Johnson about his unpublished Latin manuscript of the *Commentaries*? Whatever Johnson had in mind, his phrase was certainly a tribute to William's erudition.

Almost a full year before Johnson's death, William had lost his lifelong friend Daniel Wray and in a letter to the Earl of Hardwicke[47] (the former Philip Yorke) he reveals the depth of his feelings. After a nostalgic reference to 'the many agreeable parties' at which they had often met as young men at the University, William continues:

> Our friend Mr Wray was quite worn out and died truly of old age; this consideration ought to make his surviving friends easy under his loss; and if it have not yet had its due weight with me, your Lp, to whom his just taste and agreeable manners & virtuous principles were so well known, will, I doubt not, excuse my weakness. I must hope that in this, as is seen in many other instances, Time will at last do what reason should have done at first & made me more thankful that I have had such a friend than disposed to repine because I have lost him.

The percentage of the population who 'died truly of old age' was very small and as Wray was asthmatic it is remarkable that he survived to the age of eighty-two. His affection for the Heberden family was demonstrated by the legacy of £500 that he bequeathed to the younger William.

The following year William was confronted with the somewhat unusual task of responding to a circular letter concerned with the health of his old friend Benjamin Franklin.[48] At the conclusion of the American War of Independence Franklin had been sent to Paris to negotiate the terms of a peace treaty with Britain and in due course was appointed first American Minister to the Court of Versailles. Unfortunately he had already begun to suffer from a stone in the bladder—a condition that gradually became more and more painful and interfered increasingly with his diplomatic duties.

In the summer of 1785 he composed a full account of his own case history and sent it to a friend in England, asking him to obtain the best advice available. This was done and in due course William received a jointly signed letter containing the opinions of his friend John Hunter and two others. William replied:

Windsor 18 Jul 1785
Dear Sir, I was this morning favoured with your letter accompanied with a case and a consultation upon it; all which I have considered

and do not find that there is anything left for me to say, unless
that I entirely agree with you, in recommending to the gentleman
not to think of an operation at such an advanced age, but to trust
wholly to the Lixivium, if he can bear it. I suppose he could find
no difficulty in taking a tea spoonful night and morning; and if
he could take two, it would be more desirable. Exercise can hardly
be wanted for health at the age of 79; it is high time to lay aside
all business which would oblige a man to go out, and use much
motion: I wish therefore your patient would confine himself wholly
to his house and garden, and avoid all riding in a Carriage . . .

Blackrie's Lixivium was a mixture of potash and quicklime
dissolved in water; but although William agrees with his colleagues
in recommending it, it is clear from the *Commentaries*[49] that its
efficacy as a dissolvent was at best very slight.

The doctors must have been aware that Franklin was on the point
of retiring. He had already left his house at Passy on 12 July;
ten days later he sailed from Le Havre, homeward bound for
Philadelphia, where he landed safely on 14 September.

In accordance with the resolution he had made many years earlier,
when attending the Duke of Leeds in the company of the ailing
Dr Mead, William finally retired from practice at the end of 1788.
It was during these closing months of his active career that he saw
three of his most famous patients.

The potter, businessman and philanthropist Josiah Wedgwood had
known William for several years; both were members of the Royal
Society and among their mutual friends was Joseph Priestley, to
whom Wedgwood had been generous in supplying retorts and other
items of apparatus for his experiments. Despite the amputation of
a leg in 1768 Wedgwood had successfully founded his Etruria works
near Stoke-on-Trent and had a London showroom in Newport Street.
For ever experimenting with new materials and new glazes, his
latest venture was an attempt to produce a replica of the Portland
Vase, a third-century Roman work made with cameo glass and
exhibited in the British Museum. Early in 1788 he had begun to
suffer from 'rheumatic headaches' and on his next trip to London
called on William for a consultation. The latter prescribed a blister
and a holiday and after a few weeks Wedgwood wrote that the blister
had been successful; the holiday however would have to be postponed
until a satisfactory replica of the Vase had been produced—an
outcome that was not achieved until the following year.[50]

One of William's next-door neighbours in Pall Mall was the artist
Thomas Gainsborough. In February 1788 Londoners were flocking
to witness a new and unusual drama in Westminster Hall, where
Warren Hastings, former Governor-General of the East India
Company, was on trial for corruption. Gainsborough went to see the
spectacle and the unfortunate results of his curiosity were later

recorded by his nephew:[51] he caught a cold 'which caused a tumour to inflame'. He then 'applied to Dr Heberden who treated it lightly, and said it would pass away with the cold. He applied to John Hunter who advised salt water poultices which greatly increased the inflammation & a suppuration followed. There seems to have been a strange mistake or neglect both in Heberden & Hunter.'

The tumour proved fatal, but whether the physicians were at fault must remain, in the absence of more precise information, an open question.

William may well have intended Gainsborough to be the last patient in his career, but there was still one more, whom he could not have refused to attend, even if he had wished to do so. In the summer of 1788 the King—who for the past ten years had resided with his large family at Windsor—suffered his first serious mental derangement—a symptom of a mysterious condition now described as acute intermittent porphyria.[52] A visit to Cheltenham was recommended and after spending five weeks there with his wife and some of the children, he seemed fully recovered. By the beginning of November however the trouble had returned, and the Royal Physician—William's former pupil, Sir George Baker—found himself faced with an unprecedented medical problem and the possibility of serious political repercussions. Sir George recorded his worries in a private journal, in which he wrote, referring to the morning of Monday 3 November:[53]

His sleep had been disturbed. He at last consented to my calling further assistance, which I had in the course of the last week often in vain solicited. I promised therefore to return in the evening accompanied by Dr Heberden.

Do these words imply that William was the only other physician whose presence the King was prepared to tolerate or that it was William's opinions which Sir George particularly respected? Whatever interpretation we favour, it is clear that at this time of the year William was at his Pall Mall house and could not therefore be expected to arrive before nightfall.

To the account quoted above Sir George added that he considered the King to be 'half-disordered—no incoherence but an excess of vivacity and eagerness . . . I dare not communicate my suspicions'. And when later he recorded the events of the same evening, he wrote: 'At nine this evening I waited on his Majesty with Dr Heberden . . . It was now too evident that his mind was greatly disturbed.'

William was in attendance again (though Sir George makes no further reference to him) probably on the evening of 5 November, and Fanny Burney gives a graphic account of the patient's behaviour, after he had been persuaded to sleep apart from the Queen in an adjoining dressing-room:[54]

The King, in the middle of the night, had insisted upon seeing if his Queen was not removed from the house; and he had come into her room, with a candle in his hand, opened the bed-curtains, and satisfied himself she was there, and Miss Goldsworthy by her side. This observance of his directions had much soothed him; but he stayed a full half hour, and the depth of terror during that time no words can paint . . . The King—the Royal sufferer—was still in the next room, attended by Sir George Baker and Dr Heberden, and his pages, with Colonel Goldsworthy occasionally, and as he called for him. He kept talking unceasingly; his voice was so lost in hoarseness and weakness, it was rendered almost inarticulate; but its tone was still all benevolence—all kindness—all touching graciousness . . . (The Queen) frequently bid me listen, to hear what the King was saying or doing . . . Nothing could be so afflicting as this task; even now it brings fresh to my ear his poor exhausted voice. 'I am nervous' he cried; 'I am not ill, but I am nervous: if you would know what is the matter with me, I am nervous. But I love you both very well; if you would tell me the truth: I love Dr Heberden best, for he has not told me a lie: Sir George has told me a lie—a white lie, he says, but I hate a white lie! If you will tell me a lie, let it be a black lie!

The King's attempt to describe his condition was not very enlightening, but was perfectly rational; and as he felt no signs of physical illness, he could hardly have added anything useful to his brief account. It is impossible to say what 'lie' he was thinking of, but as he had already suffered one relapse, he might well have disbelieved any bland assurances of a speedy and lasting recovery. Fortunately for all concerned, he was soon well again and remained in good health for the remaining years of the century.

As the King was not only the last of William's patients but also the most prestigious, we may wonder what personal contacts they had during the many years of robust good health that His Majesty had enjoyed throughout most of his reign. Apart from his respect for William as a physician, there were two spheres of special interest which both men had in common.[55] The first of these was literature. Although the King was not a bookish man, he read (when he could spare time from his many duties) both for instruction and improvement and collected books on a grand scale. These were housed in the royal library[56] where men of letters were permitted to browse or study, and where Dr Johnson was introduced to the King in 1767.

In the sphere of religion, the King was totally committed to the doctrines of the Established Church of England; no man, he believed could be good or happy without faith, and any atheistical tendencies were socially destructive and dangerous. He attended prayers and services in his royal chapels with the utmost regularity and considered it his prerogative to decide on the appointment of suitable candidates for Bishoprics and other senior ecclesiastical positions.

Although the King was always conscious of his royal dignity, his manner was generally affable and he enjoyed talking to people of all ranks and degrees on informal occasions. William would have been present on many such occasions, particularly at Windsor and he records one instance in a letter[57] written in September 1787 to the Revd John Douglas, who had just been appointed Bishop of Carlisle in the place of the late Edmund Law:

> My Lord, Give me leave to appear in the crowd of your friends and to trouble your Lp with the congratulation of my family as well as of mine, upon the present happy occasion. But I request no notice may be taken of this letter, unless you should think it worth any when I see you in Windsor, which I am glad to hear is likely to be soon. The King spoke to me as he was going to his chapel and told me how much he was pleased with having made you a Bishop: his Majesty added that he was only sorry for one thing & of that indeed he was ashamed, that he had not made you sooner. I wish you may enjoy this Bishopric (or a better) as long as your predecessor and am, my Lord, your Lordship's most humble servant
>
> W Heberden

The tone of the letter is revealing: it clearly implies that William was a familiar figure in the chapel; that the King knew all about his friendships among senior clerics and that there had probably been many earlier conversations between them that were never recorded.

For other sidelights on life at Windsor we can refer again to Fanny Burney (friend of Dr Johnson and Mrs Thrale), who had won fame for her first novel *Evelina* long before her appearance at Court. On the advice of her father, she had accepted in 1786 the supposedly prestigious appointment of Second Keeper of the Robes to Queen Charlotte; the job in fact proved tedious and uncongenial and she was thankful to be allowed to retire from it five years later with a small pension. But the time at Court had not been wasted and in her lively and observant diary she records some of the more carefree moments and quotes from the conversations of her party guests some unflattering opinions of the medical profession in general and William in particular. On one occasion dinner was followed by whist:[58]

> Mr Hamilton, who had now given his place at the whist-table to Mr Bateson, related to us a very extraordinary cure performed by a physician, who would not write his prescriptions, 'Because', said he, 'they would not appear against him, as his advice was

out of rule; but the cure was performed, and I much honour, and would willingly employ such a man'.

'How!' exclaimed Mr B---y, who always fires at the very name of a physician, 'what! let one of those fellows try his experiments upon you? For my part, I'll never employ one again as long as I live! I've suffered too much by them; lost me five years of happiness of my life—ever since the year—let's see, '71, '72 . . . One of those Dr Gallipots, now—Heberden attended a poor fellow I knew. 'Oh,' says he, 'he'll do vastly well!' and so on and so on, and all that kind of thing: but the next morning, when he called, the poor gentleman was dead! There's your Mr Heberden for you! Oh, fie! fie!

Miss Burney describes another party in 1787 at which one of her guests was a choleric Colonel:[59]

'. . . Somebody related that, upon the heat in the air being mentioned to Dr Heberden, he had answered that he supposed it proceeded from the last eruption in the volcano in the moon. 'Ay,' cried Colonel Manners, 'I suppose he knows as much of the matter as the rest of them: if you put a candle at the end of a telescope, and let him look at it, he'll say, what an eruption there is in the moon! I mean if Dr Herschel[60] would do it to him; I don't say he would think so from such a person as me.'

'But Mr Bryant[61] himself has seen this volcano from the telescope!'

'Why, I don't mind Mr Bryant any more than Dr Heberden: he's just as credulous as t'other.'

Up to this point in our narrative, the members of William's family have hardly been mentioned. The reason for this omission is simply the regrettable lack of any written record of a personal nature. Certainly William considered that family matters were of no concern to the outside world—a point of view which, however frustrating to a biographer, would have been shared by many of his contemporaries. As the role of women was usually subordinated to men's interests, it is not surprising that our information about the two Marys—William's wife and daughter—is scanty; for a brief glimpse of both of them we are once again indebted to Miss Burney, who describes her first introduction to them in 1786 soon after her appointment at Court when she was fearful of upsetting Mrs Schwellenberg, from whom she took her orders:[62]

While I was drinking coffee with Mrs Schwellenberg, a message was brought to me, that Mrs and Miss Heberden desired their compliments, and would come to drink tea with me if I was disengaged.

To drink tea with me! The words made me colour. I hesitated,—I knew not if I might accept such an offer. With regard to themselves, I had little or no interest in it, as they were strangers to me, but with regard to such an opening to future potentiality,— there, indeed, the message acquired consequence.

After keeping the man some minutes, I was so much at a loss, still, to know what step I had power to take, that I was induced to apply to Mrs Schwellenberg, asking her what I must do.

'What you please!' was her answer; and I waited nothing more explicit, but instantly sent back my compliments, and that I should be very glad of their company.

This was a most happy event to me: it first let me know the possibility of receiving a friend in my own room to tea.

Both mother and daughter are sensible women. I had met them one morning at Mrs Delany's, and they had then proposed and settled that we were to meet again.

The following year Miss Burney records:[63]

Another day I invited Mr Bryant to dinner . . . Before tea, as he wished to go on the Terrace, I accompanied him thither, where we met the Heberdens . . .

Of William's wife, who survived until 1812, the records have nothing further to tell us, and the only guide we have to her physical appearance is a silhouette, cut in 1786, which shows her with a straight nose and firm chin, wearing a mob-cap. Her daughter Mary had her portrait painted by Gainsborough,[64] in or about 1777; we see a handsome young woman with a string of pearls in her hair and a curling lock falling over her left shoulder; more pearls adorn the border of her low-cut gown and a pearl pendant hangs from a clasp on her bosom. In her late twenties she was married to the Revd George Leonard Jenyns, Canon of Ely and went to live at Bottisham Hall in Cambridgeshire.[65]

William's eldest son Thomas had been sent to school at Hackney, where he proved himself a sufficiently good scholar to be admitted at the age of 15 to his father's college as a pensioner. He decided to enter the Church and after taking his MA was ordained priest at Exeter in October 1778. The very next day the Bishop, Dr Ross, appointed him a Prebendary 'out of friendship', remarks Cole, 'to his Father'. In due course he received other life-long appointments as Prebendary of Chichester, Prebendary of Wells and Residentiary Canon of Exeter. In addition he held the living of Bridestow with Sourton from 1779 to 1786 and then became Rector of Whimple, where he remained for the rest of his life. For much of this period he was also Vicar of Bishops Nympton, for 52 years beginning in 1782.[66]

Thomas's various appointments cast an interesting light on the state of the Church of England and the attitudes of the clergy. The great majority of people—including Cole—would have upheld the right of a parson to get part of his living from sinecures. Thomas's emoluments, in addition to his stipends, would have included rents, tithes and accommodation and we can be certain that he could afford to live very comfortably.

Thomas's two marriages are noteworthy, as both his brides were from the families into which William, his father, had married. In December 1784 he married Althea Hyde, daughter of the Revd Francis Wollaston, Rector of Chislehurst, Kent.[67] She died two years later, following the birth of her second daughter. Thomas married again in April 1794, and his bride was Mary, daughter of Joseph Martin, Banker and MP for Tewkesbury.

Of William's three sons by his second wife, the career of his namesake, the future royal physician, will be described in an appendix. The lives of the other two were tragically brief; George died while still a schoolboy from some unrecorded accident or illness;

William Heberden the Younger, aged about 14. A pastel sketch in the style of John Taylor.

Charles (the youngest) was at Charterhouse; he was admitted a pensioner at his father's College in 1789, took his BA and won the Chancellor's Classical Medal in 1793. In the same year he was admitted to Lincoln's Inn and called to the Bar. On the threshold of his promising career, he was, like his brother George, struck down by some unknown cause and died at his father's house in Pall Mall on 13 March 1796.

The main events in the life of the surgeon-physician Thomas have already been recounted; to complete the picture of William's family, we must now give a brief account of the youngest brother—John. He was admitted Attorney in the Court of Common Pleas in February 1733/4[68] and was in due course appointed Signer of the Writs in the Court of King's Bench, a position he held for the rest of his working life. We know nothing of the details of his professional career, although he evidently prospered financially; one event in his life, however, adds a welcome touch of romance to an otherwise unexciting story. At some point, probably late in 1740, he met a girl named Elizabeth, daughter of John Robinson of Lincolnshire. For reasons unrecorded the couple decided to get married with the minimum of fuss, formality or delay; the venue chosen for the

William Heberden the Elder, from a silhouette, (Francis A Countway Library of Medicine, Boston, Massachusetts.)

ceremony, which was performed on 13 January 1740/1, was St George's Chapel, Mayfair, near Hyde Park Corner.[69] This chapel, only some ten years old, had been built for the sole purpose of conducting wedding ceremonies (for an appropriate fee) without requiring the production of a marriage licence or the calling of banns. Although such marriages were legal, and the contracts binding, they were naturally frowned upon for encouraging unauthorised elopements, shot-gun marriages and 'extemporary thoughtless unions'.[70]

But if they married in haste, there is no reason to suppose they repented later. True, they suffered the common misfortune of losing three children in infancy, but the fourth, a daughter Amelia, survived her parents, though she never married. For a time the family lived in Norfolk Street near Thomas Birch; after that, we hear nothing more of them until in 1786 John died, a widower; to Amelia he left his 'house and gardens at Lambeth and Chambers in the Temple, with the leases and the contents'; to his housekeeper and to his daughter's servant, annuities of £30 each; the remainder he left to his trustees to provide an annuity of £400 for his daughter and thereafter to divide equally 'all my estate remaining amongst my niece and nephews Mary, Thomas, William, George and Charles'.

For the elder William's physical appearance as a young man or even in middle age, we have to be content with Cole's description, quoted earlier, that he was tall and thin with 'a florid good countenance'. The earliest likeness of him to survive is a silhouette (probably cut at the same time as his wife's) which shows a profile of his head and shoulders. A second silhouette is more informative;[71] we see William seated on a ladder-back chair with a quill pen in his hand, writing at his three-legged desk, with its adjustable sloping top. He is wearing a tie-wig, frock coat, knee-breeches, stockings and buckled shoes.

It was not until 1796 that he had his portrait painted[72] and although we could wish that this had been done at an earlier stage in his life, we can be confident that the picture is accurate and perceptive. The artist was William Beechey, RA, who painted several members of the Royal Family and was highly esteemed for his ability to achieve likenesses which conveyed something of each sitter's individuality. William is shown sitting in a leather arm-chair, his head turned slightly to the left, his eyes looking straight at the artist, his lips just parted, as though about to speak. The expression shows the suggestion of a smile and brings out both the humorous side of his nature, as well as the sadness which overshadowed him in the year of Charles's death.

Chapter 9

The Commentaries and the Final Years

William's major work—*Commentaries on the History and Cure of Diseases*—was written in Latin and completed in August 1782. The task must have been spread over a period of many months; until William settled into his house at Windsor, he was still in full-time practice and was at the same time busily engaged in those other activities which we have already described. Thus, it seems unlikely that he could have found many spare hours for uninterrupted writing. In his 'Preface' he explains how the work evolved:

> The notes from which the following observations were collected were taken in the chambers of the sick from themselves or from their attendants, where several things might occasion the omission of some material circumstances. These notes were read over every month, and such facts as tended to throw any light upon the history of a distemper, or the effects of a remedy, were entered under the title of the distemper in another book, from which were extracted all the particulars here given, relating to the nature and cure of diseases. It appeared more advisable to give such facts only, as were justified by the original papers, however imperfect, than either to supply their defects from memory, except in a very few instances, or than to borrow anything from other writers.

Although the original case-notes no longer exist, we can judge their general style from the transcription of the notes on Mr Baker which William sent to the Revd William Cole.[1] As for the 'other book' in which the significant features of each case were entered, William is referring to his *Index*—the original series of volumes which he preserved (and no doubt often consulted) throughout his long career. These volumes were probably destroyed when William had completed his fair copy.

We would naturally have expected William to publish his *Commentaries* with the least possible delay; his failure to do so is hard to understand or to justify. He states his attitude in the opening paragraph of his 'Preface':

> Plutarch says that the life of the vestal virgin was divided into three portions: in the first she learned the duties of her profession; in the second she practised them; and in the third she taught them to others. This is no bad model for the life of a physician ... I am willing to employ the remainder of my days in teaching what

GULIELMI HEBERDEN

COMMENTARII

DE

MORBORUM HISTORIA

ET

CURATIONE.

Γέρων, καὶ κάμνειν οὐκέτι δυνάμενος, τοῦτο τὸ βιβλίον ἔγραψα, συντάξας τὰς μετὰ πολλῆς τριβῆς ἐν ταῖς τῶν ἀνθρώπων νόσοις καταληφθείσας μοι πείρας.

ALEX. TRALL. Lib. XII.

LONDINI

VENEUNT APUD T. PAYNE, MEWS-GATE;

TYPIS MANDAVIT S. HAMILTON,
Falcon-Court, Fleet-street.

MDCCCII.

Title page of the 1802 Latin edition of the Commentaries.

I know to any of my sons who may choose the profession of physic; and to him I desire these papers should be given.

William confirms his intention in a pencilled note on the flyleaf of the work:

I desire this book may be given to Mrs Heberden for the use of any of our sons who shall study physic. WH.

Of his four sons then living, Thomas was already ordained, while George, Charles and William were still too young to have chosen their careers. How could their father apparently be content to allow the distillation of a lifetime's experience to gather the dust unread? There is no satisfactory answer to this enigma; perhaps William felt that he had already made his most important contributions in the pages of the *Medical Transactions* and that the other subjects dealt with in the *Commentaries* had been adequately covered by other writers. But whatever the true explanation, we are left with the impression that he seriously undervalued the merits of his own work and was quite unable to appreciate that he had written a medical classic.

The credit for translating the *Commentaries* into English and for publishing both the Latin and English versions in 1802 belongs to William the younger. We do not know when he began the work of translation or whether he ever succeeded in persuading his father that publication was desirable; but there can be no doubt that the *Commentaries* soon acquired a European reputation;[2] editions were published in Frankfurt and Leipzig, and in 1831 the work was re-issued—again at Leipzig—in a series of medical classics. Meanwhile the fourth English edition had been printed and American editions were later to appear in Boston and Philadelphia.

The work consists of 102 chapters, varying greatly in length. The first two deal with diet and general patient care, and the remainder (apart from some observations on the waters of Bath and Bristol) with specific diseases and ailments arranged, like the *Index*, alphabetically under their appropriate Latin names.[3]

It would be unreasonable to expect all the chapters to contain nuggets of wisdom. Thus, with regard to that common affliction of labouring men who had to rely on their own physical strength to move heavy loads, William has nothing to say except that 'Ruptures require no other remedy than a proper bandage or truss'.[4] But despite the fact that there were many conditions for which William could offer little or nothing in the way of improved remedies or cures, the work deserves our admiration for its independence of outlook and freedom from dogma, for its acute observations and accurate descriptions of symptoms. Many of the clinical contributions contained in the book are original, and in his oration to the

---

CAP. 28.

De Nodis Digitorum.

NUNQUAM rite intellexi naturam tumorum, ✦qui interdum nascuntur, ad pisi magnitudinem, prope tertium digitorum articulum.   Nihil certe illis commune est cum arthritide; quoniam in multis reperiuntur, quibus morbus ille est incognitus.   Per hominis ætatem manent; vacant omni dolore, neque spectant ad exulcerationem.   Proinde deformitas major est, quam incommodum : quanquam motus digitorum aliquantulum impeditur.

Chapter 28 of the Commentaries—*on 'Heberden's Nodes'.*

Heberden Society in 1961, Lord Cohen of Birkenhead mentions at least twenty instances.[5] Two of these—the description of angina pectoris and of the symptoms of chicken-pox—have already been mentioned. Among many other examples, we may begin·by quoting William's description of what are still known as Heberden's Nodes:[6]

> What are those little hard knobs, about the size of a small pea, which are frequently seen upon the fingers, particularly a little below the top, near the joint? They have no connexion with the gout, being found in persons who never had it: they continue for life; and being hardly ever attended with pain, or disposed to become sores, are rather unsightly, than inconvenient, though they must be some little hindrance to the free use of the fingers.

It is worth noting that William cannot tell us what the nodes *are*; he simply draws our attention to them and tells us what they are *not*.

In another chapter he gives the earliest description of an unusual children's complaint:[7]

> Some children, without any alteration of their health at the time, or before, or after, have had purple spots come out all over them, exactly the same as are seen in purple fevers. In some places they

were no broader than a millet-seed, in others they were as broad as the palm of the hand. In a few days they disappeared without the help of any medicines. It was remarkable, that in one of these, the slightest pressure was sufficient to extravasate the blood, and make the part appear as it usually does from a bruise.

He gives an accurate description of ringworm,[8] which he knew to be infectious, and recommends the following treatment:

The best method which I know, is to cut off the hair where the distemper has spread over a great part of the head, and to keep it anointed with the tar ointment, covering it with a hog's bladder.

William made some penetrating observations on the subject of lunacy:[9]

Great anxiety of mind, whatever may have been its origin, is a principal cause of insanity . . . It is an inveterate opinion, which my experience has uniformly contradicted, that madness is influenced by the moon . . .
Great violence is probably done to the brain, when a man is deprived of reason, the prinicipal characteristic of his nature: but the parts of the brain subservient to animal life, seem so distinct from those which are essential to the exercise of reason, that insanity has in many instances been no hindrance to the enjoyment of good health in all other respects. Those who have been cured of lunacy, are very apt to have relapses; and some divide their whole lives between madness and reason. Such as never return to the use of their senses, are alternatively under the dominion of spirits either too drooping or too elevated; and in each of which states it is not uncommon to have them pass several months together: they appear most reasonable in the melancholy fit.

The longest chapter in the book is on gout. Apart from being extremely painful and very common, its causes were obscure, and the remedies available were either useless or at best unreliable. But the factor that induced William to devote so much space to the subject was the widely held, but entirely groundless belief that gout was 'antagonistic' to other diseases, and that it was to be welcomed, rather than dreaded:[10]

. . . people are neither ashamed, nor afraid of it; but are rather ambitious of supposing that every complaint arises from a gouty cause, and support themselves with the hopes that they shall one day have the gout, and use variety of means for this purpose, which happily for them are generally ineffectual.

William contends that this belief is refuted by experience and brings up his case-notes to support his arguments:[11]

Now, among those gouts which I have had an opportunity of seeing, I find by the notes which I have taken, that the patients in whom they have supervened other distempers without relieving them, or where they have been thought to bring on new disorders, are at least double in number to those in whom they have been judged to befriend the constitution; and it has appeared to me, that the mischief which has been laid to their charge, was much more certainly owing to them, than the good which they had the credit of doing.

In his account of asthma William lists numerous remedies that had brought relief to some cases and been useless or positively harmful in others; he also noted the effects of environment and how these varied with the individual patient:[12]

Several asthmas cannot bear the country air, and are much more tolerable in great towns; but the far greater number are impatient of cities, and are always easiest in the country. Cold fresh air is a general relief; but I have known more than one asthma, the fits of which were moderated by sitting before as great a fire as could be borne. Sometimes any change of air is beneficial. More than once an asthma has been more tolerable in England than in warmer climates; but the contrary to this is most generally experienced. So summer is to not a few the time of their breathing with most difficulty; though winter be most generally the dangerous season . . .

William discusses palsies and apoplexies together in the same chapter 'as they are only different degrees of the same distemper'. Of palsies he had seen 'a very great number' and his lengthy and illuminating account of the many ways in which patients could be affected suggests that Dr Johnson's experience was somewhat unusual:[13]

. . . The faculties of the mind are enfeebled in all possible degrees, as well as those of the body. When a person therefore has been struck on the left side, and has at the same time lost his voice, there is no certainty of his being able to signify his feelings, or his wants, by writing. They, who have been put upon this, have sometimes been able to do it, though in a confused manner; and the same person on different days would either write intelligibly, or make only an illegible scrawl . . .

In another passage we are reminded of William's comments on the *Bills of Mortality*:[14]

All sudden deaths are put down to the account of apoplexies; though some of them be unquestionably owing to ruptures of great blood vessels, to suffocations from inundations of phlegm, or from the breaking of abscesses in the lungs, and other causes of immediate death, very different from those by which genuine apoplexies are produced.

The chapter on measles (of which William notes that there was an epidemic in 1753) contains an unusually detailed account of an individual case. The patient was a young woman, and her illness was of a 'regular and middling sort'; William visited her at least once every day for a fortnight and seems to be quoting verbatim from his case notes. For example, the account for the seventh day reads:[15]

Bleeding yesterday gave some relief. The night was a little quieter; but the fever and anxiety are very little abated. The eruption in the face is paler. The skin begins to itch in a troublesome manner.

Who was this patient who received such close attention during a minor illness? Could she have been William's daughter?

The chapter on depression contains several memorable passages:[16]

. . . it appears to be a misery much harder to be borne than most other human evils, and makes every blessing tasteless and unenjoyable . . . Our great ignorance of the connexion and sympathies of body and mind, and also of the animal powers, which are exerted in a manner not to be explained by the common laws of inanimate matter, makes a great difficulty in the history of all distempers, and particularly of this . . . It is the condition of this malady to make the patient hopeless of a cure: but neither reason nor experience justifies his despair. For every part of the body, as far as our senses can judge, is whole and uninjured by his sufferings, great as they are; and the mind and animal powers are indeed oppressed, and cannot exert themselves, but their abilities are all entire . . . Many in a lowness of spirits are not indisposed to raise them by wine and spirituous liquors; and they are encouraged and pressed to do it by their well-meaning but ill-judging friends. No words can be too strong to paint the danger of such a practice in its proper colours. The momentary relief is much too dearly bought by the far greater langour which succeeds; and the necessity of increasing the quantity of these liquors in order to obtain the same effect, irrecoverably ruins the health, and in the most miserable manner.

Opium is a much safer antidote, provided (as William emphasised in his second Gulstonian lecture) that the dosage is carefully regulated:

My experience has often taught me, how safely, and consistently with business, a course of taking opium may be continued for a considerable part of a man's life; and how practicable it is to be weaned from the habit of it: while everybody's experience must have shown them the danger of persisting in a course of drinking immoderately, and the almost impossibility of ever reclaiming a sot.

In another chapter opium is recommended as a means of securing 'euthanasia' — a word William uses (as the context makes plain) in its strict and original sense:[17]

Under the protection of an opiate . . . the patient's strength has been kept up by some refreshing sleeps, and even in hopeless cases in which the dying person is harrassed by unspeakable inquietude, he may be lulled into some composure and without dying at all sooner may be enabled to die more easily.
    Lord Verulam[18] blames physicians for not making the euthanasia a part of their studies and surely though the recovery of the patient be the grand aim of their profession, yet where that cannot be attained, they should try to disarm death of some of its terrors and if they cannot make him quit his prey, and the life must be lost, they may still prevail to have it taken away in the most merciful manner.

William's skill in differentiating between similar or related conditions is evident in his chapters on rheumatism.[19]

The Rheumatism is a common name for many aches and pains, which have as yet got no peculiar appellation, though owing to very different causes. It is besides often hard to be distinguished from some, which have a certain name and class assigned them: it being in many instances doubtful, whether the pains be gouty, or venereal, or strumous, and tending to an ulcer of the part affected.
    There are two different appearances of the rheumatism, one of which may be called the acute, and the other the chronical . . .
A pain with a swelling fixed in a single part, as the knee, or wrist, without ever removing to any other, is hardly to be called rheumatic, and is more likely to be a cramp, or strain, or strumous, that is, to have a tendency to an ulcer from some internal cause. An exception however must be made in regard to the sciatica, which is of the rheumatic kind, though it be fixed in the same

part: as for the lumbago, it seems to be rather a cramp or strain
. . . Pains of the hips are well known to arise sometimes from a
morbid state of the joint, of a very different nature from the
rheumatism.

William regrets that 'chronical rheumatism' is not distinguished
'by a peculiar name, which might prevent its being confounded with
other disorders'. Today we call it arthritis, a term not available to
William, as it was already in use as the Latin name for gout.

William judged 'patent medicines' on their merits; the Portland
Powder[20] which had for a time been highly regarded as a remedy
for gout. . .

. . . is one of a great crowd of specifics of which the rise and reign
and fall have all happened within my memory. It rose into favour
too fast and too high to keep its place; but it appears to me to have
sunk into a state of discredit and neglect, as much below its real
merit, as the first praises were above it . . . The Portland powder
lost its reputation partly by the largeness of the dose, which,
though almost too great for anyone, was indiscriminately given
to all, and partly by having all the natural ill effects of the gout
imputed to it . . .

On the other hand, in the chapter on whooping cough he
remarks:[21]

As for the numberless specifics which are everywhere to be met
with, I have nothing to say in their favour from my own
observation.

In spite of his dismissive attitude towards these reputed remedies,
he was fully aware of the psychological effect of novelty and drily
observes that 'new medicines and new methods of cure always work
miracles for a while'.[22] In another chapter he writes:[23]

The difficulty of ascertaining the powers of medicines, and of
distinguishing their real effects from the changes wrought in the
body by other causes, must have been felt by every physician: and
no aphorism of Hippocrates holds truer to this day, than that in
which he laments the length of time necessary to establish medical
truths, and the danger, unless the utmost caution be used, of our
being misled even by experience.

Animals could sometimes give interesting—and possibly useful—
information on the effects of drugs or poisons. One of the medicines
recommended as 'friendly to the nerves' was the root of wild
valerian:[24]

Most cats are fond of gnawing it, and seem to be almost intoxicated by it into outrageous playfulness; and the nerves of cats afford a very tender test of the powers which any substances possess of affecting the nerves. The poisoned darts of the Indians, tobacco, opium, brandy, and all the inebriating nervous poisons, are far more sensibly felt by this animal than by any other, that I know, of an equal size.

When medicines are of no avail and everything possible has been done as will be most conducive to putting the body into the best general health[25]

the whole hope must be placed in that power, with which all animals are endowed, not only of preserving themselves in health, but likewise of correcting many deviations from their natural state. And in some happy constitutions this power has been known to exert itself successfully, in cases that have appeared all but desperate.

William was a firm believer in the virtues of fresh air:[26]

In every fever it is of the utmost consequence to keep the air of the patient's chamber as pure as possible. No cordial is so reviving as fresh air; and many persons have been stifled in their own putrid atmosphere by the injudicious, though well meaned, care of their attendants. The English seem to have a very extraordinary dread of a person's catching cold in fevers, and almost all other illnesses; the reason of which I could never rightly comprehend. The sick do not appear to me to be particularly liable to catching cold; nor do I know that a cold would be so detrimental, as not to make it worth while to run the risk of it for the sake of enjoying fresh air . . .

His views on diet and other disciplines in the sick-room were tolerant and relaxed:[27]

Many physicians appear to be too strict and particular in the rules of diet and regimen, which they deliver as proper to be observed by all who are solicitous either to preserve or recover their health. The too anxious attention to these rules hath often hurt those who are well, and added unnecessarily to the distresses of the sick. The common experience of mankind will sufficiently acquaint anyone with the sorts of food which are wholesome to the generality of men; and his own experience will teach him which of these agrees best with his particular constitution. Scarcely any other directions besides these are wanted, except that, as variety of food at the same meal, and poignant sauces, will tempt most persons to eat more than they can well digest, they ought therefore to be avoided by all who are afflicted with any chronical disorder, or wish to keep free from them. But whether meat should be boiled or roasted, or dressed in any other plain way, and what sort of vegetables should be eaten with it, I never yet met with any person of common sense (except in an acute illness) whom I did not think much fitter to choose for himself, than I was to determine for him. Small beer, where it agrees, or water alone, are the properest liquors at meals. Wine or spirits mixed with water have gradually led on several to be sots, and have ruined more constitutions than ever were hurt by small beer from its first invention . . .

There is scarcely any distemper, in every stage of which it may not be safely left to the patient's own choice, if he be perfectly in his senses, whether he will sit up, or keep his bed. His strength and his ease are chiefly to be attended to in settling this point; and who can tell so well as himself, what his ease requires, and what his strength will bear?

No account of the *Commentaries* could be adequate if it omitted William's conclusion:

It might be expected that the experience of fifty years spent in the practice of Physic, would have taught me more, than I here appear to have learned, of distempers, and their remedies. I readily confess my knowledge of them to be slight, and imperfect; and that a considerable share of this imperfection is chargeable upon my want of ability to make a better use of the opportunities I have had: but at the same time it must be allowed, that some part must be put down to the very great difficulty of making improvements in the medical art. This is too evident from the slow progress which has been made, though men well qualified by their learning, experience, and abilities, have for above two thousand years been communicating to the world all they could add by just reasoning to the facts collected by attentive observation. Whoever applies himself to the study of nature, must own we are yet greatly in the dark in regard even to brute matter, and that we know but little of the properties and powers of the inanimate creation; but we have all this darkness to perplex us in studying animated nature, and a great deal more arising from the unknown peculiarities of life: for to living bodies belong many additional powers, the operations of which can never be accounted for by the laws of lifeless matter. The art of healing therefore has scarcely hitherto had any guide but the slow one of experience, and has yet made no illustrious advances by the help of reason; nor will it probably make any, till Providence thinks fit to bless mankind by sending into the world some superior genius capable of contemplating the animated world with the sagacity shown by Newton in the inanimate, and of discovering that great principle of life, upon which its existence depends, and by which all its functions are governed and directed.

William was the least conceited of men, and his readiness to admit his failures is evident throughout the *Commentaries*. Could he (as he suggests) have made a better use of his opportunities? No doubt his sociable nature and wide interests deflected him from concentrating single-mindedly on medical problems; without these distractions he might—perhaps—have made some new discovery; but any hypothetical gain must be offset by the special qualities of sympathy and understanding—nurtured by the variety of his friendships and interests—which are so frequently evident in the pages of the *Commentaries*.

William's lament at the lack of progress made 'by the aid of reason' refers, of course, to remedies or 'specifics', which had almost invariably been discovered by accident. In looking to the future, he excusably failed to appreciate that further 'illustrious advances' would depend as much on developments in technology and a general increase in the understanding of nature, as upon the emergence of some 'superior genius'. Happily this note of pessimism was later replaced by a much more optimistic attitude, expressed in one of his letters to Dr Percival.[28]

As both the content and the arrangement of the *Commentaries* owed so much to William's system of indexing, it is worth pausing for a moment to look more closely at the single-volume *Index* that is still preserved. It is immediately obvious from the tidy arrangement and the consistency of the handwriting that this is a fair copy—a fact confirmed by William, who notes under the heading *Intestinorum Dolores*: 'In this *Index* some cases have been omitted.'

We must assume that in undertaking the laborious task of transcription William was motivated by the hope that one of his sons would follow in his footsteps; yet the amount of information likely to be useful to a medical student is more limited than we would expect; notes on symptoms are abundant, but accounts of remedial measures are extremely sparse. A possible explanation may be inferred from the hundreds of voucher numbers, stretching back to the early days of William's Cambridge practice. Even if the vouchers had been destroyed, the case-notes (headed with their voucher numbers and filed numerically) may well have been preserved, to provide all the information a student could need regarding William's therapeutic routines. Finally, what are we to make of the scatter of names that identify many of William's patients from the 1760s onwards? A high proportion of them (as we have seen earlier) were titled, and though some of them were already dead, it is tempting to suppose that William was in effect saying to himself, 'If a son of mine should follow physic, here are some of the households where my name will be remembered to his advantage.'

Among William's continuing interests in this closing period of his life was his old University. His three sons had entered St John's as pensioners—Thomas in 1770, William in 1784 and Charles in 1789—and it was natural that his active mind should make comparisons between his own experiences of University life and theirs.

During the second quarter of the century, when Cambridge was virtually William's home, he came to know its many faults and failings at first hand; and because so many of these were remediable, it was undoubtedly a grave disappointment to him to realise that as the century approached its end, no significant reforms either in the field of behaviour and attitudes or in the curriculum had been achieved. On the contrary, some aspects of University life were distinctly worse than they had been fifty years earlier, and William had little doubt where the chief blame for these continuing blemishes should be placed—on the shoulders of the Senate, who had the power, but not the will, to act.

At his advanced age he might have been excused for taking no active steps in the matter, but his feelings were too strong to give way to inertia and in 1792 he published an anonymous pamphlet of 53 pages entitled *Strictures upon the Discipline of the University of Cambridge, Addressed to the Senate.*[29] After some general reflections on the responsibilities of the University's senior members, William directs his opening salvo against the decline of religious observance since his own student days fifty years earlier:

It is undeniable that then the Master, the Tutors and the generality of the Fellows of each society, never omitted attending the College prayers either in the morning or evening, where the service was performed in a manner that might tend to fix the naturally wandering attention of the younger part of the congregation;

'Modern politeness' has effected a very different picture:

When are the Fellows, or even the Tutors, now seen at the morning service in chapel? An attendance to which they are urged, not more by the duties of their station in College, than by the voice of religion, and often by the sanctity of their profession as clergymen. But those who dare publicly to slight their God, and suffer their indolence to overcome their obedience to the ceremonies of the Church, of which they have solemnly entered themselves as protectors, are not likely to be persuaded to it by any considerations of propriety or good example . . .

Nor is this all. The service is frequently performed in that slovenly manner, which reflects equal disgrace upon the minister, and upon those who, by their absence, may be said to connive at it. This daily indecency naturally hardens the minds of the audience, and a young man generally leaves College disgusted with all the holy rites of his Church, which he considers as the cloke of hypocricy, and the justly-exploded remnant of ancient superstition. All reverence for the profession, the service, and possibly the doctrines of religion, is nearly obliterated, if not entirely effaced from his mind; and the first stab not only to his orthodoxy, but to his principles of piety and morality, is given him from the hand which is supposed to be stretched out to defend him . . .

William deplores the modern custom of dining out, which he considers to be one of the chief causes of 'the enormous expense attending a liberal education, by which many of the middling ranks of people, particularly clergymen of small preferment, are either deterred from bringing their sons up to learned professions, or are nearly ruined in their exertions to effect it'.

He refutes the suggestion that expenses of this sort are voluntary; on the contrary they are unavoidable to those who wish to live in the same manner as their friends and associates.

Nor would the advantages of a College education be much felt by him, who had passed his regular time here, and attended his due quota of lectures and school exercises, without joining in the company of his fellow students, who are so nearly and naturally connected with him. It is not the authors that are read here, and which are accessible any where, nor the declamations, the disputations, the examinations necessary to be gone through, that form the superior excellence of an education in the University; but the knowledge of the world, and the enlarged ideas gained by the initiation into so extensive a society, the emulation inseparable from the number of students, and the mutual information resulting from the daily conversation of persons eager after the same pursuits, and inflamed with the same love of learning.

William takes a poor view of the increased popularity of card games—an amusement that 'choaks conversation' and encourages idleness and gambling.

Whatever sneers some may be inclined to cast on the objection made to trifling conversation, I am not ashamed to repeat that I think it a very great and disgraceful nuisance. To suppose that in the usual companies which meet in College, there are none capable of keeping up a rational chain of conversation, would be an insult upon the understanding of the University. Whence comes it, then, that the sensible part suffer themselves to be overwhelmed by the boisterous folly of those to whom ignorance seems to give, rather than take away, confidence?

During the century certain Statutes had been abolished as obsolete; William criticises the Senate for abolishing some that should have been retained and for retaining others 'respecting ceremonies, which, as they are now become mere shadows of forms, serve only to render the mode of education ridiculous'.

> Among such may be reckoned the ingenious regulations of 1750, respecting the dress of the students . . . It is unworthy and absurd of a grave Senate of an University, to descend to descriptions of particular modes of dress, to forbid one sleeve and recommend another. Leave such trifles to the animadversion of particular tutors or friends, or leave them, if you will, to the sense or caprice of the wearer; a sober behaviour is of far more consequence than a grave-coloured suit, and a red waistcoat a very small crime in comparison of gaming, drinking or irreligion.

Having dealt with questions of discipline, William goes on to lambast the Senate for its failure to reform the 'system of studies'. A fundamental weakness is the precedence given in the curriculum for the BA degree to the study of mathematics; other subjects such as classics, morals, metaphysics and logic are also taught—but mathematics is the only subject in which a pass is indispensably necessary to the taking of a degree. Inevitably many students will find to their disappointment that their degree has little or no practical value:

> This key, which they naturally imagined would open to them the way to any station or any profession, which their choice should fix on, is found upon trial to gain them admission nowhere; they are refused holy orders; they must study for the bar, they must attend the Hospitals. Even their boasted honours are unknown out of the sphere in which they moved. Like an European cast among savages, their titles convey no ideas of respect, their passports are unintelligible, and their claims to superiority ridiculed.

As the majority of students are 'designed for the Church', should Divinity be made a compulsory subject for all? William replies:

> The University was intended for the reception of students of all kinds; it is not a nursery for clergymen, for lawyers, or for physicians; it is an extensive school for all ranks, for all professions, calculated to give to each that sort of learning which is alike necessary for all.

But this does not mean that religious knowledge is necessary for the clergy alone; indeed practical religion ought to be the first object of every man's life. For laymen, however, this object is more promoted by the perusal of the Scriptures and the expositions of the practical parts of them, by persuasion to good behaviour united with good example, and by a regular observance of the external duties of religion, than by being examined in the works of the most acute speculative theologian.

William goes on to comment on the 'impious idea that less preparation is necessary for admittance into the sacred profession than into any other'—a view that has brought the clergy into contempt 'for their ignorance and their immorality' and has been the cause of 'the rapid increase of Dissenters of every denomination, whose ministers are men of tried abilities and known steadiness'.

For the student body in general all the subjects of study . . .

> should be subjects of common utility, such as tend to open the mind, enlarge the ideas, and lay a firm foundation of general knowledge ready for the reception of any superstructure. And, doubtless, for this purpose natural philosophy was admirably chosen, as it opens the widest field for the exertion of the faculties; it teaches at once the strength and weakness of human reason, as it shews to what lengths the enlightened genius of Newton could push his researches, and yet how many of the most obvious phaenomena are beyond the utmost stretch of our curiosity or conception: it frees the mind from prejudice and hasty opinions, and discovers to it, its own powers. Or should these advantages be reckoned imaginary or trivial, it boasts of far nobler perfection, in being able to raise the soul to the contemplation of the wonders of the creation, while it displays the immense scheme of the visible world, as harmonious as it is vast, and yet teaches that this scheme is but a point in comparison of the boundless universe.

The notion that students should be offered a choice of examination subjects receives William's warm support as

> this would at once take away the necessity of entering so deep into one particular science, and would besides cut off all pretences from the indolent, who now hide their idleness under the excuse of dislike for that one study, which is the principal one requisite.

His final stricture concerns 'the corroding rust of inactivity, with which the resident Fellows of Universities are too frequently incrusted':

> A foreigner would scarce believe that fewer works of learning are published from our Universities, than from the same number of men of liberal education anywhere in the kingdom; and yet this is an undoubted fact. Since the act of Parliament in 1781, which gave £500 annually to each of the Universities towards the promotion of learning, Oxford has produced but very few learned publications from its own body, and Cambridge, I believe, none . . .

William's pamphlet seems to have elicited no positive reaction from the members of the Senate to whom it was addressed; and it would indeed have been surprising if the protests of a single individual had stirred them to action. But though William's message fell on stony ground, his *Strictures* are still valuable for what they tell us about the state of the University, and about William's own practical attitude to all the matters under discussion.

Most of his observations are so plainly expressed that comments are superfluous; only two points might be questioned: first, whether University life in William's student days was in fact any more disciplined than it was when the *Strictures* were written. One cannot help suspecting that from his recollections of those happy and fruitful College years, some of the less favourable aspects of manners and conduct have conveniently faded.

The second point concerns William's views on conversation, which might at first glance seem to be pedantic. Fortunately, he had far too much humour and common sense to suppose that all conversation should be conducted at the level of serious discourse; nevertheless in the context of the times, conversation was an art to be cultivated by all civilised men as one of the pleasantest ways of filling those acres of time which now might be taken up by radio, TV, commuting, office routines and a thousand other time-consumers. Remembering again his own student days, William would have regarded Time as a commodity as precious as gold and it would have pained him to think that a minority should waste their own and others' opportunities by mindless rowdyism.

As for William's devastating critique of the 'system of studies', his views must have been shared by many University graduates, as well as by parents ambitious for their sons' careers, who could only regard the system as an expensive monopoly, unresponsive to changing conditions. It is hard to believe that the *Strictures* had no influence; perhaps William may be allowed some crumb of credit for the introduction in 1822 of the Classical Tripos, which brought to an end the overwhelming dominance of mathematics.

Because of his many accomplishments and interests William had no difficulty in filling the days of his retirement happily and productively. But for many others, as he knew from personal observation, the imagined joys of retirement often proved illusory. He addresses the subject, with his usual lucidity in a short undated essay,[30] which begins:

> There is perhaps hardly any state of life which requires more uncommon talents, a happier temper & more peculiar preparation in order to its being properly filled up & enjoyed, than retirement; & yet the prevailing notion seems to be that everyone is fit for it & that it has a manna-like sweetness which must be grateful

to every taste. This error, for such I think it will appear, is by no means confined to speculation; it every year influences the practice of many citizens who are betrayed by it into a state, perhaps the most comfortless of any that can befall an innocent mind. This evil is the more to be lamented, as it happens chiefly to the most industrious & deserving; to such as have been most successful in improving the manufactures & extending the trade of their country, which of course by their deserting its service is deprived of a pair of able hands, it may be of a good head, or perhaps of both . . .

Every man's importance is proportioned to his power & usefulness; & he who deserts the only station in which he could be useful, voluntarily makes himself, as far as he can, a cypher in the creation & is contented, like some ignoble herb, to live without being minded & to dye without being missed.

The use of recreation is to fit us for business & not that of business to fit us for recreation. To have a whole life of holidays is the sure means of never enjoying any . . .

William's remarks did not of course apply to the thousands who had to keep on working to avoid penury; but besides the 'most industrious and deserving' he must have had in mind those 'gentlemen of leisure' who lived parasitically on their inherited wealth and did very little to justify their existence.

His explanation of the timing of his own retirement is given in a letter written in August 1794 to Dr Thomas Percival:[31]

I have entered my 85th year; and when I retired, a few years ago, from the practice of physic, I trust it was not from a wish to be idle, which no man capable of being usefully employed has a right to be, but because I was willing to give over, before my presence of thought, judgment, and recollection were so impaired, that I could not do justice to my patients. It is more desirable for a man to do this a little too soon, than a little too late; for the chief danger is on the side of not doing it soon enough.

Percival (born in 1740) was a Dissenter and thus debarred from attending an English university; instead he enrolled at the newly formed Academy in his home town of Warrington in Cheshire; he then went to Edinburgh to study medicine, but before taking his degree came south to spend a year in London; it was during this visit that he was elected FRS and his friendship with William began. After further study he finally set up his practice in Manchester, where he used his talents to promote improvements in sanitation, the building of public baths and other good causes. In 1794 he was putting the finishing touches to a book on medical ethics — a labour that had been interrupted by the death of his son; and it was to this

event that William refers at the beginning of the letter from which
we have already quoted:

> Your being able to resume the work you had in hand, makes me
> hope that your good principles, with the aid of time, have greatly
> recovered your mind from what you must have suffered on
> occasion of the great loss in your family; and your attention in
> the further prosecution of it, will powerfully assist in perfectly
> restoring your tranquillity. What you have already communicated
> to the public, with so much just applause, shews you to be
> peculiarly well qualified for drawing up a Code of Medical Ethics,
> by the just sense you have of your duties as a man, and by the
> masterly knowledge of your profession as a physician. I hope it
> will not be long before the sheets already printed come to my
> hands; and I return you many thanks for intending to favor me
> with a sight of them.
>   The pleasure of a visit from one of Dr Haygarth's merit, whom
> I have long known and esteemed, would probably give me spirits,
> and make him think me less broken than I am.

William's reaction to the proposed visit of John Haygarth—a
former student of St John's and now physician to Chester
Infirmary—suggests that his own tranquillity had temporarily
forsaken him. If so, why should we be surprised? It is too easy to
assume that because William's life had been outwardly so successful
and his circle of friends so wide, he was therefore invariably buoyant
and cheerful. Apart from his own personal bereavements, he must
often have felt desperately frustrated when attending patients
doomed by some 'distemper' for which no cure was available.
Moreover he had by now outlived nearly all his contemporaries and
despite his continuing good health and mental alertness, there must
have been moments when he felt depressed by the passing of the
years.

Within a few weeks all traces of gloom had evaporated; Percival's
book had been delivered to Pall Mall, where William found it on
his return from Windsor in October. As soon as he had read it, he
wrote to the author complimenting him on his achievement and
assuring him that 'if your judicious advice and rules were duly
observed, they would greatly contribute to support the dignity of
the profession, and the peace and comfort of the professors'. Then,
to keep his Manchester friend *au fait* with recent developments in
the capital, he continues:

> There has lately been established, in several of the London
> hospitals, a plan of courses of lectures in all the branches of
> knowledge useful to a student in physic. Such plans, if rightly
> executed, as I have no reason to doubt they will be, must make

London a school of physic, superior to most in Europe. The experience afforded in an hospital, will keep down the luxuriance of plausible theories. Many such have been delivered in lectures, by celebrated teachers, with great applause; but the students, though perfectly masters of them, not having corrected them with what nature exhibits in an hospital, have found themselves more at a loss in the cure of a patient, than an elder apprentice of an apothecary. I please myself with thinking, that the method of teaching the art of healing, is becoming every day more conformable to what reason and nature require; that the errors introduced by superstition and false philosophy are gradually retreating; and that medical knowledge, as well as all other dependent upon observation and experience, is continually increasing in the world. The present race of physicians are possessed of several most important rules of practice, utterly unknown to the ablest in former ages, not excepting Hippocrates himself, or even Aesculapius. I am, dear sir,

Your affectionate, humble servant,

W Heberden.

William here takes a much more optimistic view of the future progress of medicine than he had expressed in his *Commentaries* twelve years earlier. The new factor which had raised his hopes was that the 'course of lectures' had been established *in hospitals*, thus forging the essential link between theory and practice. Examples could be seen at the London Hospital, where Dr Blizard's medical school had opened in 1785; at Bart's, John Abernethy (elected Assistant Surgeon in 1787) lectured on anatomy, physiology and surgery with such success that a new lecture hall was built for him four years later; and in Southwark, Guy's and St Thomas's had joined forces to become the United Hospitals of the Borough and offered courses by distinguished lecturers from about 1791.

Physically, William remained active until his mid-eighties; he took daily walks and managed during the winter months to put in an occasional appearance at the weekly Dinner Club. In 1796 he had walked the short distance from his house in Pall Mall to the Chapel Royal, St James's Palace to attend a service. While there he fell and fractured his thigh — an accident that disabled him for the rest of his life. At the next Annual General Meeting of the Dinner Club, members were informed of his resignation:[32]

Dr Heberden on account of his advanced age and the infirmity occasioned by an accident is deprived of the satisfaction of attending the meetings of the Club and desires to withdraw his name.

Thus ended a cherished association that had lasted nearly fifty years.

Despite his loss of mobility, his cheerfulness, according to Pettigrew,[33] was in no degree disturbed, for when he was fast approaching the age of 90, he observed, that though his occupations and pleasures were certainly changed from what they had used to be, yet he knew not if he had ever passed a year more comfortably than the last.

William died at his house in Pall Mall on 17 May 1801 and was buried in the parish church at Windsor, where a tablet to his memory can be seen on the south wall of the nave. In his Will, which he had drawn up four years earlier, William left his wife the house at Windsor, together with the 'furniture and plate' of both houses. His son William received the Pall Mall house, the tithes from the Gloucestershire farms, plus £10 000 invested in 'the 4% consolidated Annuities'. Thomas was left all the other freehold and leasehold properties—presumably those in and around Cricklade. William's daughter Mary got £1500, and Thomas's daughters Althea and Elizabeth £500 each. Among the smaller bequests, Sir George Baker received £20 to spend on some memento; and the two surgeons who had attended William free of charge at the time of his accident were rewarded with £50 each 'for their friendly assistance'. The servants too were remembered, although their number is not revealed, as only three are mentioned individually. From the extensive library William's wife was invited to take 'as many of my English and French books as she shall chuse'; the rest were to be divided between the two sons. The residue of the estate 'not already settled' also went to William's wife.

The value of William's estate, though very considerable, was by no means exceptional for a physician of his distinction. It is clear that his fortune had been built up partly from professional fees and partly from the connexions formed through his two marriages. Probably some additional capital had come his way in legacies from wealthy patients, anxious to show their appreciation of his skill and care.

We need not doubt that William had ample business acumen; but this was controlled by his religious convictions, which prompted him to be a generous giver; various instances of this have already been mentioned, and the point is emphasised by Pettigrew:[34]

> Dr Heberden's charity to the poor was more extended even than his protection of literary men. There was scarcely a public institution to which he did not liberally subscribe and his private donations were numerous and large.

Although we can all make our own assessments of William's character and personality from the material already presented, there is one more voice to be heard—that of a much younger physician, Dr WC Wells (1757-1817), who had never met William but had heard a great deal about him from friends in the Royal Society and other sources. Wells was actively involved on the side of the Licentiates in their continuing dispute with the Fellows of the Royal College of Physicians and had supported a certain Dr Stanger in his action against the College by a letter of no less than 186 printed pages, dated July 1799, addressed to the Lord Chief Justice. As we might expect, Wells regarded the motives of those physicians who had consistently opposed reform as thoroughly discreditable; by contrast he viewed William's behaviour throughout the earlier disputes of the 1760s and 1770s as above reproach and in the following passage[35] he seems to set him up as a model practitioner, in order to highlight by implication the shortcomings of those he is attacking:

But Dr Heberden, my Lord, stands, in a manner alone in his profession. No other person, I believe, either in this or any other country, has ever exercised the art of medicine with the same dignity, or has contributed so much to raise it in the estimation of mankind . . .

Were I, my lord, possessed of talents adequate to the undertaking, I should here endeavour to describe, at full length, the character of that illustrious man. In this attempt, I should first mark his various and extensive learning, his modesty in the use of it, and philosophical distrust of human opinions in science, however sanctioned by time, or the authority of great names. I should then exhibit him in the exercise of his profession, without envy or jealousy; too proud to court employment, yet underrating his services after they were performed; unwearied, even when a veteran in his art, in ascertaining the minutest circumstances of the sick, who placed themselves under his care, taking nothing in their situation for granted, that might be learned by inquiry, and trusting nothing of importance that concerned them to his memory. To demonstrate his greatness of mind, I should next mention his repeatedly declining to accept those offices of honour and profit at the British Court, which are regarded by other physicians as objects of their highest ambition, and are therefore sought by them with the utmost assiduity. I should afterwards take notice of his simple, yet dignified manners, his piety to God, his love for his country, and his exemplary discharge of the duties of all the private relations in which he stood to society; and I should conclude, by observing, that his whole life had been regulated by the most exquisite prudence, by means of which his other virtues were rendered more conspicuous and useful; and whatever failings, he might as a human being possess, were either shaded or altogether concealed.

Perhaps in his opening sentences Wells has allowed his pen to run away with him and we may question his later assertion that William refused a Court appointment on more than the one occasion described in an earlier chapter. But Wells's tribute—even if the trumpet is slightly overblown—surely reflects something of the veneration with which William was widely regarded in the final years of his long life.

As the new century unfolded, William's reputation was enhanced by the publication of successive editions of the *Commentaries*; and when the time came, as it was bound to do, for the work to be relegated from its place amongst current textbooks, there still remained in its pages ample material of interest and value to ensure that William's name was not forgotten.

In 1937 he received a posthumous honour when the Committee for the Study and Investigation of Rheumatism (formed the previous year) changed its name to The Heberden Society—thus recognising the contributions that William had made by describing and differentiating the various rheumatic conditions. The Society's library is housed in the Royal College of Physicians, in a room bearing William's name;[36] his portrait hangs outside the door in company with the portraits of many famous Fellows of the College, past and present. In what better company could William have wished to be remembered, than among his forerunners and successors— all of them participants in the unending struggle to push back the frontiers of ignorance?

Appendix

William Heberden the Younger

The active career of William Heberden Junior was comparatively brief and his achievements were overshadowed by those of his father; yet he deserves to be remembered not only for translating and publishing his father's *Commentaries*, but for his persistent (though unavailing) efforts to secure more tolerable treatment for the King during the years of his derangement.

William was born at Cecil Street on 23 March 1767 and was sent to school at Charterhouse; from there he proceeded to St John's College, Cambridge as a Pensioner and distinguished himself both in classics and mathematics. On receiving his BA in 1788, he was elected to a Fellowship and in December of the same year he entered the medical school of St George's Hospital in London.

In order to circumvent the rigidity of the Cambridge University statutes, which would have delayed the taking of his medical degrees, he was incorporated on his MA at Oxford—a ploy which enabled him to take his MB in 1792 and led to his appointment the following year as physician at St George's. The year 1795 was his personal *annus mirabilis*: he secured his MD, acquired a house in Dover Street, Mayfair, married an heiress (Elizabeth Catherine Miller)[1] and received his first Court appointment, as Physician Extra-Ordinary to the Queen. He was already FRS and within a few months had been elected FRCP.

William could hardly have achieved these goals so soon without considerable background support. Unlike his father—the impoverished sizar from Southwark—he was 'aided by every favouring circumstance of education, position, and family connection'. At Charterhouse he was among the sons of other affluent families and received 'parental encouragement' from the former Carthusian Daniel Wray.[2] Both in his classical and medical studies, his father was available as a willing and helpful tutor and was able to introduce his promising son to everyone at Court, from the King downwards. With the tide running so strongly in William Junior's favour, his rapid progress is not surprising.

In 1801 William published his first work—a pamphlet entitled *Observations on the increase and decrease of different diseases and particularly of the Plague*. His observations were based on statistics derived from the *Bills of Mortality* and supplemented his father's work in the same field.

The important and onerous task of translating and publishing the *Commentaries* was completed the following year, and William

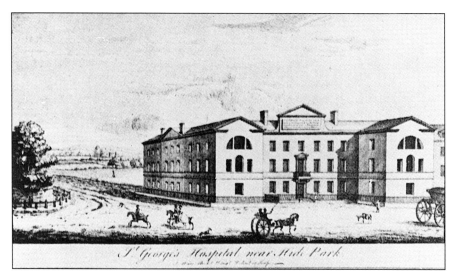

St George's Hospital, Hyde Park Corner in 1760—a view from the north-east.

followed this with a short work of his own entitled *An Epitome of Infantile Diseases.*[3]

He contributed only two papers to the *Philosophical Transactions* of the Royal Society.[4] The first—'On the Influence of Cold upon the Health of the Inhabitants of London'—was read in March 1796. January of that year had been exceptionally mild, whereas the preceding January had been unusually severe. The object of the paper was to disprove the widely held belief that unseasonably mild winter weather was more harmful to health than 'bracing cold'. William's arguments were supported by tables of mean temperatures and mortality figures for the two contrasting months, and demonstrated that the cold month was almost twice as lethal as the mild one.

His second paper, read thirty years later, was again concerned with the subject of temperature. It gave an account of the 'Heat in July 1825, together with some Remarks upon sensible Cold'. By the latter, William meant 'the degree of cold perceptible to the human body in its ordinary exposure to the atmosphere'. The whole paper was based on a series of careful observations made at his home in Datchet, near Windsor.

At the Royal College of Physicians William took his turn as Censor on two occasions and delivered the Harveian Oration in 1809. He contributed five papers to the *Medical Transactions*, all of which he read in the brief period 1807-14. The most interesting of these was 'The Mortality of London',[5] a sequel to the article he had published in 1801. By quoting figures for christenings and burials, he demonstrated the gradual improvement over the past century in the expectation of life and pointed out some of the main causes:

William Heberden the Younger, from a lithograph by JS Templeton.

The meeting-room of the Royal Society in Somerset House, (The Royal Society).

The very aspect of the city in every direction will suggest a reason for this in the widening of its streets, in the removal of nuisances, the opening of confined quarters, the erection of public squares, the construction of better drains and that universal diffusion of water pipes which . . . convey away the impurities of life.

In another paper—'Some Observations on the Scurvy'[6]—he develops his theme: 'Cleanliness and ventilation' are 'the principal agents in producing this reform'

and to this may be added . . . the increased use of fresh provisions and the introduction of a variety of vegetables among the ranks of our people. The same spirit of improvement which has constructed our sewers and widened our streets and removed the nuisances with which they abounded, and dispersed the inhabitants over a wider surface and taught them to love airy apartments and frequent changes of linen, has spread itself into the country, where it has drained the marshes, cultivated the wastes, enclosed the commons . . . Few have adverted with the attention it deserves to the prodigious mortality occasioned formerly by annual returns of epidemical fevers, of bowel complaints and other consequences of poor and sordid living to which we are entire strangers.

Despite the proliferation of medical charities during the latter half of the eighteenth century, very few of them offered help to poor patients who were unfit for work after their discharge from hospital. William's response to this problem was to submit a plan which led in 1809 to the founding of The Charity for Convalescents of St George's Hospital.[7] The Charity provided clothes and journey-money, sometimes a visit to the seaside and surgical appliances when required.

William had resigned his hospital appointment after serving ten years, but further Court appointments soon followed: first he was named Physician Extra-Ordinary to the King, then Physician-in-Ordinary to the Queen and finally (in 1809) Physician-in-Ordinary to the King.

The King's spontaneous recovery from his alarming illness of 1788/89 had unfortunately enhanced the reputation of the 'specialist', the Revd Doctor Francis Willis, director of his own mental asylum, whose methods of treatment, widely approved at the time, were repressive, coercive and punitive; and when the King's illness returned in 1801, Willis accompanied by his two sons was again called in to take charge. The King recuperated at Weymouth and remained in good health until his next attack in February 1804.[8] It is at this point that William enters the scene.

As soon as the physicians—William, Sir Francis Milman, Sir Lucas Pepys and Doctor Reynolds—had informed the Prime Minister Addington that the King seemed to be afflicted with his old complaint, Addington sent for the Willises. This action was entirely contrary to the wishes of the King, who on a number of occasions since his recovery from his last illness had begged his two sons, the Dukes of Kent and Cumberland, that if he should again be afflicted, they would use every means in their power to prevent anyone of the Willis family from being placed about him. The brothers had promised to do their best to carry out their father's wishes and when the Willises arrived, they barred their way and reported the matter to Addington.

The following day Addington consulted William and Milman, and their views were reported in a letter to the 3rd Earl of Hardwicke from his half-brother Charles York:[9]

. . . The Physicians (Milman and young Heberden) have been consulted on the necessity of calling in either the Willis's or some other Person of that description and I am told that they are of opinion that in the present state of the King's health, such a measure would in all probability produce *convulsions* which might be *fatal*.

After some further days of indecision, Addington reluctantly dismissed the Willises and called in another 'specialist',

Dr Samuel Foart Simmons, whose régime involved tying the King in a strait-waistcoat every day.

Despite this treatment, the King made steady progress towards recovery[10] and by the end of August was well enough to travel to Weymouth for a period of convalescence, during which he was able to enjoy the pleasures of sailing, sea-bathing and riding. William followed him a few days later—presumably at the King's personal desire—and on 9 September had a lengthy conversation with Lord Camden, in which he gave his views on the current state of the patient's health. Camden wrote a report[11] to the Prime Minister the same evening, quoting William's opinion:

> . . . that the King is advanced very much in his recovery, since he has been here—that those irritations of temper to which he had been subject subside gradually, that the hurry and agitation of spirits, are also subsided except when called forth by extraordinary exertion, as was the case yesterday when the King gave a fete on his Wedding Day, and that except want of rest at night, he [William] observes nothing either in the King's state of health or manner that he thinks is not as it ought to be and he authorized me to state it as his opinion 'that things wore a most flattering aspect'.

William's optimistic forecast was justified and before the end of the year, the King was fully restored to health.

For the next five years, the King maintained his good health and William was free to carry on his practice in London. Then, late in October 1810, exactly 50 years from the day of his accession, the familiar symptoms of the King's malady re-appeared. Sir Henry Halford at once called in William and Dr Baillie and having informed the Prime Minister Perceval, they insisted 'that no resort should be had to any means of restraint, as in the prior instances, lest that which appeared to be now subsiding should be aggravated and exasperated'.[12]

But the physicians' good intentions were frustrated the same evening by the King's 'extremely violent' behaviour[13] and they were very reluctantly obliged to send for Dr Simmons. The King, who had suffered under the Simmons régime in 1804, heartily disliked him and had made his physicians promise that in the event of another attack, 'he should never be left entirely alone with any medical person specially engaged in the department of insanity'.[14] When therefore Simmons arrived at Windsor, accompanied by his son and four assistants, and demanded 'sole management of the King', his demand was refused and he immediately left.

The physicians (who at all stages of the King's illnesses had to conform to the decisions of the Privy Council) now agreed on a compromise solution: that the King 'should be under no coersion or management not superintended by the ordinary physicians', whose task would be to 'control and govern, but to have some of the mad people under them'. William therefore sent for an apothecary who had recently retired from St Luke's Hospital, and when he arrived with his three assistants, they were instructed[15]

> that they were not to be afraid of employing the necessary means of restraint, but were at the same time never to lose sight of the King's rank, that they were to conduct themselves with respect but firmness, that they were to use no familiarity and no unnecessary violence, that they were not to wait for the discretion of the physicians for the employment of the means placed in their hands, but that they would always be liable to the inspection of His Majesty's physicians, one or more of whom would be constantly in attendance.

Hardly had the new routine been established, when Perceval, totally disregarding the views of the physicians and the Princes, brought in Dr Robert Willis,[16] advocate of all the repressive methods which William so deplored.

Meanwhile the official bulletins had to be issued each day regarding the King's condition, and the wording of these was always entrusted to William—'a task of some difficulty when curiosity was awakened on the one hand and prudence was necessary on the other'.[17]

Apart from his mental derangement, the King was now suffering from a bowel complaint and other physical symptoms, and on 28 November the Privy Council (following a precedent set in 1788) summoned each of the physicians in turn to give their individual answers to a number of questions regarding the King's health and his prospects of recovery. William gave his definition of the King's illness as:[18]

> . . . not merely the delirium of fever; nor is it any common case of insanity; it is a derangement attended with more or less fever, and liable to accessions and remissions . . . connected with his bodily health . . . the whole frame has been more or less disordered, both body and mind . . . a peculiarity of constitution, of which I can give no distinct account.

The Council, faced once again with the question of advising whether a Regency should be established, decided for the moment to take no action; and the physicians, with Willis in their midst, had to accept their frustrations as best they could. William voices his own feelings in a letter from Windsor Castle dated 30 December[19] to a friend:

I am necessarily so much confined here, that I have altogether
relinquished London . . . I fear the present state of parties will ill
admit of that tranquillity which is always so desirable for an invalid.

In February 1811 the physicians were again questioned by the
Parliamentary Committee and in the light of their answers a Bill
was approved giving temporary powers of Regency to the Prince of
Wales.

The same month William wrote to Perceval[20] to report that the
King had seen the Prince of Wales for nearly two hours and had
been 'much gratified with the interview'.

On the whole [the letter continued] His Majesty seems to be going
on quite well; but he is now at a period of his illness, when it is
very necessary he should be gradually brought more & more to
the exercise of his natural faculties; and this can hardly be done
without occasionally producing some additional excitement. We
have reason to believe that the communication of public affairs,
which was first made to His Majesty through you, has contributed
in no small degree to fix his attention, and make his former errors
subside from his mind.

William's advice regarding the exercise of the King's natural
faculties was disregarded, and the patient, after showing signs of
a temporary improvement, relapsed once more into frequent
delusions. The Willis régime of 'restraint' and the exclusion of all
sources of excitement was rigorously followed and by the middle of
May William felt obliged to address the Queen's Council
independently of his colleagues and express his total opposition to
a form of treatment that seemed to him both futile and inhumane:[21]

It is now more than six months, that His Majesty has been
indisposed; and it is become of great moment that his Majesty's
mind should, if possible, be roused from its disordered actions,
and not suffered to degenerate into a state of habitual error . . .
it becomes a duty to present to it fit occasions of exertion, if we
would have it resume its natural tone . . . At present there is not
one moment of the day passed by His Majesty in his usual manner;
scarcely one moment that he is not reminded of his unhappy
situation, without being assisted to extricate himself from it . . .
The very same restraint, which at one time was calculated to allay
irritation, becomes at another a cause of increasing it. When the
King was well, his day was spent . . . in the following manner . . .

At this point, William gives a typical day's programme, listing
the King's activities hour by hour from the time he rose at 7, until
his bedtime at 10 pm. He continues:

Of this rational and tranquil course of occupation or amusement, seasoned with that sweetness which is the effect of liberty and free choice of everybody (much more then to a King) not one particular is at present permitted him. Instead of it, his Majesty is either led about under the direction of another; or watched and examined by his family during a formal visit; or left to converse with his Physicians, or his Pages, or to amuse himself with the excursions of his own imagination. He has no business to call forth his judgment, no friendly intercourse to relieve his mind, no amusement to recreate his spirits, no company to vary his thoughts, no music to solace his cares: added to which He has no sight to arrest his attention, or to give importance or employment to his solitude . . . If we would have done with schemes & trifles, we must surely not content ourselves with telling the King of his errors; but must study to place him in a situation, that may call forth the energies of his mind, and divert the wanderings of fancy, not by vain expostulation, but by objects of natural interest.

William's letter had some effect, but not for long; the King was allowed to go out riding in Windsor and to see his family, but when he relapsed at the end of May, the Queen laid the blame squarely at William's door and the repressive measures were reintroduced. Worse still, the Queen's Council ordered that 'nobody be suffered to communicate with the King but with the consent of Dr Willis and in his presence'.

Although the tide of opinion was running so strongly against him, William decided to protest once again—independently of his colleagues and at the risk of arousing their displeasure. Accordingly on 12 September 1811 he despatched the following letter[22] to the Archbishop of Canterbury, in his capacity as Head of the Queen's Council:

. . . The state most to be dreaded is that of permanent delusion and imbecillity; and the danger of this seems to be much increased by his Majesty's want of sight, which precludes the most copious source of real images, the most familiar subjects of natural contemplation. Surely then it is not unreasonable to employ every method that can be employed with safety to avert such a calamity and to let slip no opportunity . . . of recalling the attention from the distractions of a disordered imagination to objects of reality and truth. It should be studied to soothe, to cherish, to comfort a mind worn by disease and disappointment, to encourage it by indulgence, by amusement, by conversation, by company, by reading, by the exertion of its own faculties . . .

Impressed, as I have been, with these sentiments, I have never hesitated to state them openly before my colleagues, though it did not become me to persevere in wilful opposition to their general wishes, or to expect for my private opinion, more weight than it might seem to deserve. But the cold acquiescence and subsequent prohibition I have met with in the only attempt that has been made since this last attack to introduce any real ideas to his Majesty's mind, or to relieve the unvaried tediousness of silent and solitary confinement, during which the imagination is left to feed on its own inventions, calls upon me for this explanation. And I beg leave to assure your Grace that I enter into it with no other feelings than those of respect and friendship towards the physicians with whom I act.

But what has in fact been done? . . . The King has been kept in a state of unedifying confinement and seclusion till the confinement itself has become a source of irritation . . .

Before I conclude this long apology, let me be permitted to say something of myself . . . I cannot be insensible to the kindness and partiality with which his Majesty has honoured me for many years; I cannot forget that I am the only one of his Majesty's ordinary Physicians at present in attendance upon him; I cannot forget that I am the only Physician of his Majesty's own calling; that his Majesty had desired me not to leave him, not to desert him; that he has told me while he would admit any additional assistance I might think necessary, he always reposed his trust in me . . .

At the end of his letter William asked permission for his proposals to be considered at a special consultation of all the physicians; but any hopes he may have had of a change of attitude, were quickly dashed; the Queen had no sympathy for his arguments and his colleagues considered his proposed consultation a waste of time.

As the months dragged on, and the physicians found themselves virtually excluded from the sickroom, Halford and Baillie realised that they were united with William in their common frustrations, and on 8 February 1812 all three signed the following letter to the Council:[23]

We . . . do most respectfully submit to your Lordships the propriety of permitting us to ascertain the state of the King's health from day to day by our own immediate personal enquiries.

We stand responsible to the Public for the proper care of His Majesty's bodily health, and we ask only for those opportunities of enquiring into it, without which it is impossible for a physician to do justice either to his Patient, or to himself. We have sufficiently shewn our willingness to bear the humiliation and indignity of being made mute spectators of His Majesty's condition without the power of contributing our services either to His recovery or to His comfort. And we might prevail upon ourselves still to endure the same degradation, were there any prospect of good to arise from the present restrained intercourse with His Majesty, which could not be obtained without so great an injury to our own feelings . . .

But the Council was not to be deflected from its earlier decisions, and the physicians' plea went unheeded.

With Willis's permission, William was able to see the King on 10 March and informed the Archbishop:[24]

> . . . I made myself known to HM and asked him how he did. The King received me with great kindness . . . asked after my family and my two eldest boys by name. He desired me to feel his pulse . . .

Apart from the frustrations involved in the management of the Royal patient, William's private life was still serene and the outlook seemed set fair. In the course of 16 years, his wife Elizabeth had produced five sons, William, Charles, George, Henry and Frederick; and four daughters, Elizabeth, Mary, Anne and Emily, all of whom survived the dangerous years of infancy and childhood. Then, on 21 May 1812, after a few days' illness, his wife died at their house in Pall Mall. This event changed the course of William's life; he gave up his London practice, retired to a house at Datchet, close to Windsor, and devoted himself to what now seemed to him his most important responsibilities—bringing up his large family and continuing his efforts to alleviate the sufferings of the King.

In July of the same year, he was protesting once more:[25]

> I am of opinion that the present medical treatment and management applied to His Majesty's case, are fundamentally and practically wrong. His Majesty appears to be in that state, from which it is not probable that any plan of management will restore him. But, though it is possible indeed that His Majesty may recover of himself, by the natural resources of his constitution, and without external assistance; yet I do believe it to be utterly impossible that the present distant and secret inspection of His Majesty's conduct can ever be in any manner conducive to the reestablishment of His Majesty's mind.

Throughout the closing years of the King's life, William continued his regular attendance and was able to see his patient from time to time, though always in the presence of one of the Willises. In a brief note to the Archbishop[26] dated 19 January 1819, he reported that he had heard the King speak 'in a manner that disclosed no degree of ill-humour'.

The King's death a year later marked the end of William's medical career, though he maintained his contacts with the Royal College of Physicians and was promoted to the status of an 'elect' in 1823. Some of his leisure was employed in translating Plutarch's *Brotherly Love* and Cicero's *Letters to Atticus*; he also wrote a dialogue *On Education* 'after the manner of Cicero's *Philosophical Dissertations*'.

In 1826 he returned to London, in order to be available with advice and encouragement to his son Henry (born 1802), a medical student at St George's Hospital. Two years later, Henry cut his hand at a post-mortem examination and died of pyaemia within a week. In 1829 George (born 1800), who was vicar of Dartford, Kent, also died and a third bereavement followed in 1833 with the death of William's eldest daughter Elizabeth, who had married the Revd Gerrard Andrewes, rector of St James's, Piccadilly.

William was by now preoccupied with religious studies; he composed his *Reflections upon the Gospel of St John* and followed this work with a translation of *The Catholic Epistles*. Finally in 1839 he published *A Literal Translation of the Apostolic Epistles and Revelations with concurrent Commentaries*.

By this time William's three surviving sons were settled in their careers; Charles had been called to the Bar; William[27] had taken Holy Orders and been presented by his father to the living of Great Bookham in Surrey; Frederick, also ordained, was now married and Vicar of Wilmington near Dartford in Kent. Anne had married the Revd Walter King, Archdeacon of Rochester. Mary and Emily remained single and lived on until the 1880s.

William (their father) had acquired a house in Cumberland Street, Marylebone, and it was there on 19 February 1845 that he died. He was buried in the parish church at Windsor.

Notes

Chapter 1
Years of Promise

1 PH Reaney. *A Dictionary of British Surnames*. (2nd edn) London: 1976.
2 Manorial Court Roll of the Manor of Idsworth. (Hampshire County Record Office, Winchester).
   Copy-holders were so called because the title to their holding was a copy of the relevant entry in the Manorial Court Roll. Although the Court Roll makes no reference to the family later than 1784, the name still survives in 'Heberden's Farm'.
3 Preserved in the library of Lambeth Palace.
4 The St Bride's parish register 'waste book' (or rough book) records the baptism on 24 September 1699 of Elizabeth Haberden Dau of Richard & Elizabeth at the Fariers in the Wilderness. A Cotchman.
5 Vestry Minutes of St Saviour's, Southwark. (Greater London Council Record Office).
6 In the baptismal register his father is described as 'Inholder'.
7 School records, preserved at St Olave's and St Saviour's Grammar School Foundation, Orpington, Kent.
8 AF Leach. History of Southwark Schools. In: *Victoria County Histories–Surrey*. HE Malden, ed. London: 1907, Vol 2(i), p 179.
9 'Southwark Fair', painted 1733. The scene includes hucksters, gamblers, freaks, a tight-rope walker, wax-works, musicians and booths for strolling players.
10 MD George. *London Life in the Eighteenth Century*. Harmondsworth: 1966, Chapter 1, p 39.
11 See Hogarth's print, 'Gin Lane'; although not published until 1751, his portrayal would have been equally valid 30 years earlier. Gin was accepted among the poor as the cheapest drug to pacify their infants.
12 MD George. *London Life in the Eighteenth Century*. Harmondsworth: 1966, Chapter 2.
13 Roy Porter. *English Society in the Eighteenth Century*. Harmondsworth, 1982, p 31.
   Richard H Schwartz. *Daily Life in Johnson's London*. University of Wisconsin Press, 1983.
14 Apprenticeship, which in Thomas's case meant living *en famille* in his Master's home, was the accepted route for any young man aspiring to become a member of the Barber-Surgeon's Guild.
15 Surrey Wills Commissary Index. September 1721. (GLC Record Office).

16 AC Buller. *The Life and Works of Heberden*. London: 1879.

17 Edward War. *A Step to Stir-Bitch-Fair*. 1700. Quoted in: Laurence and Helen Fowler, compilers. *Cambridge Commemorated, An Anthology of University Life*. Cambridge: 1984.

18 Edward War. *A Step to Stir-Bitch-Fair*. 1700. Daniel Defoe visited the fair and mentions it in his *Tour Through the Whole Island of Great Britain (1724-6)*.

19 DA Winstanley. *Unreformed Cambridge*. Cambridge: 1935, p 202.

20 DA Winstanley. *The University of Cambridge in the Eighteenth Century*. Cambridge: 1922, p 8.

21 DA Winstanley. *The University of Cambridge in the Eighteenth Century*. Cambridge: 1922, p 16.

22 DA Winstanley. *Unreformed Cambridge*. Cambridge: 1935, p 44.

23 Preserved in the Cambridge University Library.

24 Autobiographical note composed by William for the Royal Society of Medicine in Paris. See Chapter 7, note 44.

25 Records of the Guild of Barber-Surgeons. (Guildhall Library). Although Surgeons still shared their Guild with the Barbers, the two occupations had for all practical purposes ceased to have any connection, and in 1745 they formally separated.

26 Thomas Baker. *History of St John's College, Cambridge*, edited and enlarged by John EB Mayor. Cambridge: 1869. Baker, who died in 1740 (see below 41-2) left his *History* in manuscript and it remained unpublished until Mayor edited it, adding supplementary material, to bring the *History* down to the 1860s.

27 Linacre (c 1460-1524) was one of the founders of the College of Physicians; he endowed lectureships both at Oxford and Cambridge.

28 Ruth Richardson. *Death, Dissection and the Destitute*. Routledge & Kegan Paul, 1987.

29 A Robb-Smith. Cambridge Medicine. In: AG Debus, ed, *Medicine in Seventeenth Century England*. University of California Press, 1974, pp 354-7.

30 See Chapter 4, 70-1.

31 Autobiographical note composed by William for the Royal Society of Medicine in Paris. Chapter 7, note 44.

32 Preserved in the *Grace Book for 1737*. (Cambridge University Library).

33 British Museum Additional Manuscript 32457. Conyers Middleton (See Chapter 2, pp 17-18) wrote in a letter dated 3 June 1738, to William Warburton (see Chapter 7, note 7):

> ... I shall be glad to see Dr Taylor here, who may chance to fall in with a Physic-Act of our friend Hebberdin which if our old Professor were in any condition to exercise him, would certainly be a good one.

Chapter 2
Building a Reputation

1 J Nichols. *Illustrations of the Literary History of the Eighteenth Century*. London: 1817, Vol 1, p 77 and Vol 4, p 524.

2 British Museum Additional Manuscript 5871.
   Cole's notes on William are printed in the 'Appendix' to: RF Scott, ed. *Admissions to the College of St John the Evangelist in the University of Cambridge*. Cambridge: 1882, pp 377-9.

3 P Toynbee and L Whibley, eds. *Correspondence of Thomas Gray*. (3 Vols) Oxford: 1935, revised 1971, letter 135.

4 The 'Preface' to the edition of 1781 described the authors as 'a Society of Friends' at Cambridge, whose names 'were an ornament to the place'. A further edition appeared in 1810.

5 Gunther. *Early Science in Cambridge*. Oxford: 1937, p 226.

6 Pettigrew. *A Biographical Memoir of Dr W Heberden in Medical Portrait Gallery*. London: 1839, Vol 3.

7 Preserved in the Francis A Countway Library of Medicine, Boston, Massachusetts.

8 Gunther. *Early Science in Cambridge*. Oxford: 1937, pp 482-9. Includes a printed version of the catalogue.

9 See Chapter 3, pp 40-1.

Chapter 3
Precept and Practice

1 William kept the first version safely and it remained in the possession of his descendants until 1963, when it was presented to the Francis A Countway Library, Boston, Massachusetts. The 'second original' is lost.

2 *Annals of Medical History*, 1928; Vol X (nos 3 and 4). In a prefatory essay, Dr Le Roy Crummer attempts to demonstrate that the manuscript he had acquired was William's original holograph. His theory is completely untenable for several reasons: the handwriting bears no resemblance to William's; compared with William's meticulous standards of accuracy and scholarship, the copy is illiterate; it is riddled with spelling mistakes, and these mistakes even extend to the names of the authors whose works William discusses; in two or three places faulty punctuation ruins the sense and in several passages words are omitted, indicating that the writer could not decipher the copy he was transcribing. Among other copies known to exist, one, in St John's College Library, was made by Erasmus Darwin in 1752; another in the Cambridge University Library, was made in 1786 by WH Wollaston, William's nephew by marriage.

3 The apothecary played an essential role in the medical system of the time and frequently acted as the poor man's doctor.

4 Pettigrew. *A Biographical Memoir of Dr W Heberden in Medical Portrait Gallery*. London: 1839, Vol 3.
Evidently Glynn's aspect could be rather forbidding:
   This morning, quite dead, Tom was found in his bed
   Although he was hearty last night;
   But 'tis thought, having seen Dr Glynn in a dream,
   That the poor fellow died of the fright.

5 English edn. London: T Payne, 1802. See Chapter 9, note 4.

6 Designed to produce a partial vacuum which would induce a blood-filled swelling.

7 An incision kept open for the discharge of noxious matter.

8 Margaret Rowbottom and Charles Susskind. *Electricity and Medicine*. San Francisco Press, 1984.
The possibility of using electric shocks for therapeutic purposes had been under investigation since the 1740s. 'Electrification' had been successful in restoring feeling and movement in certain cases of paralysis and an English surgeon had used the same means to cure an eleven-year-old boy who had suddenly been smitten with blindness.

9 *Scarborough 966-1966*. Scarborough and District Archaeological Society, 1966, pp 63-5.

10 VC Medvei and JL Thornton, eds. *The Royal Hospital of St Bartholomew 1123-1973*. London: 1974, p 137.
The editors refer to a three-page manuscript in the Bodleian Library, Oxford, written by the chief Physician Peirce Dod FRCP, entitled 'Reasons against increasing the number of Physicians in St Bartholomew's Hospital'. One of his arguments was that the necessary staffing level could be maintained by the employment of temporary assistants. 'Several young gentlemen from our own Universities' had acted as assistants from time to time, among them' William Heberden . . .'

11 British Museum Additional Manuscript 5824, f 110.

12 Roy and Dorothy Porter. *In Sickness and in Health*. London: Fourth Estate, 1988, Chapter 14.
Georgian attitudes to death are discussed.

13 British Museum Additional Manuscript 32457.
Correspondence of Dr C Middleton.

14 RJ White. *Dr Bentley*. Eyre & Spottiswoode, 1965.

15 JH Monk. *Life of Bentley*. 1833, Vol 2, p 413.
Monk was writing at a time when the craze for bleeding had reached a peak.
Roderick E McGrew. *Encyclopaedia of Medical History*. Macmillan, 1985, p 33.

16 British Museum Additional Manuscript 6269.
Dissertation on Daphne, with letter to Dr Mead; transcribed by John Ward.

17 College Annals. (Library of Royal College of Physicians).

18 *Antitheriaca, or an Essay on Mithridatium and Theriaca*. Printed (but not published), Cambridge: 1745.

19 Ronald D Mann. *Modern Drug Use*. Lancaster: MTP Press Ltd, 1984, pp 307-9.

    A modern assessment of William's Essay.

20 H Pemberton MD. *The Dispensatory of the Royal College of Physicians, London*, translated into English. London: Longman and Shewell, 1746. Quoted in: G Watson. *Theriac and Mithridatium*. London: Wellcome Historical Medical Library, 1966, pp 142-3.

21 College Annals.

22 Sir Hans Sloane (1660-1753) bequeathed his library and collections of botanical specimens to the nation, to form the nucleus of the British Museum. In the volume of his lecture notes on Materia Medica, William recorded:

    'Sir H Sloane told me that he had been possessed of an amethyst with a drop of water inclosed in it. In a hard winter this drop froze, & burst the amethyst.'

23 *A Short Account of the Late Donation of a Botanic Garden to the University of Cambridge by the Revd Dr Walker, Vice-Master of Trinity College with Rules and Orders for the Government of it*. Cambridge: 1763.

    Hazel Le Rougetel. Early Chelsea/Cambridge Association in Botany. In: *Garden History*, Winter 1979: Vol 7 (No 3); pp 49-52.

24 J Nichols. *Illustrations of the Literary History of the Eighteenth Century*. London: 1817, Vol 2, p 146.

    Includes a letter from William to Dr Birch asking him to introduce the young poet Mr Mason, 'the Author of *Musaeus, a Monody on the Death of Mr Pope*' to 'a breakfasting at the Doctor's.'

25 WF Bynum. In: GS Rousseau and Roy Porter, eds. *The Ferment of Knowledge*. Cambridge University Press, 1980, p 243.

26 W Macmichael. *The Gold-Headed Cane*. (2nd edn) London: John Murray, 1828, pp 169-73.

    In the full text of Hulse's letter the name of the offender (says Macmichael) had been effectually erased before it came into his hands. It is unfortunate that the information that William Heberden the Younger divulged about his father was so limited in scope and so discreet; his attitude is summed up in his reply to someone who had asked for further biographical details:

    A domestic and literary life afford few materials for history. When Dr Macmichael was preparing his *Gold Headed Cane* I gave him all the information that occur'd to me on the subject of my Father, and I cannot do better than refer you to the 2nd edition of that work.

    Yours truly,   W Heberden

(Original manuscript in the Library of the Royal College of Physicians).

27 Dr Peter Shaw (1694-1763) began practice in Scarborough and later published a pamphlet on the spa waters there. On coming to London he was admitted LRCP and in 1752 was made Physician-Extraordinary to George II, whom he attended on his journeys to Hanover.

28 In 1748 George II and his newly-appointed Minister of State, the Duke of Newcastle, were both closely concerned in the negotiations which brought the war of the Austrian Succession to an end. Hulse's PS implies that they were already in Hanover and that Shaw was in attendance, although he had not yet received his formal appointment as royal physician.

Chapter 4
Cecil Street

1 Sir A Geikie. *Annals of the Royal Society Club.* 1917.
The Club was closely connected to the Royal Society, to which it soon became formally attached.

2 LCC Survey of London, 1937: Vol 18 (part 2); p 123.

3 J Nichols. *Illustrations of the Literary History of the Eighteenth Century.* London: 1817, Vol 2, p 147.

4 British Museum Additional Manuscript 32457.

5 British Museum Additional Manuscript 32457.

6 Roy Porter. The Patient in Eighteenth Century England. In: A Wear, ed. *History of Medicine in Society.* Cambridge University Press (in press).

7 Peter Cunningham, ed. *Horace Walpole's Letters.* London: 1857-59, Vol 2, p 214.

8 Roy and Dorothy Porter. *In Sickness and in Health.* London: Fourth Estate, 1988, p 239.

9 British Museum Additional Manuscript 32457.

10 Pettigrew. *A Biographical Memoir of Dr W Heberden in Medical Portrait Gallery.* London: 1839, Vol 3.

11 British Museum Additional Manuscript 4326, ff 198-201.

12 Better looking.

13 Appendix to: RF Scott, ed. *Admissions to the College of St John the Evangelist in the University of Cambridge.* Cambridge: 1882, p 379.

14 College inventory.

15 TR Thomson, ed. *Materials for a History of Cricklade.* Oxford: for Cricklade Historical Society, 1958-61, p 62.

16 Bristol Record Office DC/E/15/2.
Tithes, originally intended as a compulsory contribution by land owners and farmers to the upkeep of their parish church and the income of the parson, might sometimes be payable to the

Dean and Chapter of the Diocese. The sale of tithes on a leasehold basis relieved them from the trouble of collecting them.

17 British Museum Additional Manuscript 4310, ff 20-9.

18 F Kilvert. *Memoirs of the Life and Writings of Bishop Hurd.* London: 1860, p 48.

19 Manuscript in the Heberden archive. (Royal College of Physicians).

20 Thomas Eaves and Ben Kimpel. *Samuel Richardson, a Biography.* Oxford: 1971, p 322.

21 Henry Pettit, ed. *The Correspondence of Edward Young.* Oxford: 1971, pp 392-4.

22 John Carroll, ed. *Selected Letters of Samuel Richardson.* Oxford: 1964, p 327.

23 Thomas Eaves and Ben Kimpel. *Samuel Richardson, a Biography.* Oxford: 1971, pp 459 and 514.

24 N Nicolson and GS Rousseau. Bishop Berkeley and Tar-Water. In: HK Miller, E Rothstein and GS Rousseau, eds. *The Augustan Milieu.* Oxford: 1970.

25 John Nichols. *Literary Anecdotes of the Eighteenth Century.* London: Nichols, Son & Bentley, 1812, Vol 4, p 596.

26 Lady Llanover, ed. *The Life and Correspondence of Mrs Delany.* London: 1862, Vol 3, p 267.
The following two extracts are from pp 308 and 313-14.

27 W Heberden. *Commentaries on the History and Cure of Diseases.* Chapter 95.

28 W Macmichael. *The Gold-Headed Cane.* (2nd edn) London: John Murray, 1828, pp 169-73.
William observed Mead's faculties 'to be so impaired, that he then determined within himself, that if he ever lived to the same age of 78, he would give up practice. And this resolution he strictly adhered to, saying that people's friends were not forward to tell them of their decay, and that he would rather retire from business several years too soon, than follow it one hour too long.'

29 J Nichols. *Illustrations of the Literary History of the Eighteenth Century.* London: 1817, Vol 2, p 457.

30 British Museum Additional Manuscript 32852, f 560.

31 Lady Llanover, ed. *The Life and Correspondence of Mrs Delany.* London: 1862, Vol 3, p 357.

32 Thomas Hinderwell. *The History and Antiquities of Scarborough and the Vicinity.* (2nd edn) York: 1811, p 205.

33 P Toynbee and L Whibley, eds. *Correspondence of Thomas Gray.* (3 Vols) Oxford: 1935, revised 1971, letter 296.

34 London, 1758.

35 See Chapter 6, note 11.

36 W Heberden. *Commentaries on the History and Cure of Diseases.* Chapter 7, section 2.

37 The original manuscript is in the Francis A Countway Library, Boston, Massachusetts. H MS C24.2.

38 These had to be specially made to accommodate an air tube which led down to a perforated plate near the floor of the still; during the heating process, a stream of air bubbles was forced through the liquid.

39 *A Description of Ventilators* and *A Treatise on Ventilators* were published in two volumes in 1743. Hales's order to the bookseller is a good example of his practical philanthropy. He had a special interest in America, as he was a Trustee for the colony of Georgia.

40 Admiral Vernon (1684-1757) had become a national hero for his capture of the Spanish colony of Porto Bello in 1739. It was routine to serve neat rum or brandy to the crews of naval vessels, and the ration of half a pint was given out about noon each day. The 'hint' was contained in Hales's *Philosophical Experiments*, published in the same year. On 4 August 1740 Vernon sent an order to the captains and surgeons of his squadron, who all agreed that 'the pernicious custom of the seamen drinking their allowance of rum in drams, and often at once, is attended with many fatal effects'. Thereafter each daily allowance of a half-pint of rum was to be diluted with one quart of water and issued in two servings, one in the morning and one in the afternoon. The new practice was soon adopted throughout the Navy.

41 Lloyd and Coulter. *Medicine and the Navy*. Edinburgh and London: E & S Livingstone, 1961, Vol 3.
    Admiral Boscawen (1711-61) was involved in expeditions to protect British colonial interests in North America. In 1755, some 2000 of his men died of fever. The ventilators installed three years later in his flagship the Namur were Hales's improved model, known as the 'ship's lungs' and depended on manually operated bellows.
    The capture of Louisburg off Nova Scotia opened the way for the final victory against the French at Quebec in 1759.

42 S Halkett and J Laing. *Dictionary of Anonymous and Pseudonymous English Literature*. London: Oliver and Boyd, 1926, i, p 374.
    The editor was at first thought to be Thomas Birch.

43 Peter R Cox. Demography. (5th edn) Cambridge: 1976, p 368.
    John Graunt (1620-74) was the pioneer of modern demography. In his *Observations*, which appeared in 1662, he analysed the causes of death shown in the bills and made an assessment of the size and trend of the population of London.

44 Petty (1623-95) was one of the most remarkable men of his time. Son of a poor clothier of Romsey in Hampshire, he studied

mathematics and medicine and served as a physician with Cromwell's army in Ireland. He developed a 'political arithmetick' intended to measure the influence of population in human affairs and produced a stream of other inventive projects on, for example, ship-building, isolation hospitals and decimal coinage.

45 Corbyn Morris (d 1779) was the author of several works on economics and statistics. He was a very able administrator and served for some years as Secretary of the Customs and Salt Duty in Scotland. He was later appointed Commissioner of the Customs, which enabled him to return to London. He was elected FRS in 1757.

46 DV Glass. *Numbering the People*. Farnborough: Saxon House, 1973, pp 12-17.

47 The New River was begun in 1613 by Sir Hugh Middleton, in order to provide Londoners with a supply of water purer than the Thames. The channels he constructed brought the water from its source in Hertfordshire via Theobalds Park near Enfield, through Highbury and Islington and thence to the New River Head in Clerkenwell.

48 'Convulsions' was a convenient term to explain—or explain away—an enormous number of infant deaths. The immediate causes of many of these doubtless included birth injuries and fevers; but the underlying causes all too frequently included poverty, dirt, ignorance, cheap gin and an attitude of indifference or despair on the part of the parents.

49 MD George. *London Life in the Eighteenth Century*. Harmondsworth: 1966, p 322.

50 Kenneth Walker. *The Story of Medicine*. London: 1959, p 226.

51 Genevieve Miller. *The Adoption of Inoculation for Small Pox in England and France*. Philadelphia: University of Pennsylvania Press, 1957, pp 169-70.

52 Royal College of Physicians. *Annals*. XII, pp 41-2.

53 *Journal Britannique*, Nov-Dec 1755: XVIII; p 483.
   The editor, Matthew Maty (1718-76) was MD of Leyden and became secretary of the Royal Society—a post later held by his son Paul (see pp 103-4).

54 William Pepper. *The Medical Side of Benjamin Franklin*. New York: Argosy-Antiquarian, 1970, p 133.
   The project was no doubt discussed at Cecil Street:
      Dr Heberden sends his compts to Dr Franklin & desires the favor of his company at dinner on Monday next Sept 29th at half an hour past three.

55 A copy of this anonymous version is in the Francis A Countway Library, Boston, Massachusetts. The text is preceded simply by a title page and a very brief (150 word) introduction.

56 Whitman M Reynolds. Inoculation for the Smallpox in Colonial America. *Bulletin of the History of Medicine*, 1948: Vol 22; pp 273-6.

57 Carroll Papers. *Maryland Historical Magazine*, 1917: Vol 12; pp 350-61.

58 D Hardinge. *Biographical Anecdotes of Daniel Wray.* London: Nichols, Son & Bentley, 1815, p 72.

59 P Toynbee and L Whibley, eds. *Correspondence of Thomas Gray.* (3 Vols) Oxford: 1935, revised 1971, letter 308.

60 P Toynbee and L Whibley, eds. *Correspondence of Thomas Gray.* (3 Vols) Oxford: 1935, revised 1971, letter 321.

61 British Museum Additional Manuscript 4310, ff 20-9. Letters to T Birch.

62 W Macmichael. *The Gold-Headed Cane.* (2nd edn) London: John Murray, 1828, p 178.

63 Letherland (1699-1764) studied at Leyden and took his MD there. He was created MD of Cambridge and then elected FRCP.

64 John Stuart, Earl of Bute, had been in effect the future King's finishing tutor, and George continued to consult him on virtually everything for some time after his accession. Like all Scots— who were still regarded with suspicion following the Jacobite rebellion of 1745—Bute was unpopular, and the feeling against him became intense when he was made Prime Minister in 1762 and negotiated the terms of the Treaty of Paris, which brought the Seven Years War with France to a formal conclusion. It was his ministry that was the target of Wilkes's attacks (see below p 82).

65 British Museum Additional Manuscript 5720, f 90.

66 *Annual Register.* 1763, pp 146-7. Prints the following two letters.

67 Richard Brocklesby (1722-97) studied medicine at Edinburgh and Leyden, took his MD at Dublin, incorporated at Cambridge and was then elected FRCP. He had very recently settled in Norfolk Street (not far from William) after serving with the army during the Seven Years War.

68 W Cowper. *Memoir of the Early Life of William Cowper.* (2nd edn) London: 1816, p 40.

69 British Museum Additional Manuscript 35607, f 200.

70 Sir William Duncan was Physician-in-Ordinary to George III and had recently been created a Baronet.

71 British Museum Additional Manuscript 37222, f 192.

72 Barker and Montgomery. *Observations . . . on the Dublin Pharmacopoeia.* Dublin: Hodges and Smith, 1830.

73 John Nichols. Literary Anecdotes of the Eighteenth Century. London: Nichols, Son & Bentley, 1812, Vol 4, p 515.

74 See Chapter 7, p 139. The following four extracts are from unpublished manuscript letters preserved in the library of St John's College, Cambridge, catalogue no 381.

75 P Thicknesse. *Valetudinarian's Guide to Bath.* Bath: 1780, p 25.

76 William reported his astronomical observations to the Royal Society. See Chapter 5, p 98.

77 See Chapter 7, pp 146-7.

78 *St James's Chronicle*. 14 February, 1767.

79 The items, numbered 3 to 6 in the inventory were: a Gregorian telescope made by Short in 1763; 'a very old small Gregorian'; a 3½ feet Transit by Sisson made in 1763; and a clock by Shelton with gridiron pendulum.

80 Thomas Baker. *History of St John's College, Cambridge*, edited and enlarged by John EB Mayor, Cambridge: 1869, p 1041. The Fellows had already shewn their appreciation of William's services by agreeing at a meeting on 27 December 1764 'to send Dr Heberden a collar of brawn every Christmas'.

Chapter 5
The Royal Society

1 Sir HG Lyons. *The Royal Society, 1660-1940*. Cambridge: 1944.

2 *Philosophical Transactions*, 1750: Vol 46; p 596.

3 See p 70.

4 Stephen Hales. *Vegetable Staticks*. London: 1727, pp 192-3.

5 Raymond Williamson. An Ancient Urinary Vesical Calculus. In: *Centaurus*, 1956: Vol 4 (no 4); pp 319-24.

6 *Philosophical Transactions*, 1764: Vol 54; p 198.

7 *Philosophical Transactions*, 1769: Vol 59; p 359.

8 G Symons and H Sowerby Wallis. The Heberden Family and Meteorology. *British Rainfall*, 1898.

9 Guildhall Library, London.

10 *Philosophical Transactions*, 1752: Vol 47; p 353.

11 *Philosophical Transactions*, 1765: Vol 55; p 57.

12 *Philosophical Transactions*, 1752: Vol 47; p 357.

13 *Philosophical Transactions*, 1770: Vol 60; p 502.

14 *Philosophical Transactions*, 1756: Vol 49; p 432.

15 *Philosophical Transactions*, 1762: Vol 52; p 155.

16 *Philosophical Transactions*, 1767: Vol 57; p 461.

17 Nicholas Munckley had also been 'created' MD at Aberdeen; he was Physician to Guy's Hospital.

18 PJ Anderson. *Officers and Graduates of University and King's College, Aberdeen, 1495-1860*. Aberdeen: New Spalding Club, 1893, p 1301.

19 *Philosophical Transactions*, 1766: Vol 56; p 10.

20 *Philosophical Transactions*, 1760: Vol 51; p 308.

21 Robert E Schofield, ed. *A Scientific Autobiography of Joseph Priestley*. Cambridge, Massachusetts: MIT Press, 1966, p 39, letter no 11.

22 J Nichols. *Illustrations of the Literary History of the Eighteenth Century*. London: 1817, Vol 3, p 754.

23 Canton Papers. (Royal Society Library).

24 E Forbes. *History of the Royal Observatory*. London: Taylor & Francis, 1975, p 149.

25 Patrick O'Brian. *Joseph Banks—A Life*. London: Collins-Harvill, 1987.

26 JC Beaglehole, ed. *The Endeavour Journal of Joseph Banks*. Sydney: The Public Library of New South Wales; and London: Angus & Robertson, 1962.

27 JC Beaglehole, ed. *The Endeavour Journal of Joseph Banks*. Sydney: The Public Library of New South Wales; and London: Angus & Robertson, 1962.

28 See p 142.

29 Council Minutes. January 1784.

30 Hutton (1737-1823) was the youngest son of a colliery labourer of Newcastle-on-Tyne. He became a schoolmaster and was later appointed Professor of Mathematics (after competitive examination) at the Royal Academy, Woolwich.

31 Blagden Papers. Letter from Robert Adair. (Royal Society Library).

32 Warren Dawson, ed. *A Calender of the Correspondence of Sir Joseph Banks*. London: 1958.
Letter from Blagden to Banks, 5 April 1784.

33 MB Hall. *All Scientists Now*. Cambridge University Press, 1984.

34 See pp 223-4.

35 Joseph Priestley. *Memoirs*. 1833 edn, p 64.

36 Robert E Schofield, ed. *A Scientific Autobiography of Joseph Priestley*. Cambridge, Massachusetts: MIT Press, 1966, letter no 123.
Priestley was living in Birmingham, though he visited London in the winter.

37 EJ Morten. Correspondence of Josiah Wedgwood 1781-95. Manchester: 1906 (reprint 1973), p 75.

38 The phlogiston theory proposed that all combustible substances contained an inflammable element called phlogiston, which was given off during combustion and absorbed by the surrounding air.

Chapter 6
The Royal College of Physicians

1 Named after Theodore Gulston or Goulston (1572-1630), who left the Royal College of Physicians £200 in his will to endow a lectureship. The lectures are unpublished; manuscript copies are among the Wollaston papers in the Cambridge University Library and in the Royal College of Physicians Library.

2 In this passage William expresses the view commonly held by his contemporaries, that as Nature exemplifies the works of God, everything in Nature must be at least potentially beneficial.

3 The herb euphorbia (spurge), noted for its acrid milky juice.

4 Bernadine Z Paulshock. William Heberden and Opium: Some Relief to All. *New England Journal of Medicine*, 1983: Vol 308; pp 53-6.

In the *Commentaries*, William mentions several situations in which he was prepared to prescribe opium and in Chapter 2 (Ratio Medendi) he recommends it as 'very commonly the most effectual means' for producing relief from pain. He also wrote a brief undated essay entitled 'Opium' in which he lists the various forms of opiate medicines and the differing reactions of patients. William's manuscript is in the Francis A Countway Library of Medicine, Boston, Massachusetts.

5 William Harvey (1578-1657) studied medicine first at Cambridge and then for four years at Padua, where he became interested in the anatomy of the vascular system. On returning to England he was elected to the staff of St Bartholomew's Hospital. His great discovery of the circulation of the blood was announced in a lecture on 16 April 1616. Later in his life he built a library and museum for the Royal College of Physicians. William Heberden recorded some personal details of the Doctor's habits in the following note, preserved in the library of the Royal College of Physicians:

1761 May 29 Mrs Harvey (great niece to Dr Harvey) told me that the Dr lived at his brother's at Roehampton, the later part of his life. That he used to walk out in a morning combing his head in the fields. That he was humoursome & would sit down exactly at the time he had appointed for dinner, whether the company was come or not. That his salt-seller was always fill'd with sugar, which he used to eat instead of salt. That if the gout was very painful to him in the night, he would rise & put his feet into cold water.

6 Bodleian Library Manuscript Eng Misc e129, p 62.

7 Named after William Croone (1633-84) FRCP and founder member of the Royal Society. He did important work on muscle physiology.

8 Thomas Lawrence (1711-83) was elected FRCP in 1744 after obtaining his MD from Oxford. He was College Registrar for nearly twenty years and President from 1767 to 1774. He attended Dr Johnson (see p 161).

9 VC Medvei and JL Thornton, eds. *The Royal Hospital of St Bartholomew 1123-1973*. London: 1974.

10 Sir George Clark. *A History of the Royal College of Physicians of London*. (3 Vols) Oxford: 1966, Vol 2, pp 549ff.

Provides a fuller account of Schomberg's case and of the whole course of the College's disputes with the Licentiates.

11 John Fothergill (1712-80) obtained his MD at Edinburgh and began to practise in the city of London in 1740. Four years later he was admitted Licentiate of the Royal College of Physicians,

being the first graduate of Edinburgh to have achieved this status. He was elected FRS in 1763. His reputation was enhanced by the publication of his *Account of the Sore Throat* (diphtheria, see p 69). His success brought him considerable wealth, which he employed for both scientific and philanthropic purposes. His chief scientific interest was botany and at his estate at Upton, near Stratford, on London's eastern outskirts, he laid out a botanical garden which Banks considered comparable to Kew. Many of his philanthropic efforts were connected with the work of the Quakers. He never married.

12 William Hunter (1718-83), son of a retired grain merchant was born in East Kilbride, Scotland, the seventh of ten children. He began his medical training as assistant to the distinguished William Cullen and then, after a year's study at Edinburgh University's Medical School, came south to London. He had several disadvantages to overcome: Scotsmen were unpopular; as a Presbyterian, he was a Dissenter, debarred from positions reserved for members of the Established Church; and he practised two crafts which were often regarded with ridicule or distaste—he gave demonstrations in anatomy and attended women as a 'man-midwife'.

By single-minded ambition and unremitting hard work he reached the peaks of success, reflected in an income of some £10 000 a year. He was a brilliant lecturer, and his Anatomy School (first in Covent Garden and later in Great Windmill Street, in the heart of the fashionable West End) did much to make surgery a respectable profession. The status of obstetrics, too, was raised by his efforts, particularly after his appointment as obstetrician to Queen Charlotte. He used part of his fortune to build up a superb collection of books and objects d'art; he was elected FRS and Fellow of the Society of Antiquaries, and when the Royal Academy was founded, he was made its Professor of Anatomy.

13 The play was the hit of the London summer season in 1768. Sir William Browne was caricatured as Dr Hellebore and was much amused by the portrayal; Fothergill was ridiculed as Dr Melchisedech Broadbrim, and was seriously offended. Foote (who had lost a leg by amputation) played a leading role.

14 I Waddington. The Struggle to Reform the Royal College of Physicians, 1767-1771. *Medical History*, 1973: Vol 17; pp 107-26.

15 J Thomson. *An Account of the Life, Lectures and Writings of William Cullen MD.* (2 Vols) Edinburgh: 1832, Vol 1, p 658.

16 See pp 134-5.

17 Sir George Clark. *A History of the Royal College of Physicians of London.* (3 Vols) Oxford: 1966, Vol 2, p 578.

18 Minute Book of the Society of Collegiate Physicians. (Royal College of Physicians Library, manuscript 2130.)

19 Papers were published by (for example) The Medical Society of Copenhagen, The Royal Academy of Sciences at Stockholm and The Royal Society of Gottingen.

20 William practised what he preached; a study of the *Commentaries* reveals many examples of his frank admission of failure.

21 4th edn, 1816.

22 *Medical Transactions*, 1768: Vol 1; p 45.

23 *Medical Transactions*, 1768: Vol 1; p 60.

24 *Medical Transactions*, 1772: Vol 2; p 1.

25 *Medical Transactions*, 1785: Vol 3; p 389.

26 *Medical Transactions*, 1772: Vol 2; p 123.

27 *Medical Transactions*, 1772: Vol 2; p 173.

28 *Medical Transactions*, 1768: Vol 1; p 469 and 1772: Vol 2; p 499.

29 Sulphuric acid, potassium nitrate and sulphate of lime.

30 Kenneth Walker. *The Story of Medicine*. London: 1959, p 155. Oil from whale-blubber. William may have heard this from John Hunter (see note 44 below) who sent a surgeon to Greenland to obtain information about the behaviour of whales.

31 TJ Matthias. *An Heroic Address in Prose to the Rev Richard Watson . . . .* 1780.
In his own home William was naturally careful to avoid the perils of untreated water. TJ Matthias (see p 141) after commenting favourably on William's 'intellectual filtering stone' remarks that 'Dr H is famous for never drinking any water but what passes through a stone of this kind.'

32 See p 219.

33 See p 70.

34 By evaporation.

35 *Medical Transactions*, 1772: Vol 2; p 216.

36 *Medical Transactions*, 1768: Vol 1; p 427.

37 *Medical Transactions*, 1772: Vol 2; p 18.
It was reprinted in the 1816 edition of the *Commentaries* as an appendix. William had already written a short treatise entitled 'The Doctrine of the Pulse' before leaving Cambridge. A transcription made by Erasmus Darwin is in St John's College Library.

38 *Sketch of the Life and Character of Messenger Monsey*. London: 1789.
Messenger Monsey (1693-1788), Physician at Chelsea Hospital, developed an intermittent pulse. According to his anonymous biographer:
As the Doctor advanced in years, an irregular stop in his pulse gave him much alarm, and he applied to Sir George Baker and Dr Heberden on the occasion. Of the last gentleman's medical skill he often expressed the highest opinion. They at first concurred with him in supposing that it arose from some

of the great vessels of the heart growing bony . . . but they afterwards altered their opinion when it was discovered that this phenomenon returned only at intervals, observing very justly that if the cause had been of so local a nature, the effect would have been permanent and regular.

39 *Medical Transactions*, 1772: Vol 2; p 59.

40 JO Leibowitz. *The History of Coronary Heart Disease*. London: 1970, p 4.
The author gives a detailed assessment of William's contribution on pp 83-95.

41 D Evan Bedford. William Heberden's Contribution to Cardiology. *Journal of the Royal College of Physicians*, 1968: Vol 2 (no 2).

42 1772: Vol 33; pp 203-4.
Apart from summarising much of the contents of *Medical Transactions* Vol 2, the issue included extracts from Diderot's *Encyclopaedia*, a review of Bougainville's *Travels* and the text of a tragedy performed at Drury Lane Theatre.

43 A Letter to Dr Heberden Concerning the Angina Pectoris; and Dr Heberden's Account of the Dissection of One who had been Troubled with the Disorder. *Medical Transactions*, 1785: Vol 3; p 1.

44 John Hunter (1728-93) had his first lessons in dissection at his brother William's Anatomy School and subsequently studied surgery under Cheselden and Percival Pott. After serving for four years overseas as a staff-surgeon, he returned to London to study comparative anatomy, a subject for which he became renowned. Unlike his brother, he had no talent for lecturing or writing; but as a surgeon he was brilliant and 'with him', to quote Dr Singer, 'surgery begins to appear at last as a real Science and not a mere applied Art'. He kept a large collection of birds, fishes and mammals at his country house near Earl's Court and was a close friend of Dr Jenner.

45 Nehemiah Curnock, ed. *Journal of the Rev John Wesley AM*. (8 Vols) London: Robert Culley, 1909, Vol 6, p 16.

46 *Medical Transactions*, 1768: Vol 1; p 23.

47 *Medical Transactions*, 1785: Vol 3; p 34.

48 Ginseng was grown in Carolina as well as in China and William had a specimen from each country in his cabinet of Materia Medica.

49 Farther Observations on the Poison of Lead. *Medical Transactions*, 1772: Vol 2; pp 419ff.
The reference occurs on p 468.

50 *Medical Observations and Enquiries*, 1776: Vol 5; p 401.

51 *Medical Transactions*, 1772: Vol 2; p 185.
Wesley in his *Journal* (see note 45 above) notes that in November 1784 at Whittlebury 'my servant was seized with a fever,

attended with eruptions all over, as big as pepper-corns. I took knowledge of the prickheat, as we call it in Georgia, termed by Dr Heberden the nettlerash.'

52 *Medical Transactions*, 1768: Vol 1; pp 469ff; and 1772: Vol 2; pp 499ff.

53 *Medical Transactions*, 1772: Vol 2; p 521.

54 See p 150.

55 *Medical Transactions*, 1768: Vol 1; p 437.

56 William's contribution begins at p 349. Fothergill did not restrict his invitations to London doctors and the contributors included William Cuming of Dorchester (see Chapter 8, p 156), Thomas Glass of Exeter, Dr Ash of Birmingham and Dr Haygarth of Chester (see Chapter 9, p 193).

Chapter 7
The Church, Literature, Correspondence

1 Minutes preserved in the City of Westminster Reference Library.

2 Manuscript in Royal College of Physicians Library.

3 A Francis Steuart, ed. *Journals of Horace Walpole During the Reign of George III from 1771-1783, with notes by Dr Doran*. London: John Lane, 1909, Vol 1, pp 9-13.

4 Lord North (1732-92) was Prime Minister from 1770 to 1782.

5 The phrase, meaning an out-dated belief, may be a reference to the goddess Diana of the Ephesians.

6 These included Law (Bishop of Durham), Green (Lincoln), Lowth (Oxford) and Newcome (see note 13 below).

7 John Nichols. *Literary Anecdotes of the Eighteenth Century*. London: Nichols, Son & Bentley, 1812, Vol 3, p 74.
   Warburton's works were widely read, but he was considered arrogant and quarrelsome. He had a high opinion of William's abilities and considered that Dr Heberden and Dr Letherland were 'the two best physicians in Europe'.

8 A Francis Steuart, ed. *Journals of Horace Walpole During the Reign of George III from 1771-1783*, with notes by Dr Doran. London: John Lane, 1909, Vol 1, pp 89-91.

9 Gerald R Cragg. *The Church & the Age of Reason 1648-1789*. Harmondsworth: Penguin Books, 1983, Chapter 9.

10 F Kilvert. *Memoirs of Bishop Hurd*. London: 1860, p 113.

11 Thomas Baker. *History of St John's College, Cambridge*. Cambridge: 1869, p 720.
   Law's letter is quoted. Edmund Law (1703-87) was a graduate of St John's.

12 Boswell. *Life of Johnson*. Oxford Standard Authors, 1953 edn, p 1015.

13 Newcome (1729-1800) graduated at Oxford and was a distinguished tutor there. He was finally made Archbishop of Armagh 'as a reward of character, principles and erudition'.

14 Manuscript in Royal College of Physicians Library.
15 The publishing of books by subscription was a common practice,
    particularly among authors of learned works. Books were often
    sold in sheets or with temporary binding and the buyer then
    had them bound according to his own taste.
16 *Gentleman's Magazine*, 1801: Part 1; p 485.
    This was a pamphlet written in the 1700s concerning the status
    of physicians in ancient Greece and Rome, a subject which had
    given rise to some heated discussion. Dr Mead had opposed
    Middleton's arguments and in order to placate him, Middleton
    refrained from publishing what he had intended to be his final
    counterblast. To this dissertation William added 'a short but
    elegant advertisement of his own'.
17 British Museum Additional Manuscript 32565, ff 28, 35 and 36.
18 A pamphlet in the form of an open letter to Bishop Warburton,
    commending his erudition.
19 In 1770 Thomas Warton brought out an edition of *Theocritus*
    in two quarto volumes. The work included an epistle from Toup
    to the editor and many notes (Vol ii, pp 389-410), also by Toup,
    dedicated to Dr Heberden.
20 John Nichols. *Literary Anecdotes of the Eighteenth Century.*
    London: Nichols, Son & Bentley, 1812, Vol 3, p 268.
    William Bowyer (1699-1777) was a sizar at St John's,
    Cambridge, but left in 1722 without a degree, in order to join
    his father's printing business. By the number and quality of
    his own writings he became known as 'the learned printer' and
    was appointed printer both to the Royal Society and to the
    Society of Antiquaries. John Nichols, who became his partner
    in 1766, later published the *Literary Anecdotes* which Bowyer
    had compiled. Bowyer was a very small man, extremely amiable
    and cheerful and always generous to people in distress. In 1776
    he suffered a severe paralytic attack 'but through the great
    attention of Dr Heberden, he in good measure got the better
    of it'.
21 Pettigrew. *A Biographical Memoir of Dr W Heberden in Medical
    Portrait Gallery.* London: 1839, Vol 3.
22 J Nichols. *Illustrations of the Literary History of the Eighteenth
    Century.* London: 1817, Vol 3, p 72.
23 W Macmichael. *The Gold-Headed Cane.* (2nd end) London: John
    Murray, 1828, p 175.
24 Thomas Tyrwhitt (1730-86) was considered one of the greatest
    literary critics of the century. His edition of Chaucer's
    Canterbury Tales was much admired.
25 Jones (1746-94), lawyer and orientalist, served as a judge in
    Calcutta.
26 Bryant wrote on antiquarian and religious subjects and
    eventually settled near Windsor.

27 The original manuscripts of the verses are in the Heberden Society archive. (Royal College of Physicians Library).

28 Lowth (1710-87) was educated at Oxford, where he became Professor of Poetry; he was a distinguished Hebrew scholar, lectured on Hebrew poetry and believed that this was the language spoken in Paradise. He was appointed Bishop of Oxford and later translated to London. FRS.

29 Jenyns (1704-87) had been a Fellow-Commoner at St John's and became MP for the county of Cambridge. He was the author of *A Free Enquiry into the Nature and Origin of Evil*—a work in which he argued that every form of life had its place in the grand scheme of the Creator and that if we could only see the whole design, we could then appreciate the Creator's benevolence. Unfortunately Jenyns's attitude to the sufferings of the poor was too complacent and thus incurred the wrath of Dr Johnson, who wrote a blistering review of the book for the *Literary Magazine* in 1757. William's daughter married Jenyns's nephew.

30 Jortin (1698-1770) was an ecclesiastical historian and critic who wrote a life of Erasmus.

31 British Museum Burn Manuscript 523, f 124.
    This Dr Taylor is not to be confused with his namesake, the friend of Dr Johnson.

32 Quoted by courtesy of Mr JRG Comyn.

33 F Kilvert. *Memoirs of the Life and Writings of Bishop Hurd.* London: 1860, p 112.

34 Mathias (1754?-1835) was at Trinity College, Cambridge and became Treasurer to the Queen. De Quincey described his poem as 'marred by much licence of tongue, much mean and impotent spite and by a systematic pedantry without parallel in literature'. Mathias was a devoted admirer of the poet Gray and of William's former pupil Dr Robert Glynn.

35 British Museum Additional Manuscript 22976, f 130.

36 Quoted by courtesy of Mr JRG Comyn.

37 Annie Ellis, ed. *The Early Diary of Frances Burney.* 1889, Vol 2, pp 130-1.

38 Joan Evans. *A History of the Society of Antiquaries.* Oxford University Press, 1956.

39 Minute Books. Vol 11.

40 School Records (see Chapter 1, note 7).

41 The manuscripts of the four letters from which the following extracts are taken are among the Blagden papers in the Royal Society Library.

42 In the *Commentaries* Chapter 31, William observes that since dysentery 'is commonly bred in camps by foul air . . . too great care cannot be taken in regard to cleanliness and fresh air'.

43 See Chapter 5, p 103.

44 Pettigrew. *A Biographical Memoir of Dr W Heberden in Medical Portrait Gallery.* London: 1839, Vol 3.
    The society instituted by the King of France was the Royal Society of Medicine in Paris. William had just been elected an Honorary Member (though the news had evidently not yet reached him) and was asked to supply autobiographical details; this he did (in Latin), and a facsimile of the document was printed by Pettigrew.

45 Although William's hopes remained unfulfilled, Blagden was eventually elected a correspondent of the Académie des Sciences in Paris on the eve of the Revolution in 1789.

46 See Chapter 6, note 11.

47 William, like many of his contemporaries, had considerable sympathy with the rebel cause, which had been so effectively championed by Benjamin Franklin.

48 The Baronet's seat was at Wingham near Canterbury.

49 Robert Lynch MD of Oxford: formerly one of Dr Radcliffe's travelling Physicians.

50 The nature of this recommendation is unknown.

51 Felice Fontana (1720-1805), Italian physiologist and naturalist.

52 Montgolfier. *Encyclopaedia Britannica.*
    The balloon constructed by the Montgolfier brothers received its lift from hot air (provided by burning straw and wool). They demonstrated it on 5 June, and it stayed airborne for ten minutes. An improved model filled with the recently discovered hydrogen was released from the Champs de Mars on 27 August.

53 Sir William Herschel (1738-1822) was born in Hanover and trained as a musician. He settled in England in 1757 and once his passion for astronomy had been aroused, he devoted much of his energy to building bigger and better telescopes. Among his few illusory observations were those of supposed volcanic outbursts on the moon. See p 170.

54 John Harrison (1693-1776) was the inventor of the chronometer. William attended him when he suffered from gout.

55 Thomas Mudge Jr. *A Description, with Plates, of the Timekeepers Invented by the Late Mr Thomas Mudge . . . and a Series of Letters Written by him to his Excellency Count Bruhl . . . .* London: 1799. The three extracts that follow are printed in this volume published by Mudge's elder son.

56 Allowance had to be made for the difference between solar and sidereal time. The star would pass the same fixed point 3 minutes 56 seconds earlier for each 24 hours that elapsed.

Chapter 8
Pall Mall

1 JP Malcolm, ed. *Letters Between the Rev James Granger MA and Many of the Most Eminent Literary Men of his Time.* London: 1805, p 308.

Ewin was a Fellow of St John's, Cambridge.

FHW Sheppard, General Editor. *Survey of London.* Published for the LCC by Athlone Press, University of London, 1960, Vol 29, pp 377-8.

2   James Paine. *Noblemen's and Gentlemen's Houses.* 1783, Vol 2, plates 76-8.

The house was demolished in 1866.

3   Peter Cunningham, ed. *Horace Walpole's Letters.* London: 1857-59, Vol 2, no 1506 (5 June 1775).

4   See Chapter 6, pp 128-9.

5   William Hunter, Letters from his Friends. Manuscript in Matthew Baillie collection. Vol 1 (no 44). (Royal College of Surgeons).

6   *Gentleman's Magazine,* 1793: LIII (no 1); pp 365-6.

7   Jessie Dobson. Eighteenth Century Experiments in Embalming. *Journal of the History of Medicine,* 1953: Oct; pp 431-41.

8   John Thomson. *An Account of the Life, Lectures and Writings of William Cullen MD.* Edinburgh: William Blackwood, 1832, Vol 1, pp 559-60.

9   GC Peachey. *A Memoir of William and John Hunter.* Plymouth: 1924.

10 PJ Bishop. *A Short History of the Royal Humane Society.* London: 1974, p 1.

Oliver Goldsmith (who studied medicine in his youth) was invited, but died before the meeting took place.

11 JP Payne. On the resuscitation of the apparently dead. *Annals of the Royal College of Surgeons of England,* 1969: Vol 45; pp 98-107.

12 Historical Manuscripts Commission, Report 15, Appendix 6, p 251.

Selwyn (1719-91) was renowned for his witty conversation—yet in the House of Commons 'he was not merely silent—but nearly always asleep'.

13 H Twiss. *Life of Lord Chancellor Eldon.* London: 1844, p 104.

14 Thomas Baker. *History of St John's College, Cambridge.* Cambridge: 1869, p 1048.

Arthur Rook and Laurence Martin. John Addenbrooke MD (1680-1719). *Medical History,* 1982: Vol 26; pp 169-78.

John Addenbrooke MD had died in 1719, leaving his money for the foundation of a hospital for poor people; but due to the dilatoriness of its Trustees it did not open until October 1766.

15 WS Lewis and A Dayle Wallace, eds. *Walpole's Correspondence.* New Haven: Yale Ed, 1937, Vol 2, p 264.

16 Manuscript in the Royal College of Physicians Library.

17 John Baron. *Life of Edward Jenner.* London: 1838, pp 39-40.

18 Boswell. *Life of Dr Samuel Johnson.* Oxford University Press, 1953, p 589.

19   RW Chapman, ed. *Letters of Samuel Johnson*. Oxford: Clarendon Press, 1952, letter 605.1.

20   RW Chapman, ed. *Letters of Samuel Johnson*. Oxford: Clarendon Press, 1952, letter 620.

21   RW Chapman, ed. *Letters of Samuel Johnson*. Oxford: Clarendon Press, 1952, letter 629.

22   K Balderston, ed. *Thraliana—The Diary of Mrs Hester Lynch Thrale 1776-1809*. Oxford: Clarendon Press, 1942, pp 389, 391, 399 and 409.

23   K Balderston, ed. *Thraliana—The Diary of Mrs Hester Lynch Thrale 1776-1809*. Oxford: Clarendon Press, 1942, pp 416 and 432.

24   Jebb was an MD of Aberdeen. He is described in Munk's Roll of Physicians as an eccentric with a wild look and an impetuous manner.

25   K Balderston, ed. *Thraliana—The Diary of Mrs Hester Lynch Thrale 1776-1809*. Oxford: Clarendon Press, 1942, p 845.

26   Walter Jackson Bate. *Samuel Johnson*. London: Chatto & Windus, 1978, pp 437 and 548.
Mr Thrale had in fact very nearly ruined himself in 1772 by investing heavily in a project to produce beer without the use of malt and hops. Some six years later he was in financial trouble again—due partly to overspending on his house at Streatham Park and partly to poor business management. After his stroke the brewery was managed by his chief clerk John Perkins, with advice from Mrs Thrale and Johnson. After Thrale's death the brewery was sold for £135 000.

27   British Museum Additional Manuscript 1310, ff 20-9.

28   J Nichols. *Illustrations of the Literary History of the Eighteenth Century*. London: 1817, Vol 1, pp 158 and 164.

29   See p 139.

30   See p 137.

31   In or about 1804 the King bought the house for Princess Charlotte.

32   John Nichols. *Literary Anecdotes of the Eighteenth Century*. London: Nichols, Son & Bentley, 1812, Vol 2, p 188.

33   Boswell. *Life of Dr Samuel Johnson*. Oxford University Press, 1953, p 1240.

34   See Chapter 4, note 67.

35   Boswell. *Life of Dr Samuel Johnson*. Oxford University Press, 1953, p 1243.

36   Lawrence C McHenry Jr. Doctor Johnson and Dr Heberden. *Clio Medica*, 1967: Vol 11 (no 2); pp 117-23. Entries in William's *Index* are quoted.

37   Sir Joshua Reynolds. On Johnson's Character. In: GB Hill, ed. *Johnsonian Miscellanies*. Oxford: 1897, Vol 2, p 221.

38   RW Chapman, ed. *Letters of Samuel Johnson*. Oxford: Clarendon Press, 1952, letter 930.

39 RW Chapman, ed. *Letters of Samuel Johnson*. Oxford: Clarendon Press, 1952, letter 932.

40 RW Chapman, ed. *Letters of Samuel Johnson*. Oxford: Clarendon Press, 1952, letter 938.

41 Boswell. *The Applause of the Jury 1782-1785*, edited by Lustig and Pottle. Heinemann, 1982, p 214.

42 RW Chapman, ed. *Letters of Samuel Johnson*. Oxford: Clarendon Press 1952, letter 1022.

43 The Bodleian reading room, approached by a stairway of 65 steps.

44 Sir John Hawkins. *Life of Samuel Johnson*, edited and abridged by Bertram H Davis. London: Jonathan Cape, 1962, p 270.
    Walter Jackson Bate. *Samuel Johnson*. London: Chatto & Windus, 1978, Chapter 32.
    An authoritative account of the sequence of events during the last few months of Johnson's life.

45 Marshall Waingrow, ed. *Correspondence and Other Papers of James Boswell Relating to the Making of the Life of Johnson*. Yale University Press, 1969, Correspondence Vol 2, p 34.

46 Boswell. *Life of Johnson*, edited by GB Hill, revised by LF Powell. Oxford: 1934-50, Vol 4, p 339.

47 British Museum Additional Manuscript 35623, f 36.

48 GW Corner and WE Goodwin. Benjamin Franklin's Bladder Stone. *Journal of the History of Medicine*, 1953: Oct; pp 359-77.

49 W Heberden. *Commentaries on the History and Cure of Diseases*. Chapter 16.

50 E Posner. Josiah Wedgwood's Doctors. *Pharmaceutical Historian*, 1973: Vol 3 (1).

51 Kenneth Garlick and Angus Macintyre, eds. *The Diary of Joseph Farington*. Yale University Press, 1978, Vol 1, p 256.

52 Ida Macalpine and Richard Hunter. *George III and the Mad-Business*. London: Allen Lane, 1969.
    The King had suffered minor attacks of the same complaint in 1762 and 1765.

53 Quoted by courtesy of Sir Richard Baker Wilbraham.

54 Charlotte Barrett, ed, with notes by Austin Dobson. *The Diary and Letters of the Countess D'Arblay (Fanny Burney)*. (6 Vols) London: 1904-5, Vol 4, pp 135-6.

55 Stanley Ayling. *George the Third*. Collins, 1972, Chapters 13 and 14.

56 In the Queen's House (later transformed into Buckingham Palace).

57 British Museum Egerton Manuscript 2185, f 128.
    John Douglas (1721-1807) FRS and FSA was a canon (and later dean) of Windsor. He was an industrious author and edited the Journals of Captain Cook.

58 Charlotte Barrett, ed, with notes by Austin Dobson. *The Diary and Letters of the Countess D'Arblay (Fanny Burney)*. (6 Vols) London: 1904-5, Vol 1, p 310.

59 Charlotte Barrett, ed, with notes by Austin Dobson. *The Diary and Letters of the Countess D'Arblay (Fanny Burney)*. (6 Vols) London: 1904-5, Vol 3, p 261.

60 See Chapter 7, note 53.

61 See Chapter 7, note 26.

62 Charlotte Barrett, ed, with notes by Austin Dobson. *The Diary and Letters of the Countess D'Arblay (Fanny Burney)*. (6 Vols) London: 1904-5, Vol 2, p 421.

63 Charlotte Barrett, ed, with notes by Austin Dobson. *The Diary and Letters of the Countess D'Arblay (Fanny Burney)*. (6 Vols) London: 1904-5, Vol 3, p 258.

64 The portrait is now in the Paul Mellon Collection, New Haven, Connecticut.

65 She had several children and died in 1832.

66 Appendix to: RF Scott, ed. *Admissions to the College of St John the Evangelist in the University of Cambridge*. Cambridge: 1882, p 297.

67 Under the terms of the marriage settlement, the bride's portion was £3000, and to this sum Thomas was able to bring a further £4000.

68 Register of Admissions. (Public Record Office).

69 Transcription of entry in chapel register. Harleian Society, Vol 15:

John Haberton of Christ Church, London and Eliz Robinson of St George's.

70 The many abuses which the system encouraged were brought to an end by Lord Hardwicke's Marriage Act of 1753.

71 The silhouette is affixed to the flyleaf of a press-run copy of the *Commentaries* (Latin version, 1802), in the Francis A Countway Library of Medicine, Boston, Massachusetts.

72 The original is in St John's College, Cambridge and a copy hangs in the Royal College of Physicians in London. A mezzotint engraving was made by James Ward.

Chapter 9
The Commentaries and the Final Years

1 See p 42.

2 Sir Humphry Rolleston. The Two Heberdens. *Annals of Medical History*, 1933: Vol 5; p 570.

3 Page referencs for the quotations that follow are to the 1802 edition. A facsimile reprint was published in New York by Hafner Publishing Inc, 1962. No 18 in the History of Medicine Series.

4 *Commentaries*, p 214.

5 *Annals of Rheumatic Diseases*, 1962, pp 1-10.

6 *Commentaries*, p 148.

7 *Commentaries*, p 395.
8 *Commentaries*, p 129.
   The complaint is referred to as 'the porrigo or scald-head'.
9 *Commentaries*, p 276.
10 *Commentaries*, p 36.
11 *Commentaries*, p 40.
12 *Commentaries*, p 65.
13 *Commentaries*, p 347.
14 *Commentaries*, p 338.
15 *Commentaries*, p 315.
16 *Commentaries*, pp 224, 225 and 235.
   William calls the condition 'the hypochondriac affection in men
   and the hysteric in women'.
17 *Commentaries*, p 273
18 Francis Bacon. *The Advancement of Learning*. 1605. Reprinted
   1974, edited by Arthur Johnston. Oxford Paperbacks English
   Texts.
   Remarks on euthanasia, p 110 of reprint.
19 *Commentaries*, Chapter 79.
   William wrote a separate chapter on 'The Chronical
   Rheumatism'; this was omitted from the 1802 edition, but
   appears as an appendix in the 1816 edition.
20 *Commentaries*, p 52.
   The powder was named after the 2nd Duke of Portland (d 1762),
   who received so much benefit from it that he bought the secret
   recipe and made it public.
   Sir Humphry Rolleston. The Two Heberdens. *Annals of Medical
   History*, 1933: Vol 5; p 573.
21 *Commentaries*, p 435.
22 *Commentaries*, p 40.
23 *Commentaries*, p 71.
24 *Commentaries*, p 357.
25 *Commentaries*, p 194.
26 *Commentaries*, p 179.
27 *Commentaries*, pp 1 and 4.
28 See below, pp 193-4.
29 S Halkett and J Laing. *Dictionary of Anonymous and
   Pseudonymous English Literature*. London: Oliver and Boyd,
   1926, i, p 374.
30 Unpublished manuscript in the Heberden Society archive. (Royal
   College of Physicians, London).
31 Percival. Retirement from Practise. *Medical Ethics* (revised
   edition, 1803).
   Includes this and the following letter.
32 Sir A Geikie. *Annals of the Royal Society Club*. 1917.
33 Pettigrew. *A Biographical Memoir of Dr W Heberden in Medical
   Portrait Gallery*. London: 1839, Vol 3.

34 Pettigrew. *A Biographical Memoir of Dr W Heberden in Medical Portrait Gallery*. London: 1839, Vol 3.

35 Pettigrew. *A Biographical Memoir of Dr W Heberden in Medical Portrait Gallery*. London: 1839, Vol 3.
    Wells, the son of Scottish emigrants, was born in South Carolina. He took his MD at Edinburgh and after being admitted LRCP, set up a practice in London. He published several important papers on medical subjects and towards the end of his life became celebrated for his Essay on Dew.

36 In 1984 the Society merged with another association to form the British Society for Rheumatology. William's name, however, remains attached to the library and the room, and is also commemorated by medals bearing his portrait which are awarded annually to the speaker of the Heberden Oration and to the leader of the clinical occasion known as the 'Heberden Round'.

Appendix
William Heberden the Younger

1   She was the only child of Charles Miller of Oving, Sussex.

2   J Nichols. *Illustrations of the Literary History of the Eighteenth Century*. London: 1817, Vol 1, p 11.

3   *Morborum Puerilium Epitome*. London: T Payne, 1804. (Latin, first publication). London: Lackington, Allen, 1805. (English translation, by J Smyth, with additional notes and observations).

4   *Philosophical Transactions*, 1796: Vol 86; p 279; and 1826: Vol 116 (part 2); p 69.

5   *Medical Transactions*, 1813: Vol 4; pp 103-18.

6   *Medical Transactions*, 1813: Vol 4; pp 65-84.

7   MD George. *London Life in the Eighteenth Century*. Harmondsworth: 1966, Chapter 1, p 329.

8   Ida Macalpine and Richard Hunter. *George III and the Mad-Business*. London: Allen Lane, 1969.
    The definitive history of the King's illness during the remaining years of his life.

9   British Museum Additional Manuscript 35705, f 105.

10 Arthur Aspinall, ed. *Later Correspondence of George III*. London: 1962, note on letter 3164.
    Prior to the King's convalescence, the Doctors had been in attendance on 110 days over the period 17 February to 1 August. The remuneration claimed was 15 guineas for a five hour day and 10 guineas for a three hour day. The daily routine began at 10.30, with a consultation to devise 'the most likely means of restoring his Majesty's health, and to settle and to sign the report of his Majesty's state, to be shewn to the public'. For afternoon and evening attendances, a shift system was in operation.

11 Arthur Aspinall, ed. *Later Correspondence of George III*. London: 1962, letter 2935.
    Camden was Lord President of the Privy Council.

12 *The Diary and Correspondence of Charles Abbot, Lord Colchester*. 1861, Vol 2, pp 282-4.

13 *The Diary and Correspondence of Charles Abbot, Lord Colchester*. 1861, Vol 2, p 288.

14 W Munk. *The Life of Sir Henry Halford*. 1895, p 143.

15 Willis Manuscript.
    British Museum Additional Manuscript 41696.

16 The Revd Francis Willis had died in 1807; his sons Dr Robert and Dr John Willis were to remain in attendence until the King's death. An anonymous versifier wrote:
    King George he has three doctors daily—
    Willis, Heberden and Baillie;
    All three extremely clever men,
    Willis, Baillie, Heberden.
    Uncertain which most like to kill is,
    Baillie, Heberden or Willis.

17 Sir Humphry Rolleston. The Two Heberdens. *Annals of Medical History*, 1933: Vol 5; p 580.

18 British Museum Additional Manuscript 41734.

19 Manuscript in Royal College of Physicians Library.

20 Manuscript in Royal College of Physicians Library.

21 Lambeth Palace Library Manuscript 2107, f 41.

22 British Museum Additional Manuscript 41735, f 33.
    In this letter William refers to his attempt to stimulate the King's interest by reading to him some items from a newspaper. Willis promptly complained and further readings were forbidden.

23 Lambeth Palace Library Manuscript 2108.

24 Lambeth Palace Library Manuscript 2108.

25 Lambeth Palace Library Manuscript 2108.

26 Lambeth Palace Library Manuscript 2108.

27 He had a large family; his fifth son, John, followed his father's calling and became Rector of Hinton Ampner, near Alresford in Hampshire; the second of John's seven sons, Ernest Arthur, became Vicar of Godley near Manchester and was the father of the present writer.

Index